Jacqueline Knörr (ed.)
Childhood and Migration

JACQUELINE KNÖRR (ED.)
CHILDHOOD AND MIGRATION
From Experience to Agency

[transcript]

This book was printed with the financial support of the Max Planck Institute for Social Anthropology Halle/Saale.

Gedruckt mit Unterstützung des Max-Planck-Instituts für ethnologische Forschung in Halle/Saale.

Bibliographic information published by Die Deutsche Bibliothek
Die Deutsche Bibliothek lists this publication in the Deutsche Nationalbibliografie; detailed bibliographic data are available in the Internet at http://dnb.ddb.de

© 2005 transcript Verlag, Bielefeld

All rights reserved. No part of this book may be reprinted or reproduced or utilized in any form or by any electronic, mechanical, or other means, now known or hereafter invented, inlcuding photocopying and recording, or in any information storage or retrieval system, without permission in writing from the publisher.

Cover layout by: Kordula Röckenhaus, Bielefeld
Typeset by: Jutta Turner, Halle/Saale
Printed and bound in Great Britain by Marston Book Services Ltd, Oxfordshire
ISBN 3-89942-384-4

Contents

Acknowledgements	7
Introduction JACQUELINE KNÖRR AND ANGELA NUNES	9
Coming of Age as "The Third Generation." Children of Immigrants in Berlin SABINE MANNITZ	23
When German Children Come "Home." Experiences of (Re-)migration to Germany – and some Remarks about the "TCK"-Issue JACQUELINE KNÖRR	51
Leaving the *Shtetl* Behind. Children's Literature on Jewish Migration from Eastern Europe JANA POHL	77
Displacement and Identity. The Memoirs of a Juvenile Deportee under Soviet Occupation VIOLETA DAVOLIUTE	95
Children Making Media. Constructions of Home and Belonging NADINA CHRISTOPOULOU AND SONJA DE LEEUW	113
Children Writing Migration. Views from a Southern Italian Mountain Village JAN C. OBERG	137

Small Heroes. Rap Music and Selective Belongings of Young Haitian
Immigrants in Montreal   155
HEIKE DROTBOHM

Liminality as Linguistic Process. Immigrant Youth and Experiences
of Language in Germany and the United States   175
H. JULIA EKSNER AND MARJORIE FAULSTICH ORELLANA

Childhood Dynamics in a Changing Culture.
Examples from the Xavante People of Central Brazil   207
ANGELA NUNES

Contributors   227

ACKNOWLEDGEMENTS

I thank all contributors of this book for their great cooperation in getting this volume together. I am grateful to many who have read the contributions and made comments highly appreciated. My special thanks go to Nina Glick-Schiller and Otto Habeck for carefully reviewing some of the articles. I am thankful to Jutta Turner for copy-editing this book thoroughly and energetically, never running out of patience and maintaining a sense of humour at all times. Andreas Hemming proofread large parts of this book and I thank him for that.

I dedicate this book to my nieces Lina Antonia and Annika Marie.

Jacqueline Knörr

INTRODUCTION

Jacqueline Knörr and Angela Nunes

Children's own views about their own childhood have long been neglected in the social and cultural sciences and so have their views of their experience of migration. This is true even when children are the ones under study and despite the fact that children make up a large proportion of migrants all over the world. The reasons for such neglect of child migrants' views are largely the same as those for the neglect of children's views in general. We will examine some of the major reasons here, but to do so we must first look at the history of childhood research in general, at the overall neglect of children's views and voices, and at the neglect of children's experiences and roles as social agents in the world they live in.

Let us start by pointing out that children were not simply ignored as objects of social and cultural studies. The first anthropological attempts to call researchers' attention to the influence culture has on children growing up of were made in the late 1920s by Mead who pointed out that children create cultural identity in a socializing process which is immersed in culture and emerging from it at the same time.[1] Based on ethnographies of non-western societies, she questioned the biological explanations for human maturation and development as stated by psychology, according to which children were not to be considered complete social beings. The contestation between cultural and biological explanations of human behaviour in general was a crucial issue in most theory (de-)construction pursued in the late 1970s and 1980s.

A more pluralistic notion of childhood and a more diachronic perspective including the idea that childhood might not always have existed as it is understood today was introduced in the early 1960s.[2] Thereby, not only biological determinism was contested but also childhood henceforth not understood as one single phenomenon but rather as a variety of phenomena influenced by and interrelated with social and cultural conditions. It is therefore of crucial importance to take into consideration the different historical, social and cultural contexts within which childhood is situated. This is especially important when dealing with childhood in societies different from those from which our dominant knowledge concerning childhood has emerged, and when investigating childhood in a comparative perspective.

---

1 Mead 1928, 1931.
2 Aries 1962.

Hardman (1973) tried to identify the obstacles that had prevented scientific progress in the anthropological contributions to childhood research, stating that none of the existing anthropological theories had revealed what this particular field of study could be. The social lives of children are a world which escapes adult understanding, she claims, this being the reason why until recently children were not considered complete social beings and not valued as phenomena worthy of the attention of social scientists. Hardman also pointed out the necessity to go beyond the common view that children are merely receivers or containers of what they are taught by adults and to view children as autonomous and creative beings producing social reality and culture. Only if we acknowledge such, she claims, can substantial knowledge about children's understanding of reality and the means by which they organize and transform it, be achieved.

Although isolated, the efforts made by Mead, Aries, and Hardman significantly contributed to a critical review of the dominant theoretical concepts about childhood at the time and thus prepared the ground for developing new and more adequate paradigms.

At the beginning of the 1980s, however, proposals emerging from Sociology, History, Anthropology, and Psychology were still diffuse and ambiguous – and far too unconnected to form the consensus needed to develop adequate theoretical approaches and methodological devices for the study of childhood.

According to Jenks (1982, 1996), the socialization models which have been in use since the 1920s have been exclusively focused on the adult social world, on the adults children were going to be. Devised without taking into consideration the social world of children, these models were not able to contribute to an understanding of childhood. Real change could only occur as a result of constituting childhood as an ontological category, which is valid in its own right rather than as a residual or transitory phase on the way to adulthood. The constant use of "growing up metaphors" through which adults, including the social scientists, tried to explain their relation with the "other" that constitutes the child must therefore be overcome. For Jenks, it is the relationship between adults and children that must change in order to achieve a true understanding of children and childhood. It must be emancipated from a view which puts adults at the centre of the social world while placing children at its margins which they gradually depart from for a more central position when passing into adulthood.

Childhood as a Social Phenomenon (CSAAP), a comparative research programme which was coordinated by the sociologist Jens Qvortrup and carried out in 19 (mostly European) countries from 1987 to 1992, marked a remarkable change in academic thought concerning the study of childhood. The project had, however, a difficult start: ideas were new, information was scant and disperse, no major precursors existed, and even among the researchers themselves it was still debated whether the academic notion of a "sociology of childhood" had a counterpart in social reality. However, the approach taken –

looking at childhood as a social phenomena in its own right – as well as the international format of the programme and its findings resulted in the recognition of the study of childhood as an acknowledged area of social and educational research.[3] Childhood was declared to be a specific form of the social structure of all (researched) societies and – in sociological terms – a permanent social category rather than a transient phase each individual has to pass through. It also became clear that children themselves have their share in the construction of childhood and society and that children are exposed to the same societal forces as adults, although in different ways – one of the major difference being their higher dependency on the conditions created – for both adults and children – by the adult world. Thus, according to the findings, children should also be regarded as a social minority suffering from marginalization and suppression.

James & Prout (1990) point out that children "must be seen as involved in the construction of their own social lives, the lives of those around them and of the societies in which they live. They can no longer be regarded simply as the passive subjects of structural determinations" (4). Meant as a reflexive tool rather than a set of fixed theoretical postulates they introduced a system of constituent elements for sociological and anthropological childhood research.[4] James, Jenks & Prout later specified four main approaches that meanwhile had become established in current childhood studies:[5]

- *Childhood as a social construction*: This approach discards concepts that until then had been considered self-evident, such as the concept of childhood as biologically determined. It inserts an epistemology of childhood in social studies. The idea of a universal childhood is substituted by the idea of a plurality of childhoods. In this understanding childhood also plays a political role in society.
- *Childhood as a world aside:* This approach emphasizes childhood as socially structured in a different way from adulthood. Therefore, it needs to be revealed, understood and analyzed by means of ethnographic research that involves children as subjects speaking for themselves.
- *Children as a minority group*: This approach has been developed in the context of an understanding of the world as unequal and discriminative, of adult power determining and deciding on childhood issues. It considers children as one of the categories of muted "others." It intends to give children a voice and aims at research which is in the interest of children rather than being just about them.

---

3 Qvortrup et al. 1994.
4 James & Prout 1990: 8–9.
5 Cf. James; Jenks & Prout 1997: 198–205.

- *Childhood as a component of (all) social structures*: This approach looks at childhood as a (universal) constituent of (all) social structures, which, nevertheless, takes different forms and meanings depending on the given society it is part of.

These four approaches also show how childhood studies can be linked to current discourses taking place in the sociological and anthropological construction of social theory, specifically by employing the notions of "agency versus structure," "identity versus difference," "continuity versus change" and "local versus global." Thus, theory developed in childhood studies has a lot to contribute to general debates in current social sciences.

The debate concerning the social and the biological impact on childhood is still continuing, however. According to Toren (1993), former concepts of child socialization should not be put aside or ignored but re-evaluated and adjusted to identify both their potentials and limitations. She argues that one of the major problems of such concepts lies in their a-historical character which ignores the fact that human cognition processes – including those of children – are in fact historical, related to the society they are part of and, thus, changing and transforming with time and with social and cultural context. Toren does not want to increase the number of ethnographies dealing with childhood as such, but stresses that children should be an integral part of studies dealing with any given society, claiming that anthropological studies which ignore children's knowledge about the society they live in are incomplete. She attributes the lack of interest in childhood to the fact that socialization is usually considered a predictable process through which children simply reproduce the adult's world.

Despite the shift towards the social world of children in more recent approaches, scientific knowledge about childhood still largely ignores what children themselves have to say about their lives and their own place in the social world. Children's explicit ways of criticizing the latter could be one of the reasons why adults are reluctant to consider their views, observations and assumptions relevant.[6]

The emergence of childhood as a social category of scientific interest and research has been compared with the emergence of women's studies as a field of research, which in the 1970s gave rise to a shift in paradigms in gender studies and theories.[7] However, the big difference is, that, unlike women, children cannot pursue ethnographic research on themselves. So it is up to adults to discover how children see the world, their social lives, their childhood. They can do so by letting children speak for themselves instead of clinging to the traditional belief in adult superiority implying that adults can think and speak for children better than they can for themselves. With regard to the practical application of such a shift in attitude adults could involve chil-

---

6   Cf. Butler & Shaw 1996.
7   See Caputo 1995.

dren in developing childhood social action programmes since only then they could be developed in ways which suit children rather than merely the interests of children as perceived by adults.[8]

What is also still largely missing is a general agreement that studies of childhood help provide more complete knowledge of particular societies and social phenomena and thereby add new perspectives to the social and cultural sciences as a whole. Speaking about anthropology in particular, Hirschfeld states:

It's worth repeating how curious is anthropology's aversion to children. [...] children are theoretically crucial: anthropology is premised on a process that children do better than almost all others, namely, acquire cultural knowledge. Nonetheless, the call to bring an anthropology of children into the main stream has been repeatedly made [...], still, a sustained, coherent, and – most critically – theoretically influential program of child-focused research has not emerged (Hirschfeld 2002: 624).

Hirschfeld points out that the actual problem is not the lack of research on childhood. What he finds surprising though is that the volume of research carried out during the last decade has not had much effect on general anthropological theory. In other words, anthropologists dealing with childhood might have done good work, but other anthropologists not interested in childhood have failed to consider the impact their findings might have on anthropological thought in general. The participation of children in social and cultural reproduction, as well as the impact of children's culture on adults' culture is still very much underestimated. He also emphasizes that children do not just learn and reproduce culture but also create and produce it. In fact, he claims "anthropology is premised on a process that children do better than almost all others, namely, acquire cultural knowledge" (624). If such acknowledgement of children's cultural competences is difficult for adults in general, it is not surprising that this is the case for anthropologists as well. Hirschfeld suggests that one possible way to overcome this resistance is to consider that children constitute themselves as a semi-autonomous subculture like so many other subcultures that constitute social life, and therefore have equal importance and deserve equal attention from social scientists.

Pierre Erny (2003) also stresses the creativity of children in the process of social (re-)production, emphasizing that it is especially pronounced in societies undergoing rapid change, where children often turn out to be the ones educating their parents more than their parents are educating them. He claims that in some such cases it would actually be accurate to speak of "children cultures" and "children societies" (15). Thus, children must be seen as both ob-

---

8   See Martins 1993; Rizinni 2002.

jects of cultural adaptation and as active subjects, who change the culture they were born into while adapting to it (at the same time).[9]

Recent research on childhood among Brazilian indigenous peoples takes the path suggested by Toren, Hirschfeld and other authors here mentioned, thus aiming at a notion of socialization which is part of an historical and dynamic process of culture.[10] Children are considered as complete beings, as social agents able to create a socio-cultural universe with its own particularities and as social agents able to critically reflect upon the adults' world.

That childhood is socially constructed is now generally accepted, but its variation in different cultural contexts still needs investigation which takes into consideration children's voices and children's actions. Studying age sets and classes socially well defined, as well as life cycles and social learning processes may very well be useful devices when trying to understand the category "child" and its social place and meaning in specific cultural contexts. However, one should keep in mind that children have something original to say and therefore their experiences, representations, feelings, and expressions should be considered a valid object of social research. According to James & James (2004) children's experiences of social life and their impact on their own childhood, future childhood generations and on adult's life is still rather unclear. In other words, childhood agency is not yet fully recognized. Children may have been discovered as actors playing roles which help them enter adulthood, but not as agents who shape those roles and imbue them with specific meanings. Children also create new roles for themselves, both as individuals and as members of wider social groups. They do so in ways which induces change in the social life of the group as a whole and in the successive generation of children (like their parents did before them). Recognizing children's agency means recognizing their experience as a potential for change. Children's agency makes a real difference for society at large.

Now what does all this imply for studying and understanding children's experiences and their agency with regard to processes of migration?

While it has been acknowledged to some extent that children's own concepts of their social world, and their thoughts and feelings should be considered when studying childhood in general and specific aspects of childhood in particular, this has had little effect on migration studies dealing with children. Little is known about children's particular understanding of (migrant) life, their concepts of their place of origin and their host society, their ways of building identity for themselves. This is true despite the fact that children

---

9 See Egli (2003) who describes such a process with regard to hereditary rules in Eastern Nepal, which to a considerable extent predestine children's perspectives but which are also changed substantially by children in the process of adaptation and "enculturation."
10 See Lopes da Silva & Nunes 2002.

make up a large proportion of migrants and despite the fact that children take on important roles in mediating between their world of origin and the host society.

Children play this role for many reasons, one being that they acquire new cultural knowledge so "exceptionally well."[11] Children are also usually more involved in the social life of their host societies than their parents through school and other child-specific institutions and contact zones (playing grounds, football fields, kindergarten, backyards etc.). Children's ways of socializing with other children and with the world around is also less constrained by prejudice and bias than those of adults. Children want to be among other children; the "others'" cultural, social or political background is far less important to them than they often are for their – or the "others'" – parents.

We want to contribute to the understanding of how children themselves experience, view and manage migration and we want to show by means of which they construct an identity for themselves which takes into account their experiences from both their places of origin and their host societies.

The question that arises first when dealing with children constructing identity in the context of migration is whether they perceive and define cultural identity for themselves at all. In the context of sociological and anthropological research on migration and multiculturality concepts have been developed which try to terminologically classify and differentiate varieties of "mixed" culture and cultural identity (hybrid, creole, transnational, global, glocal etc.). Do such concepts also fit the reality of migrating children or is their perception of culture more dynamic and flexible than that of the researchers on the one hand and of the adults they usually research on the other?

One of the key issues raised in the context of identity as created by migrant children is the view children have of both their respective culture of origin and their host society. How children construct an identity for themselves, a sense of home and belonging and a sense of origin and descent which takes into account both contexts in which they find themselves is critically important. Another question is to what extent and by which means a relationship is maintained to the place of origin and whether and how it changes in the course of migration. How is this relationship represented in social interaction among children, between children and their parents, and between children and their social environment? It is important to get insight into children's observation concerning the social and cultural changes taking place that affect themselves and their families in the process of migration. What changes do they perceive, what do they think of those changes and how do they deal with them? What do they relate their observations to? Who do they perceive as initiating these changes and do they perceive themselves as agents of change within their families and their new social environment?

Another important issue is the process of social and cultural integration in society as a whole. How is it influenced by the dynamics of interaction of a

---

11 Hirschfeld 2002: 615, 624.

particular cultural background of the society of origin on the one hand and the integration strategies and practices of a particular host society on the other?

The role of social milieus and peer groups is an important issue when dealing with children experiencing and managing migration. How do peer group environments, socialization at home and school interact or contradict each other? And how do children deal with these different social milieus and the demands they put on them?

One experience almost all migrants of all ages have is xenophobia. How do migrant children cope with a lack of acceptance, with hostility and exclusion? How do children make use of existing institutions to overcome frustrations resulting from such experiences and how do they create new social niches where they can feel at home? How do they express processes of cultural orientation, integration, disintegration via music, writing, media, and forms of creative discourse? Are there gender specific differences concerning the construction of identity in the course of migration? How do different motivations and reasons for migration influence the course that migration and integration take?

We cannot deal with all these issues with the same degree of thoroughness in this volume, nor can we answer all the questions raised here. What we can do, however, is shed light on some of the major issues related to children's experience of migration. There can be no doubt that cultural identity and social practices learned and generated in childhood have an important impact on the course of social and cultural integration in youth and adulthood. Therefore, the investigation of these processes is not only of scientific interest but can also give important impetus to the development of strategies and modes of integration that appeal to children and serve their needs.

The approach we take is both comparative and interdisciplinary, the contributors having different theoretical and methodological backgrounds, and dealing with different social and cultural settings with regard to both place of origin and host society.

Sabine Mannitz' contribution presents the results of ten months of ethnographic fieldwork and subsequent interviews over a period of four years with adolescents from immigrant families in former West-Berlin. She points out that migration research has often stressed the adverse circumstances of immigrants in Germany. The so-called second and third generations in particular are seen as having the problem of living betwixt and between two cultures. This perception situates immigrants and their children in a structural conflict and creates the impression that they must choose between two competing cultures. But contrary to this model, Mannitz finds that her informants in Berlin face no such gap. While conforming in many instances to the idea of bounded groups and their unequivocal social identities – the idea that foreigners differ from Germans in their culture – children generally manage to act in both of these settings, applying practices of mediation and eventually creating a new transnational space for the management of identifications. However, despite their competency in double agency, they have to cope with the fact that neither their migrant parents nor the wider German society is willing to legitimize their melange of identifications as a viable strategy. This is significant beyond the individual level, since creating an intersecting space for imagining collectivity may be a first step towards developing new codes of coexistence for the society as a whole. According to Mannitz, with transnationalization challenging the nation-state's previous *raison d'être*, the ways in which migrants construct their multiple affiliations might thus become centrally instructive.

Jacqueline Knörr deals with a group of (re-)migrant children and youths hardly mentioned in migration studies, namely children of Western background brought up in a non-Western environment before "returning" to a "home," which in many cases has never been or is no longer home to them. She deals with German children coming to live in Germany after having spent most of their childhood in Sub-Saharan Africa. Many of these children spent most of their social lives in German and/or international expatriate environments. In the context of dealing with some of their typical features she critically examines the notion of "TCK" – "Third Culture Kid" – a notion which has been used for some time now to denote children brought up as (children of) expatriates. Knörr looks at what it means to be brought up as a white child in Africa and how this experience affects (re-)migration to Germany. Upon "return" these children often find themselves in a dilemma: they are expected to be the same – speaking the same language and looking the same as everyone else – while their experiences, views, and ways of life are usually quite different from those of children and youths who have spent all their lives "at home" in Germany. Their difference is often neither recognized nor appreciated by teachers, peers, or their own families. What makes it even harder for them to find some comfort in their situation is the fact that compared to other groups of "real" migrants, it is usually more difficult for them to find others around them who share their experiences and problems. Knörr looks at the views and attitudes these children and youths develop in the course of (re-)integration and at some of their ways "in to" and "out of" German society – which include social isolation, self-exotization, multiple identifications, and idealization of one's former "real" home back in Africa.

Jana Pohl analyses the image of the *shtetl* in American children's literature. The *shtetl* was a predominantly Jewish community which corresponded to the size of a village or small town. The *shtetl* image has a long and rich tradition in American children's literature. It accommodates the manifold recollections of Jewish-American writers, whose autobiographical experiences are often related to their subject. To many Eastern European Jews who left their home and migrated to North America around the turn of the last century, the *shtetl* stands for their culture, their place of origin. In contemporary children's literature the image of the *shtetl* is linked to migration, the two concepts both being central to the collective identity of American Jews of Eastern European descent. By connecting the – memorized – *shtetl* image with migration, those stories embrace memories of both childhood images of the country of origin and images of the target country.

Violeta Davoliute's analysis of the diaries and memoirs of young victims of the Soviet deportations of non-Russian minorities during WWII offers unique insights into the effects of migration in its extreme forms, both on individual and collective identity. As the initial solidarity of ethnically defined group victim status breaks down in the multinational *Gulag* environment, the child's sense of cultural and even personal identity is tested and transformed under extreme duress. Davoliute's article considers the experience of Dalia Grinkevičiūtė, deported from Lithuania to the Russian far north at the age of 14. Her "early" memoirs, written when she was 21, capture her immediate apprehension of the ethical and cultural dilemmas facing the deportees individually and as a group. Her youthful reflections on women's recourse to prostitution, religious and bourgeois morality, national identity under conditions of Russification and Sovietization, and questions of ethics and justice in captivity defy any simple categorization. Believing her memoirs to have been lost, Grinkevičiūtė wrote a second version as a mature adult. A comparison of the "early" and "mature" versions of her memoirs helps to identify the immediacy of the early work discovered only after Grinkevičiūtė's death in 1989.

Nadina Christopoulou and **Sonja de Leeuw** discuss the findings of a European research project on "Children in Communication about Migration" (*Chicam*) and compare them with existing theories on culture and identity. The research was carried out in six European countries and focused on the social and cultural worlds of refugee and migrant children. It explored the potential uses of media and communication technologies as means of empowering migrant children and enabling them to realize their potential. Christopoulou and De Leeuw focus on "family relations" to investigate the relationship between media, migration and childhood. They analyze how children see themselves positioned within these relationships, and explore how their perceptions are articulated in the process of making media productions. Using examples from the media work done by the children they analyze the children's conceptions of "home" and cultural identity in the context of family relations as they are being re-established in the new country.

Jan C. Oberg's contribution deals with more than 200 essays on local history and the tradition of migration written by children themselves. The children under study describe their life-worlds located between Tramonti – a small mountain community near the Amalfitan Coast (Southern Italy) – and "the North." They tell of past times rich in tradition when "innumerable cows stood in the cowshed," of "times long gone [when] one could meet people here with pure hearts free of the manifold problems that plague humanity today." They tell of migration as the fiend raging in Tramonti, destroying the ideal life of the past. But they also tell of fast cars and pizzerias, of the wealth of the North, and of the freedom which their migrant relatives bring with them to Tramonti on their summer vacations. The children's narratives fluctuate between idealization of migration and disapproval of it. However, more than reflecting inner conflict their stories reveal how creatively children manage to deal with heterogeneous environments and how actively they take part in the production of culture.

Heike Drotbohm aims at exploring how children of the second generation of Haitian immigrants in Montreal, Canada, perceive and define their position between Haiti, as their parents' reference culture, and Canada, as their host society. Through the analysis of the songs of one particular local Haitian rap group "family conflicts" and "black power" are identified as core issues with regard to the construction of personal and ethnic identity. Drotbohm finds the lyrics reflect the social realities of Haitian children in Montreal from different points of view and pinpoint the transnational dimension of Haitian ethnicity in Montreal. From the children's perspective, Haiti serves either as a negative stereotype, referring to their parents' difficulties in coping with everyday-life in Canada or as an imaginary homeland, which helps to develop ethnic consciousness and pride in Haitian community life in Montreal.

H. Julia Eksner and **Marjorie Faulstich Orellana** address the conjunction of "liminal" and contradictory aspects in the lives of immigrant children and youths. In analyzing how children's experiences of immigration in Germany and the United States are translated into linguistic practices, they present a critical appraisal of liminality, a concept describing individuals' subjective experiences of in-betweenness. Liminality has been used in a variety of ways in anthropological, sociological and sociolinguistic theory. The authors examine several uses of the concept, including both its original application and the various ways it has been expanded and adapted, highlighting its efficacy in some contexts and pointing to its limitations in others.

Angela Nunes' ethnographic research does not deal with children living through a migration process but with children who belong to the Xavante, an indigenous group of people in Brazil who were prevented from maintaining their semi-nomadic way of life which had determined their existence for centuries. They now settle permanently, suffering the consequences of the sudden and violent change they endured in all aspects of their social life. With a great deal of effort, however, the Xavante are reacting, though, and finding innovative ways to mend what was almost destroyed. Their hopes lie in their children. They say children can better bridge the past with the future and that children have a wisdom adults have lost. Nunes' article reveals how children actively and creatively participate in the process of reconstructing the social life of a migrant people who have been forced to settle down.

References

Ariès, Philippe 1962: *Centuries of Childhood: A Social History of Family Life*. New York: Knopf.
Butler, Ian & Ian Shaw (eds.) 1996: *A Case of Neglect? Children's Experiences and the Sociology of Childhood*. Aldershot: Avebury.

Caputo, Virginia 1995: Anthropology's silent 'others:' a consideration of some conceptual and methodological issues for the study of youth and children's cultures. In: Amit-Talai, Vered & Helena Wulff (eds.): *Youth Culture*. London & New York: Routledge: 19–41.

Egli, Werner M. 2003: Ich heiße Bahadur – Erbrechte und Lebensperspektiven von Kindern in Ostnepal. In: Egli, Werner M. & Uwe Krebs (eds.): *Beiträge zur Ethnologie der Kindheit. Erziehungswissenschaftliche und kulturvergleichende Aspekte*. Studien zur Ethnopsychologie und Ethnopsychoanalyse, Vol. 5. Münster: Lit Verlag: 129–143.

Erny, Pierre 2003: Einleitung. In: Egli, Werner M. & Uwe Krebs (eds.): *Beiträge zur Ethnologie der Kindheit. Erziehungswissenschaftliche und kulturvergleichende Aspekte*. Studien zur Ethnopsychologie und Ethnopsychoanalyse, Vol. 5. Münster: Lit Verlag: 5–20.

Hardman, Charlotte 1973: Can there be an Anthropology of Children? *Journal of the Anthropological Society of Oxford* 4 (2): 85–99.

Hirschfeld, Laurence 2002: Why don't anthropologists like children? *American Anthropologist* 104 (2): 611–627.

James, Allison & Alan Prout (eds.) 1990: *Constructing and Reconstructing Childhood: Contemporary Issues in the Sociological Study of Childhood*. Basingstoke: Falmer Press.

James, Allison, Chris Jenks & Alan Prout 1997: *Theorizing Childhood*. Cambridge: Polity Press.

James, Allison & Adrian James 2004: *Constructing Childhood: Theory, Policy and Social Practice*. New York, Basingstoke: Palgrave Macmillan.

Jenks, Chris 1982: *The Sociology of Childhood: Essential Readings*. London: Batsford.

Jenks, Chris 1996: *Childhood*. London & New York: Routledge.

Lopes da Silva, Aracy & Angela Nunes 2002: Contribuições da etnologia indígena Brasileira à antropologia da infância. In: Lopes da Silva, Macedo & Angela Nunes (eds.): *Crianças Indígenas: Ensaios Antropológicos*. São Paulo: Global, Mari e Fapesp: 11–33.

Martins, José de Souza (ed.) 1993 [1991[1]]: *O Massacre dos Inocentes: A Criança Sem Infância no Brasil*. 2a. edição, São Paulo: Ed. Hucitec.

Mead, Margaret 1928: *Coming of Age in Samoa: A Psychological Study of Primitive Youth for Western Civilization*. New York: William Morrow & Sons.

Mead, Margaret 1931: *Growing Up in New Guinea: A Comparative Study of Primitive Education*. New York: William Morrow & Sons.

Mead, Margaret 1955: Theoretical setting – 1954. In: Mead & Wolfenstein: *Childhood in Contemporary Cultures*. Chicago: The University of Chicago Press: 3–20.

Nunes, Angela 2004: *Brincando de Ser Criança: Contribuições da Etnologia Indígena Brasileira à Antropologia da Infância.* Tese de Doutoramento, Departamento de Antropologia, ISCTE. Portugal.

Qvortrup, Jens et al. (eds.) 1994: *Childhood Matters: Social Theory, Practice and Politics.* Aldershot: Avebury.

Rizzini, Irene (ed.) 2002: *Pesquisa em Acção: Crianças, Adolescentes, Famílias e Comunidades.* Rio de Janeiro: Editora Universitária Santa Úrsula.

Toren, Christina 1993: Making history: The significance of childhood cognition for a comparative anthropology of mind. *Man* (N.S.) 28: 461–478.

COMING OF AGE AS "THE THIRD GENERATION." CHILDREN OF IMMIGRANTS IN BERLIN

Sabine Mannitz

Migration research focusing on immigrants in Germany[1] has often stressed the adverse circumstances of an altogether unintended immigration process and the problematic effects of political ignorance that has prevailed in the field of integration for decades. Owing to the lack of political visions for full incorporation, the situation of the so-called second and third generations of immigrants in particular has been considered problematic. In this reading, the offspring of the immigrant population has been depicted for the most part as being trapped in a miserable structural conflict of living between two cultures. This perception insinuates that extraordinary personal and emotional crises are an inevitable part of their coming of age in Germany, forcing them to choose between competing cultures – if such a choice is deemed possible at all. This perspective is not restricted to any particular position in the fields of migration or integration policies. It has been disseminated, for instance, by (well-meaning) pedagogues, whose major aim is to assist children with migration backgrounds to catch up in German schools and to make good for their supposed deficits and disadvantages.[2] Although a number of authors have come to criticise these tendencies of culturalist reification in pedagogy since the late 1980s,[3] it is still a powerful discourse. The situation of immigrant youths is interpreted on these grounds from the point of view of collective shortcomings in the cultural realm, and culture tends to be conceptualised as a stock of conventions acquired in childhood and governing the behaviour of a person thereafter. The scenario of inevitable crises resulting out of cultural

---

1 My research sample draws upon families that immigrated into the former Federal Republic of Germany (FRG)/West Germany. Hence, Germany refers to the FRG/West Germany whenever the period before 1990 is at issue.
2 See for example Mertens 1980; Jerusalem 1992; Schrader, Nikles & Griese 1979. They understand enculturation as a phase of irreversible identity formation in primary socialization.
3 See Bukow & Llaroya 1988; Prengel 1993; Bukow 1996; Hamburger 1997.

clashes appears as an almost natural consequence.[4] The rigid concept appears as a misrepresentation not only in view of recent findings in the scholarship of ethnicity but also in view of the adolescents' own views and personal experiences which I studied. Nevertheless, the hegemonic discourse of cultural difference will in some way influence their perceptions of self and other and shape their scopes of agency in contesting their identities.[5] In other words, it will unquestionably be within the prevalent discursive "landscapes of group identities" (Appadurai 1991) that the children and grandchildren of immigrants have to negotiate their own possible identifications.

And yet, what does it mean to come of age in such a setting, being seen as the second or third generation of foreign immigrants? While the political discussion in Germany has recognised the necessity of future immigration for several years, little attention has been devoted to the ways in which immigrants and their children actually experienced their lives in Germany since the 1960s. From an anthropological point of view, this dimension is of particular relevance. Studying the ways in which indigenous majorities come to terms (or not) with immigrant populations and vice versa may reveal practical solutions developed through social interaction. This is impossible when assuming that in the course of primary socialization, "culture grows into *soma*" (Schrader, Nikles & Griese 1979: 58), as if a mental mould came to function as a behavioural prison.

This contribution presents empirical findings that challenge the established assumption of migrants' identity conflicts developed in the scholarship of cultural essentialism. In the study of ethnicity, there has been a growing number of works since the 1990s that falsify the traditional paradigm which defined ethnic identity as a given and, instead, illustrate the situational and contextual, hence fluid, character of ethnic as well as religious or other social identifications.[6] Contrary to primordialist hypotheses, processes in social identification are far more complex. Identities can be internally heterogeneous and culture appears as an interactive field of discursive contestations.[7] Evidently, the very falsification of cultural essentialism applies not only to the biographical situations of migrants. However, their certainties are challenged

---

4   This faction within "intercultural pedagogy" argues for the most part without presenting any corresponding empirical data (see Bründel & Hurrelmann 1995; Gemende et al. 1999; Czock 1993; Schepker & Eberding 1996). Multiculturalism is based on the same concept, in principle, i.e. considering people as representatives of a collective rather than as individuals. It does, however, invest the idea of distinctiveness with a positive rather than a negative bias. For a critique see Leggewie 1989; Radtke 1995; 1996; Bommes 1996; Baumann 1999. Treibel (2003) provides a systematic review of the different conceptual approaches to migration in German scholarship.
5   Mills 1997: 17.
6   See, e.g., Hall 1990; Eriksen 1993; Al-Azmeh 1993; Barth 1994.
7   See, e.g., Hall 1990; Schiffauer 1991; Hannerz 1992; Kaschuba 1995; Baumann 1996, 1999; Rogers & Vertovec 1995; Baumann & Gingrich 2004.

more often and to greater extents than those of indigenous populations whose cultural or ethnic particularities are hardly ever contested. Given the expectation that international mobility becomes more and more relevant in the future, it is therefore long overdue to consider the immigrant experience.

The essay deals with a number of adolescents from labour immigrant families in Berlin who developed various forms of transnational identification and displayed a notable competence in double cultural agency under the circumstances of a prevalent culturalist, and negatively biased discourse. To study these phenomena in context, I will briefly sketch the contradictory trends that mark the post-war history of immigration on the one hand, and the political ambitions to foster a post-national collective identity in the Federal Republic of Germany on the other. I will then look into the daily routines in a school as one prominent site where cohabitation norms are foregrounded in the lives of children and adolescents.[8] Even if they reject what is suggested to them, the interaction is part of the dialectical process by means of which young people become familiar with hegemonic boundary concepts and define their own positions. In order to specify how educational norms may influence the process of social integration in general and to demonstrate the position of migrant minorities in relation to the indigenous German majority in particular, I shall review the general character of education for citizenship in Germany. Following an account of the normative agenda, the question of how immigrant diversity is handled practically in a school in Berlin will be introduced. Finally, I will present the identity-related practices applied by adolescents from immigrant families. How do these young people cope with the ambivalent messages regarding possible options of associating and dissociating themselves? Apparently, they partly conformed to and partly subverted the common narrations about them. I shall argue that such ways of conflating competing identity models are typical acts of transnationalization in that they refer to imagined "social fields that cross national boundaries," and thereby aim to "reconfigure space" when positioning themselves (Basch et al. 1994: 22, 28–34). This resourceful double agency unfolded, however, as stigma management, to cope with a lack of recognition. Moreover, it remains as yet tied to an imagined transnational space that differs from the dominant imagery of "us" and "them" in Germany. These limitations are discussed in the conclusion.

---

8   The empirical data were collected during ten months of fieldwork in a secondary school in Berlin-Neukölln during the 1996/97 term, and from interviews I conducted with young people from migrant families (15–17 and 20–22 years of age) between 1998 and 2001. The interviewees had been pupils in the above mentioned school while I was doing research there. The initial fieldwork was part of the research project, "State, School, and Ethnicity" funded by the Volkswagen Foundation 1996–1999. All direct citations, whether single terms or whole sentences are those of the people who interacted in the setting of this school. Given the limited space, they cannot be portrayed here as individuals and the findings are only quoted very briefly. For more details see Schiffauer et al. 2004.

Background: The reception of labour immigrants in postwar Germany

Although the hiring of foreign labourers has been part and parcel of the economic and social recovery of West Germany after World War II, immigration has never been acknowledged favourably by German politics and society in general. Instead, the project of hiring labourers from abroad on a temporary basis gradually developed into *de facto* immigration, unintended on the part of both Germans and so-called "guestworkers." The resulting demographic multinationalization has therefore only waveringly begun to enter *collective consciousness*.[9] The ambivalence is reflected in the prevalent conceptualization of migrants and immigration in Germany. It also influences the circumstances under which children of immigrants come of age in Germany. Even though we are talking here not only of the sons and daughters but meanwhile also of the *grand*sons and *grand*daughters of the first generation "guestworkers," these offspring are still perceived – e.g. in media discourse and in school textbooks – as "second and third generations" of foreigners rather than as equal fellow citizens. The following brief account will illustrate the historical background of this perception scheme.

Beginning in the early 1960s, West Germany suffered a dramatic shortage of labour because the closing of the border between the two German states prevented people in the Eastern parts from entering the Western zones or commuting in between them. To solve this problem, the recruitment of foreign "guestworkers" (*Gastarbeiter*) was seen as necessary and useful. Labour immigration was supposed to work by rotation, with eventual repatriation being taken for granted – both by the German public and by most migrant workers as well. When Germany's economy took a downward turn in the early 1970s, the federal government favoured reducing the number of foreign workers. A recruitment freeze and return incentives were introduced, but this resulted, contrary to the intentions, in increased immigration since many people used the remaining window of opportunity for the immigration of relatives, fearing that more restrictions would follow.[10]

Irrespective of the actual settlement of the "guestworkers" in West Germany, the official political doctrine that Germany was not an immigration country continued until the end of the 1990s. The fact that a considerable number of foreign nationals had become part of the population surely needed to be dealt with; however, no concepts were developed regarding any long-term incorporation of immigrants, and state authorities continued to respond on an *ad hoc* basis. The outcome was a mixture of partial inclusion and exclusion. The legal foreigner status entailed restrictions, particularly in terms of rights to formal political participation. With regard to most requirements and routines of daily life however – the job market, civil society institutions, the

---

9   Schiffauer 1993: 195–198.
10 Münz, Seifert & Ulrich (1997) provide a detailed account.

education system and most welfare benefits – few exclusions were made. Hence, the presence of foreigners acquired a form of normalcy despite the lack of official efforts encouraging the former "guestworkers" to remain in the country and become German nationals. West Germany was thus "[...] not only an ambivalent *de facto* immigration country with an inclusive welfare policy and an exclusive citizenship policy. The foreign population developing out of the earlier "guestworker population" had unexpectedly and without any corresponding convergence on the part of the obstinate immigration country developed into an immigration situation" (Bade 2000: 338).

There are reasons to criticise this unsystematic handling of the situation, as evidenced by political omissions and failure to take the initiative in responding to a *de facto* immigration process. Yet in spite of the range of missed opportunities to improve the immigrants' reception in Germany through political and legal measures, it seems inadequate to conceive of this immigration history in terms of failure. The present situation does not correspond to the goal of temporary residence that once motivated both German politics and the labour migrants themselves. Yet their extensive inclusion into German civil society and their near equal entitlement to the benefits of the welfare state has had the effect that the immigrant population in Germany has achieved high levels of societal participation. In some respects this surpasses what countries with more inclusive integration policies, such as the Netherlands, have accomplished.[11] While most immigrants remained excluded from formal political citizenship in Germany, they were included on nearly all other informal levels of participation in public life. State school education is a good example of this ambivalent situation.

Education for citizenship under pressure

Schools function as important communication channels between the state and its citizens as well as between various social groups. Schools are a relay point between generations, between public and private and, last but not least, between majorities and minorities. It is hence an important site for integrating social differences, for transmitting shared rules and restrictions, civic norms and values and for promoting a collective imagery of one's own group vis-à-vis others. Among other things, school teaches children how merit can be earned, how conflicts should best be handled and how participation in the polity should be practised in a given society. As part of this education for citizenship, schooling promotes particular ideals from preferred argumentative styles to the norms and limits of the country's civil and political culture; in brief, it functions as a force for enculturation.[12] Because of this role in organising socialization in accordance with the principles of the common social and politi-

---

11 Thränhardt 2000.
12 Bourdieu & Passeron 1977; Gellner 1983; Harker 1984; Baumann 2004.

cal order, schools are excellent places to study the projections and also the changes in how a nation defines itself and others.

Historically, state citizenship education followed a nationalist programme, which both reflected and produced "cleavages based on nation and language" (Finaldi & Shore 2000: 2). This model of projecting and creating collective identities as national ones has been highly effective in constructing, shaping, and reproducing nations and "their" states as reified actors of early modernity.[13] Social cohesion was created by stressing collective traits of one's own nation in contrast to those of other nations. However, several developments have led to an undermining of the conventional nation-state arrangement combining social and civic rights with territorial consolidation and the political sovereignty of its "imagined community," as Benedict Anderson has phrased it (Anderson 1991). In the field of education across Europe, major changes resulting from increased societal heterogeneity, whether intended or not, and of the political project of transnationalization within the European Union can be noted. In theory, this eases the incorporation of newcomers.

Twentieth century Europe has undergone various processes that might be regarded as instances of denationalization: increased immigration has made populations more multi-ethnic and multi-national; the project of European unification qualifies the national nature of collective identities; and, as has been said for Germany, many forms of legitimate representation as well as political participation are no longer tied to the formal condition of nationality.[14] In the wake of these changes, schools must initiate new cognitive processes: whether their pupils are German nationals, long or short term residents, recently arrived refugees, with or without expectation of repatriation – in short, irrespective of their students' origins – schools are expected, at the very least, to prepare adolescents for their lives as possible future citizens. Their aim of enculturation has thereby come to relate to the political culture of civil society, rather than to the nation-state itself:

> [N]ation-state schools are no longer schools of nationalism, yet we continue to recognize that state-directed schooling is always related to identity-shaping purposes within the framework of the nation-state. [...] Civil enculturation in its currently observable form strives hard at managing the seemingly paradoxical: to inculcate pupils with a civil culture that is nationally specific, yet normatively open to all regardless of their backgrounds, identifications or possible loyalties (Baumann 2004: 10–13).

In order to serve this purpose, educational representations of nationhood and their collective symbols have undergone remarkable changes in Western Europe in the second half of the 20th century. With the integrative forces at work in the European Union, the traditional fortifications of the nation concept appear to have been rethought. Although adhering to locally and nation-

---

13 Gellner 1983; Anderson 1991.
14 A sampling on this topic from the social sciences might include Sassen 1996; Soysal 1994; Joppke 1998; Koopmans & Statham 1999; Kastoryano 2002.

ally specific understandings, there is a general trend towards a "Europeanization" of issues.[15] Symbols of national identities or national "heroes" figure less prominently than they did 50 years ago. Present-day teaching materials throughout Western Europe clearly demonstrate a retreat from the notion of national identities revolving around fixed sets of attributes, traditions and cultural heritages.[16] Negative stereotypes of other European nations have also been largely removed from these media. Furthermore, increasing emphasis is put on broadly defined ideals such as those of the Enlightenment and liberal democracy.Abstract principles are stressed of democracy, human rights and social justice in order to foster a European identity in the schools.[17]

In (West) Germany, the trend towards denationalization of civic education took a variety of forms since the end of World War II. The totalitarian experience left nationalism so discredited that the only feasible projection for regaining a positive self-image and some political influence after 1945 was placed in the European context. This can clearly be seen in the normative agenda to guide socialization in state institutions. The federal state of Berlin, for example, features a rejection of national arrogance in its constitutional preamble, and this tone is noticeable throughout the educational programme of the city-state. Already in the seventh grade teaching of geography[18] many topics are related to the common economic, political and social space of the European Union. Europeanization and globalization are treated as "World Studies" in grades 9 and 10, which combines social studies, history, civics, geography and economics.[19] Children are to be given an introduction to European and global interrelatedness, international dependencies and migration issues, all of which are meant to contribute to the students' abilities to participate in democracy "in a society of rapid social change," and irrespective of their nationalities.[20]

However, such lofty ambitions are difficult to translate into practice, and it does not make matters easier that education policies are ideological battlefields in themselves. Moreover, curricula and textbook supervision fall into the legislation of the respective federal states in Germany and are subject to a

---

15 This is one result of the project, "Rethinking Nation-State Identities in the New Europe: A Cross-National Study of School Curricula and Textbooks" (www.one-europe.ac.uk, funded by the Economic and Social Research Council of the UK 1999–2002), in which I was involved as a Research Officer. Our study was focused upon history and civics textbooks and curricula from four European case countries since the 1950s. The idea of Europe has entered teaching programmes extensively as a theoretical concept while the specific appropriations vary from country to country. For examples from the French and the German case-studies see Bertilotti, Mannitz, & Soysal 2005.
16 See Bertilotti, Mannitz & Soysal 2005.
17 See Pingel 1995: xi–xii, 2001.
18 Geography Curriculum: Rahmenplan Erdkunde 7, 2001.
19 World Studies Curriculum: Rahmenplan Weltkunde 9 & 10, 2001.
20 Syllabi of Political Education: Zur Zielsetzung und Praxis Politischer Bildung in der Berliner Schule, 2001.

diversity of funding measures, meaning that schools are located not only in very different social, but likewise in very different institutional and financial environments. The extent to which revised textbooks can actually be found in schools depends on a number of variables also. In most of Berlin's schools the equipment is substandard and outdated, since the city-state has been near bankruptcy for many years. Many of the textbooks used in the school where my research took place dated from the early 1980s, and some were unchanged reprints from even older editions. Thus, the impressive normative rhetoric at the official level as well as with regard to the latest textbook editions is not implemented at the level of school socialization.[21] Furthermore, the ambition to strengthen a European rather than a national consciousness seems to be limited by the fact that the vision of an integrated Europe is far from the everyday experience of school children.

The gap between the normative discourse in favour of transnationalization in civic education planning on the one hand and social reality on the other is noteworthy. Yet, it does not render the overall tendency obsolete. Lessons have been drawn from the experience of nationalist hubris in Germany, so that children are no longer being socialised in terms of the "banal nationalism" (Billig 1995) in its traditional meaning of spreading nationalist symbols of identity by way of everyday routines. Nevertheless, the nation-states are still important. They act as gatekeepers for the brokerage of rights, they constitute social sites for agency and are the most tangible interlocutors for the civil public. Young people need to learn how to pursue their interests within this national public in which the relevant argumentative methods are as particular as the national political cultures and their civic conventions. Indeed, the study on "State, School, and Ethnicity" carried out in various European countries[22] was able to confirm that pupils are socialised within nationally specific fields and standards of discourse, which are, however, understood now as being compatible with the broader concepts of Europeanness.[23] In the German case, especially, collective self-reference is no longer based on any nationally codified concept but on the post-war conception of being part of the Western world of democracies. In other words, a shift has taken place from explicit nationalism to implicit, more instrumental forms of establishing collectivity. This shift has not simply ruled out the relevance of national boundaries. It instead produces its own peculiar boundary effects.

The fact that parts of the agenda are denationalised while others are not results in a complex set of competing expectations. The main tension stems from the fact that, "the nation-state school has [...] [in the meantime] taken on two missions at once: it is expected to perpetuate a sense of nation-state continuity but also to integrate non-nationals and first-generation citizens into the democratic project of equalizing chances" (Baumann 2004: 1). The different

---

21 Leclerq 1995: 13–14.
22 See note 12 for more information on the study.
23 Schiffauer et al. 2004.

layers of belonging, entitlement and incorporation are thus multiple and somewhat contradictory. Diversity and the crossing of national borders appear to be cherished on the rather abstract and vague level of a desirable European community formation. With regard to concrete labour immigrant populations, they are received less enthusiastically, especially when the immigrants are not (considered) Europeans. As a result, adolescents can be expected to come to terms with competing discursive strands today which delineate and assess diversity from different angles.[24] Even though being nationally specific, these fields of discourse must not be mistaken for any straightforward pressure towards, e.g., "Germanization." After all, young foreigners also participate in and influence the interaction taking place. Besides, owing to the particular ambiguity prevailing with regard to immigration in Germany, no programmatic assimilation policy has been developed here.

Immigrant Diversity in a Berlin School

Although all children encounter axiomatic rules and social concepts most systematically at school, this does entail special consequences for those from immigrant families. For one thing, they are confronted personally with dominant conceptualizations and evaluations of collective difference. These take their most tangible form in the treatment of migration-related topics in teaching and in the practical handling of immigrant diversity in everyday school life. In both respects, the site of my study in Berlin was marked by assessments that run counter the quoted programme ideal in "world studies," which largely represents the vision of "one-world" without prejudices.

The history and geography textbooks used in the school I studied depict a world of harsh differences. When dealing with migration and the most relevant emigration countries[25] the latter are frequently qualified as underdeveloped and divided by acute inner conflicts, a negative performance often related to parochial cultural traditions such as the caste system in India[26] or clan loyalties in sub-Saharan Africa[27]. An example that affects the image of Turkish immigrants explicitly is the grade 8 geography textbook. The chapter dealing with Turkey starts with the statement that the country suffers from severe development contrasts. It goes on to explain that the people who made their

---

24 See Mannitz 2004.
25 Geography textbooks tend to present selected countries because of their emigrant populations these days. This has the twofold motivation (1) to improve knowledge about the immigrants and enhance mutual understanding and (2) to facilitate identification by pupils of migrant origin with the teaching programme. Both of these intentions may be counteracted by the stereotypical way in which the emigration countries are presented, that is, largely in terms of shortcomings and deficits (see Lütkes & Klüter 1995; Stöber 2001).
26 Brodengeier et al. 1996: 99.
27 Krauter & Rother 1988: 44.

way to Germany beginning in the 1960s came from the least developed parts of Turkey. Different from their fellow nationals in Istanbul, these migrants are said to have very little in common with Central Europeans:

> Inhabitants of Istanbul have more in common with Central Europeans than with the inhabitants of eastern Anatolian villages. [...] In the 19th century, [...] most reforms remained restricted to Istanbul and the western parts of the country. [...] The Turkish Republic tried to overcome its inferiority in relation to the European industrial nations independently. [...] The extreme imbalance was to be levelled out. However, the new state's limited economic power prevented any considerable success. [...] Finally, a rural migration drift started. Urban conglomerations like Istanbul and the Marmara region were the main destinations of this internal migration. After 1961, many migrants tried to find work in the industrialised countries of Central and Western Europe (Krauter & Rother 1988: 56–59).

In the same vein, migration is portrayed in many cases as being triggered mostly by push factors. Pull factors are hardly ever mentioned. While migrants are thus associated with poverty and other problems intrinsic to the country or the region of origin, the permanent presence of immigrants in Germany is presented as having imported problems. This is an issue brought forward in subjects like history or social studies also. In the history textbook used at the school of my research, it reads as follows in the volume for grade 9:

> *Other difficulties* resulted from the large number of immigrants, of foreigners and returning emigrants [*Aussiedler*] of German descent from Eastern European countries, who streamed into the Federal Republic. Almost five million foreigners lived here in 1990 including 1.5 million Turks. Many came because they expected better living conditions than in their home countries. Others requested asylum because they were being persecuted for political or religious reasons at home. *They were all looking for housing and work. Additionally, there are language barriers, the clash of cultural differences and problems of integration* (Ebeling & Birkenfeld 1991: 109; emphasis added).

In other words, immigrants appear as recipients who reap advantages from being in Germany, while Germans are not explained how they gain from the presence of immigrants. From these elements a problematic causal chain suggests itself: The immigrants' cultures of origin involve poverty and backwardness, these being the cause of both emigration and the burden which immigrants bring with them. Thus, an implicit concept of culture as a fixed collective disposition lacking internal diversity may legitimise a low opinion of the others, who altogether appear to represent backward mentalities.[28] Theo-

---

28 More details are discussed in Mannitz & Schiffauer 2004. Our findings have been confirmed by other research projects. See, e.g., the study by Hormel & Scherr 2004, or the reports on the study "Images of others" carried out at the University of Frankfurt/Main. The latter analysis shows that the image of immigrant youths as betwixt and between (*zwischen zwei Stühlen*) is an established metaphor in teaching materials for social studies in junior secondary schools

retically, this negative message is still open to discussion and even invalidation through critical use of textbook representation in teaching. But my participant observation carried out in classrooms over a period of ten months did not reveal many instances of such a critical approach.

The secondary school in the Berlin borough of Neukölln had large numbers of pupils from various foreign nationalities, those from Turkish, Lebanese and (former) Yugoslavian families being most numerous. How was their presence understood to affect daily school life? The briefest answer is that they were considered a major problem. Many teachers expressed the view that the "oriental pupils in particular" posed great difficulties because of their "completely different" upbringing and culture. In the same vein, these students' knowledge of other languages was not seen as any asset or useful skill but rather as a handicap that hindered their participation, social integration, and individual chances for success in German society. The immigrant parents, moreover, tended to be perceived by most of the teaching staff as mere sources of obstruction. They were believed to follow a counter-productive agenda, focusing all of their attention on their own cultural milieu instead of taking part in the wider society and assisting their children to do the same in school. The negative cliché of migrant youth occupying a space "between," or even as "torn between" different cultures was reproduced in many instances. A number of teachers went a step further and complained about the altogether negative impact of the large number of foreign pupils on their German peers, the effect being a "reactionary assimilation process" among German pupils, as one teacher put it. According to him, the German pupils were adapting to a higher level of aggression and other bad habits introduced by the foreigners. He argued that the Germans had behaved better and had achieved more when the foreigners had been less numerous.

To contextualise this negative appraisal, one needs to take into consideration that schools with high rates of pupils from immigrant families are often situated in socio-economically weak or "high risk" neighbourhoods. This is also the case in Berlin. A combination of high rates of unemployment and welfare recipients, bad housing conditions and populations consisting of many and rather poorly skilled immigrants characterised the outlying districts of Berlin where most pupils resided. Such difficult social conditions render an impact on school since pupils from underprivileged families of whatever nationality tend to lack linguistic and social skills, which are important prerequisites for successful schooling. Yet, quite different from approaches chosen in other European countries – e.g. in France, the UK or in Sweden – where additional resources are allocated to counterbalance negative circumstances from home and cope with the particular challenges immigrants are facing, in Germany most schools in "high risk" neighbourhoods are usually not better but even more poorly equipped than average. This issue has received increased at-

---

(Höhne, Kunz & Radtke 1999, 2000). As regards the negative image of migration and nomadism see Treibel 2003: 43 ff.

tention since the publication of the latest OECD PIZA study (Baumert et al. 2001). Children from immigrant families proved to be significantly less skilled than their German peers in reading and comprehension of the German language. And they came up much worse than pupils from comparative immigrant groups in other countries of the OECD survey. This results in a serious disadvantage. For the pupils concerned, opportunities are limited if they lack the basic prerequisite of mastering the residential country's *lingua franca*. Conversely, Germany obviously missed chances of making good use of its human resource potential.[29]

In Berlin, the poor material situation of the school and the substandard living conditions at home created stress for both teachers and students. It resulted in many teachers willingly accepting the thesis of cultural differences as the outstanding explanation for the difficulties encountered. The cultural otherness of their "oriental pupils" easily ruled out alternative explanations such as the impact of social class or individual problems, be it in the context of a student's social behaviour, his or her lack of progress in class, or a girl's refusal to join a class outing. Aggressive behaviour was less interpreted as indicating pressure deriving from deprived living conditions but more as expressions of role models rooted in "other cultures." One of the teachers explained to me as follows why the presence of the "oriental pupils" had negative effects in his view on the overall situation in school: "Especially among foreign pupils, behaviour is following backward role models. [...] There is almost no possibility of solving conflicts verbally, no willingness to compromise. And with our large proportion of oriental students, there are many failings in the area of tensions between male and female teenagers."

A more empathetic colleague of his judged that these pupils were victims of circumstance:

Turkish parents fail insofar as little value is placed on acquisition of the German language. Our students' Turkish parents throw their children into the German school system without any assistance. Turkish boys especially are often confronted with such unreal expectations from their parents that many are in danger of breaking down. This pressure naturally produces behaviours that we feel to be very unpleasant. [...] My opinion is that the Turkish Parents' Association fails completely.

A third teacher, reacting to two Turkish students whom she heard talking in their mother tongue, was explicit on why integration of the Turks in Germany failed: "You speak Turkish, you stay in your own circles, you go shopping only in Turkish shops. Integration cannot work like that!"

---

[29] The causes of this lose-lose-situation are numerous but experts agree that the socio-economic origin of a child determines school success to an extraordinarily high degree in the German school system. If their social backgrounds are substandard, pupils from migrant families seem to be subject to twofold processes of systemic discrimination of the disadvantaged and of the institution's incapability to cope with heterogeneity as such.

As these examples show, the foreign students, and especially the "oriental" immigrants among them, were perceived as incapable of fulfilling the model proposed for them. In the view of the quoted teachers, the Turkish families represented the cultural antipode to modernity and civilization, and as such were assumed to reproduce outdated gender roles, condone oppressive educational methods and authoritarianism, and insist on maintaining various peculiar cultural traditions – all of which were regarded as irreconcilable with the ambitious aspiration to follow the universalistic ideals of Europeanised Germany.

To some degree, this juxtaposition of the underdeveloped Orient vis-à-vis the advanced Europe sounds familiarly similar to arguments compiled thirty years ago in defining orientalism.[30] But unlike the ambivalence of conventional orientalism, which combined negative stereotyping with an idealization of the mysterious and fascinating Orient, comments and assessments made by numerous German teachers contained no positive connotations at all. Whenever labour immigrants and their children were at issue, a self-evident cultural hierarchy prevailed: the "oriental" immigrants were seen as a specific group of foreigners, whose different cultures were reminiscent of earlier stages in communal life, resulted in social divisions and a backlash in the "host society" – namely the quoted "reactionary" influence of German peers. According to many teachers' understanding "the orientals," more so than other immigrant groups, were basically reluctant to adopt anything of the modern German lifestyle. They may not even be wrong in some of their assessments of individual students or families. However, such judgements were readily transferred to larger groups of foreigners, i.e. "the Turks" or "the orientals." The collective image of these others was that of notorious troublemakers, the reason being their different cultural backgrounds.

The teachers' integration efforts were, however, not directed in favour of any "culture" flagged as German either. From their side[31] there was clearly no sympathy with narratives of German (or any other) national culture and traditions. Their ideals drew upon the universal value of social modernity, rationalism, liberalism and pluralism, nothing particular to Germany. Nevertheless, since these ideals were perceived as being rooted in the historical experience of central Europe, in the shape of the Enlightenment and the European spirit of overcoming a terrible nationalist past, the "orientals" not sharing this experience seemed destined to remain a negative contrast group.

---

30 Said 1978.
31 Many of the teachers had been influenced by the anti-authoritarian student revolts and the social movements that followed in the 1970s. Negative evaluation of Germanness is not restricted to this political generation but it appears as a strong common outlook. Besides, the revolts may have contributed also to establishing reserved views of the nation in the wider society. By the end of the 1990s, a representative survey on German national identity noted an altogether "strong push in a negative direction" (Rossteutscher 1997: 624).

Yet in effect, the ill-famed children from migrant families appeared to be both insiders and outsiders at the same time. While they represented essential otherness in the dominant narration, the routine of everyday life implied that one had to come to terms with them as *de facto* fellow citizens. This led to expectations among teachers that their "foreign" pupils would somehow have to surmount their otherness. And again this carried ambivalent implications: How can an individual overcome his or her cultural otherness when this is understood as being a "mentality" or an iron cage of a collective cultural disposition? Opinions and expectations of teachers and peers varied on this point. Each possible positioning meant social compliances and breaches, and pupils could hardly avoid or remain disengaged from such confrontations. These combined factors make school a place where interactions take place at different levels of integration and disintegration: standards of articulating one's position are established within the existing power relations whilst being subject to continuous contestation also.

Creative conflations:
The foreigner experience as an asset

Neither the experience of relatively consistent negative stereotyping of their own backgrounds, nor the overall critical representation of Germanness prevented my young interlocutors in Berlin from remaining both in the foreigner category and from becoming German in some ways. I shall try to explain why.

Children from migrant families do not only encounter the idea of cultural differences and collectively attributed mentalities in school. At home, many are confronted with similar concepts when their parents insist on preserving certain cultural boundaries in relation to "the Germans," boundaries that are stressed out of fear of losing their children in a cultural sense as a minority. Having grown up with these complementary ideas, discourses, practices, and expectations relating to cultural difference, the adolescents I met in Berlin reproduced the hegemonic concept frequently. They claimed that different cultural collectivities based on nationality or religion were matters of fact and articulated this assumption through contrasting comparisons. The range varied though: in some cases the "individualist Western lifestyle" was pitted against "our countries that are bound to religion, customs, and tradition," or "modern Muslims" were contrasted with "traditional Muslims." In other cases what mattered most was the difference between "Christian Europe" and "the Muslim world," or that between Christian and Muslim foreigners in Germany. Yet another contrasting dualism was that between Germans from West Berlin and "the Nazis from the East." In spite of these bold and generalising classifications, the students' personal experience of cultural distance and their own identifications differed from situation to situation. Being a foreigner, being from West Berlin, being a Muslim or a Turk had different meanings under different social circumstances. Sometimes the Germans served as the main contrast group, sometimes the same person who had just quoted the boundary between Turks and Germans as significant described the own family with strongest feelings of alienation, like 19-year-old Mehabal: "I come home and everything is completely different from outside. At home the things that matter are basically very unimportant to me, really very, very unimportant and of no significance!"

Despite the apparent confusion, a general argumentative pattern marked these narrations: although the view that cultural differences existed between the home and German public spaces was widely conformed to, the children of immigrants themselves did not want to be forced into any exclusive category. The reason for this was that switching between the two "worlds" or "cultures" and acting in both was not regarded as a trap or a major problem. The overwhelming majority did not see themselves as victims of circumstance but as protagonists of an unforeseen interim stage. There was a shared feeling that none of the pre-defined characteristics attributed to them matched their own mixed experiences. Thus, students from immigrant families of all kinds often preferred to resort to the vague common identity of being "foreigner." While being also aware of their friends' various origins, the national or ethnic differences tended to be levelled out within this residual in-group of "the foreigners." In one discussion involving young people from Turkish, Palestinian, Greek, Albanian, Croatian and Sri Lankan families, participants all agreed that their "foreign parents" had raised them differently than Germany parents had raised their peers. The main boundary was hence drawn along the line of nationality yet it was understood as being related to processes of cultural reproduction.

The home and the social world outside seemed to represent a discrepancy of expectations to all children from migrant families, yet one that could be handled according to situation. The "foreign" adolescents agreed that they encountered difficulties now and then, requiring extra competence in mediation and placing considerable demands on them psychologically when they refused to fulfil the role their families expected of them, namely that of future guardians of their parents' original culture in the diaspora. Nevertheless, confidence in their own capacity to ultimately master these expectations prevailed over frustration. They made a virtue of commuting between diverse spheres, of managing stigmatization and were very well aware of their competence with regard to double "cultural" agency. The fall-back category of the "foreigner" served this purpose on numerous levels: It functioned to appease their parents' fears of the next generation's Germanization by stressing a certain distance from "the Germans." At the same time, it was a means of maintaining a distinct position vis-à-vis the indigenous German population while not stressing one's own *particular* origin, i.e. possibly one's special stigma if belonging to the "oriental" category of immigrants. The extended concept of "the foreigners" also fostered solidarity among the different national minorities. As a common denominator, it allowed its members to take a joint stand substantiated by similar, shared experiences of exclusion.

While many pupils in the multi-national networks of "foreigners" had no objections against the general assessment that national groups possessed different mentalities, they did not take this personally. Truly problematic cultural otherness was, in their view, embodied by their elders and relatives "back home." They generally found it hard to bear their parents' home environments for more than short periods of time. 20-year-old Hashim explained his feelings of alienation this way:

Living here in Germany, we see many things differently. When I try to question some things over there [i.e. in Kosovo], I am always told, 'No, we don't do that, that doesn't suit us, it's not our tradition and culture, that's a matter of honour, we don't do things like that...' Living in Germany has given me a different way of thinking. When I imagine what I would have been like, had I grown up in Kosovo..., I would have had a completely different idea of the world, absolutely! The people there think completely differently.

Similar to this young man, many other children of immigrants saw their very competence in questioning matters, discussing and searching for compromise as the core of a cultural change that their own generation but not the one of their parents had undergone in Germany. A girl from a Greek family put it like this: "I am in any case convinced – and that is exactly what my parents mean by 'behaving German' – that you must also be able to compromise, otherwise it doesn't work." About her parents she thought: "They are not used to discussing things or finding interim solutions."

Personal development and the ability to tolerate controversy, to discuss and solve conflicts by accepting compromise was seen as a chance, which their parents had never had, let alone family members who had not emigrated, because these attributes were conceptualised as typical of German life. In the words of a girl from a Tamil family, "One can develop much better here than in our own countries." Accordingly, the notion of mentality recurred regularly when these young people spoke about their parents' countries of emigration where they regarded socialization circumstances as being altogether limited. In effect, the emigration societies appeared as if frozen in a state of timeless traditionalism, not allowing for any dynamic change.

The "narrow-mindedness" of relatives who had never been abroad and their "weird expectations and distorted ideas" about life in Germany bothered many young people and gave them the impression that the "authentic" cultures of the emigration countries were, in fact, as backward as the German school textbooks portrayed them to be. Hashim once commented that, "countries that are economically weak are always bound to religion, customs, and tradition." This nexus of culture as a locational factor for poor economic circumstances, which in their turn are assessed as being responsible for conflicts and instability, sounds quite familiar: It is one of the recurrent lines of argument followed in the teaching about underdeveloped countries, traditional culture and the push-factors for migration. The pupils had obviously got the message and applied it to the countries of their families' origin. Just as their own parents and relatives were judged as holding on to traditional norms and being unable to discuss controversial subjects, their original national societies were regarded as a whole as carrying the same deficiency. Traditions appeared hence as a kind of "tied and tagged baggage" (Baumann 1999: 94), which limits the scope for possible development. Given the rather negative evaluation attached to cultural traditions, my interlocutors showed hardly any interest in them. However, since the young people saw themselves as "foreigners" in Germany rather than as representatives of a particular national, ethnic or religious group, the suggested parochialism of traditions was of no real concern for their own self-images.

And yet, in situations of conflict between "foreigners" and "Germans," the allocation table with the reified categories turned out to reach a dead end. The underlying imbalance in power relations suddenly became visible when the so-called foreigners felt they were being provoked to justify themselves or their supposed original cultures. While German students were able to use the negative bias of "traditional cultures" against "the foreigners," the latter in turn had difficulty in defending concepts they could not fully subscribe to, nor were they willing to accept the stigmatization for themselves. If their German peers saw no necessity to seek intersecting commonalties, such situations were prone to result in a breakdown of communication and to reconfirm the *cliché* of the Germans being a bounded contrast group, even in the eyes of those "foreigners" who represented supposedly German ways of behaviour at their homes.[32]

In line with the stereotypes prevailing at school, many pupils from migrant families accused their parents indeed of insisting on the maintenance of group boundaries and traditions that had lost any meaning among their own peer-group. Being different from "the Germans" did not imply identification with any particular group of origin and vice versa. This was a matter of family conflict. To some extent many of the young "foreigners" felt they had, in fact, become "Germanised" as their parents noticed with displeasure. Yet any direct identification with "becoming German" was inconceivable. This was not just because their German peers denied them access to their in-group but also due to the ambivalent feelings about Germanness in itself. As one young woman explained: "One cannot feel one is a German, and somehow I don't *want* to think of myself as German, since the idea of being 'typically German' is a deterrent in itself!"

It appears the "foreign" adolescents were thoroughly enculturated into the prevailing discursive conventions of German self-reflection and had fully internalised its negative connotations. The latter make identification as German difficult for native Germans as well as for immigrants. Since hybridity is not (yet) foreseen in the conceptualization of Germanness, immigrants are, however, confronted in the public with an either/or option with regard to their identification as Germans and as members of a nation they or their parents

---

32 See Mannitz 2001.

originated from. The boundaries of Germanness cannot be blurred or shifted as easily as is the case, for example, with Britishness.[33] And the option of Europeanness remains a restricted category for most of the "foreigners" not only because of its remoteness from daily business, but also because it continues, in its dominant interpretations, to exclude those denizens with "oriental" origins.

The self-positioning as being "foreigners in Germany" is a remarkable way out of this conceptual dilemma for it draws upon assumed otherness as a resource, which the Germans do not have at their disposal to deal with the altogether negative meanings of Germanness. In one classroom discussion one Kurdish girl explicitly described this as an advantage: "Since we, the foreigners, also know another mentality, another culture, we can decide which one is better or appeals to us more. As a result, there is always this longing for the culture that one likes best. I think Germans do not have this choice."

One of her classmates, a girl from a migrant family as well, commented on the same issue: "Sometimes one feels, like, Where do I belong ultimately? Should we have to found a new state for all who are 'half German,' or what?!"

This was not the only positioning strategy; partial identification with various other factors was another solution. Among such factors were the identification with the neighbourhood they lived in, with certain groups like the "good" anti-fascist, pro-immigrant Germans, with the old West before German unification; and with the economic success of West Germany, to name just a few.[34]

The everyday reality of the children with migration backgrounds was obviously far more complex than what the concept of clearly delimited cultures was able to convey, in spite of the fact that everybody made use of it. The "foreign" pupils had learned to conceive of themselves as being the others in Germany, while at the same time being insiders in everyday social life and, what is more, insiders on the level of the conceptual and argumentative "tool kit" (Swidler 1986), they used in making themselves understood. The ways in which the adolescents made sense of the world, voiced their arguments and handled the notions of cultural difference reflected the discursive assimilation

---

33 Legal amendments regarding nationality only took effect in the year 2000 and it will take time before they are integrated in the public self-image. With the new laws, a civic understanding replaced the ethno-national tradition that bolstered the popular understanding of Germanness as an equation of demos and ethnos "with higher evaluation of the ethnos" (Hoffmann 1996: 252). Before the amendment, naturalization of immigrants was exceptional unless they could demonstrate ethnic German ancestry. The current conditions are explained under www.einbuergerung.de.

34 For more examples see Mannitz 2004. In her study on the ways in which young migrants handle the particular burden of German history, Viola Georgi (2003) has likewise documented the difficulties inherent in the latent German integration demands.

process they had undergone growing up in Berlin. They were able to deploy available discourses on and about themselves, both conforming to and subverting the existing narratives. Their difficulty was thus not in handling the multi-level reality of their lives, but in coping with the fact that their creative conflation, which went beyond the conventionally imagined communities of national societies, found no apt recognition, neither from their families nor from their German surroundings; at home, as much as in school, they were expected to show sentiments of *unambiguous* identification and commitment. Yet even though nationality was in this way associated with culture, emotional ties and collective identity on all sides of the hegemonic categorization, this did not quite match the mixed experience of distance and simultaneous belonging of many adolescents. Their way out of this situation was the "foreigner" identity that makes use of the existing terminology but equips it with new meanings of transnational experiences.

Owing to the then rather restrictive German nationality legislation, most of the "foreign" pupils were in fact foreign nationals at the time of my fieldwork. Their own classifications, although citing the familiar reifications of alterity, were, however, fluid enough to transcend the rigid container model of national groups and "their" cultures, which still occupies the dominant imageries despite the decline of explicit nationalism. The following quote is a typical illustration of this conflation. It was made by one of the young women I continued to meet for interviews after she had left school. Her family had emigrated from Sri Lanka in the 1980s and she had come to Berlin at primary school age. When reflecting upon her coming of age in Berlin, her argument presupposes a classical model of multi-cultural diversity with distinct cultural communities, yet the underlying notion of otherness is reassessed positively as meaning a collective resource in terms of enrichment that entails special opportunities in learning tolerance: "We had the advantage of enrichment through all the cultures. I have got to know so many cultures in school, [...] and therefore I will never be able to claim that I have something against somebody from this or that culture. After all, I got to know these people; they had the same problems I had, and we could talk to each other about that!"

From this point of view, the immigrants appear as indispensable agents of social change because they embody plurality in society. This young woman was not the only one to discover such a positive side in the ascription of otherness. In search of possible ways out of the nationally codified dilemma of conceptual exclusion, the "foreign" youth made a virtue out of the attribute of being others with different cultures. It was thus the very diversity in a "multi-cultural" school setting as the emic vocabulary labelled it – which their German teachers regarded as a major source of distress and problems – that had made these pupils accept the relative meaning of difference to such an extent that they could reassess the collective value of heterogeneity and conclude, in the words of a teenage girl from a Greek family, that "every person is different. That has nothing to do with nationalities."

Conclusion

Although cross-border relations mark the contemporary world to an unprecedented degree and may in the long run further undermine the nation concept, the boundaries of nationally defined societies, cultures, and citizenship models are still powerful categories in terms of perceptions, recognition and access to privileges. West Germany has always been a country of immigration, but the presence of immigrants has largely remained a white space in the collective imagination. Not even the large scale *de facto* consolidation of the former "guestworker" immigration had led to any straightforward policy of formal inclusion in Germany till the end of the 1990s. Until a Social Democrat-Green coalition supplanted the conservative coalition in 1998, much of the normative political discourse depicted labour migrants in Germany as foreigners destined to return to their home countries rather than as immigrants expecting to somehow become part of the permanent denizenry. Owing to this long-standing policy of denial, the conceptualization of the immigrants recruited in the heyday of the booming economy developed at a different pace than that of much of the societal inclusion process, which Germans and foreign residents were experiencing together in West Germany. Yet even this situation was left surprisingly uncontested for most of the past forty years. Looking back, it seems as if both indigenous Germans and immigrants preferred to practice a "muddling through" (Lindblom 1959; Geertz 1973) instead of taking positive action and risking public strife.

However, the 1990s brought several catalytic moments that drew attention to the question of how cohabitation could be improved. Above all, the German unification put issues of national identity onto the agenda, triggering discussions on internal cohesion in German society, on membership, belonging, and entitlements within the polity and on the place of unified Germany in the project of an increasingly integrating Europe. In the wake of these debates, the post-war trend towards the denationalization of German self-definitions was reconfirmed, its most tangible expression being the amendment of the nationality laws in the year 2000. Debates on how to manage and organise immigration have nevertheless remained a site of ideological battles where fears of different cultures and traditions that immigrants might bring with them have repeatedly resurfaced along with fears of the economic charge that a decided integration policy would imply. Compared to neighbouring immigration countries, the German public appears to be not only little experienced in facing the challenges of diversity, it also seems little confident in its own integrative potential.

The characteristic uneasiness which Germans display vis-à-vis immigrant others takes the shape of a culturalist discourse. This discourse is negatively biased and it poses particular constraints on the project of integration by way of the civic socialization in school, which is post-national in theory but continues to reflect ethno-national boundaries in the face of a "multicultural" reality. In fact, coping with immigration and furthering ideas of post-nationalism do not appear as two sides to the same coin but as separate projects in the German setting. Despite the fact that Germanness has lost credit with the experience of dreadful nationalism, cultural heterogeneity is hardly deemed a positive alternative vision, neither in public discourse on the whole nor in the topical discussions concerning the presence of immigrant children in schools. Owing to the difficulties in promoting Germanness and furthermore enhanced by the absence of a clear policy in favour of immigration, the struggle in reconciling the ambitions in favour of post-nationalism with the desire of enculturating newcomers within the bounds of the national society may be more complicated here than in other European countries.

While the European nation-states continue moving towards some form of transnational commonality (and by doing so may in future shift the imagined boundaries to fence Europe off), national concepts of sameness still matter in the articulation of internal collectivity. Even though the symbolic boundaries of national communities have been recast by the project of Europeanization, the nation-states have not become altogether insignificant. Shifts towards universalistic learning contents and participation-oriented methods have gained importance, but each nation follows its own distinctive path of fitting its self-definition into the European framework. Consequently, the layers of discourse regarding nationality, social identities and viable options for collective as well as individual positioning have both multiplied and become more contested. Normative orientations toward desirable modes and balances of social, national, and international integration compete with and partially they also contradict one another. This is not restricted to the tense moments between the national and the transnational layers of citizenship in the contemporary European Union but likewise appears to affect the terms of recognition within national societies.

The complexity of these competing projects no doubt influences the processes of socialization of both children with and without immigrant backgrounds. The young people whose practices I studied in Berlin constructed their identifications using strategic elements from many topical areas, from the debates over East and West Germany and the issue of internal unity to the distinctions between Europe and the Orient, Christianity and Islam, urban Berlin and rural Turkey and so forth. Yet their self-positioning was not expressed through taking offensive positions *in favour* of one particular group allocation. Instead, the young "foreigners" defined themselves through various forms of "othering" (Abu-Lughod 1991) – fencing oneself off, stressing cultural but also individual differences which is not part of the image of clearly bounded groups. In the desire to define their place *within* German society they went beyond existing social boundaries and ultimately confirmed their identification with the more fluid and intersecting categorization of the "foreigners" than with either of the conventional nation-state informed concepts. By deploying this identity, one escapes the supposedly self-evident recourse to nationally defined groups or cultures and opts directly into the intersecting cleavages. As a mode of identification, this strategy refuses to meet the expectation that immigrants would have to acquire national identity first in order to qualify as members of a post-national community thereafter. Nearly all students whom I interviewed declared themselves to be both German and "foreign" to some degree, thus both subverting the existing classifications while simultaneously making use of them. The "third generation" of immigrants thus appeared as embedded agents of a much larger shift towards the transnationalization of identities and lifestyles than is foreseen in education programmes focused upon the construction of a post-national sense of citizenship.

According to the young people's accounts, their mixed attitude was not particularly welcome by their parents, many of whom felt the need to preserve some cultural distinctiveness. But it was no less problematic for many German teachers who felt responsible for promoting the values and standards of liberal democracy in Germany and had difficulties with their pupils' concept of maintaining their ties with the other home culture at the same time. For both teachers and parents, the notion of a genuine emotional – albeit situational – identification with selected aspects of both groups was beyond imagination. It questioned the certainties they had grown up with themselves. Identification with the national collectivity was traditionally supposed to link the political system of the state with its people as loyal custodians and sovereign of "their" nation-states. Blurring national identities, of course, challenges this basic premise; yet it also entails opportunities to overcome various forms of polarization resulting from the categorical concept of different nationalities with distinct cultures co-existing, at best, side by side.

The way in which the adolescents included in this research came to terms with the competing assessments and discourses deserves acknowledgement as a form of self-empowered agency. Creating a transnational space for either imagining or escaping collectivity is an important first step toward developing new codes of coexistence. Of course, while pacifying animosities based on national differences within the "foreigner" community, the core identification with attributed otherness does little to erase the persistent conceptual divide between indigenous Germans and the immigrant population. Ultimately, many of those who see themselves – in cultural terms – as foreigners in Germany are also foreigners in the formal judicial sense, which still qualifies the spectrum of possible claims and political rights. As long as the German majority does not make comparable efforts to transcend the conceptual limitations underlying this very imbalance in hegemonic discourse and societal practice, the offspring of the immigrant population will be left alone with their stock of knowledge. To put it the other way round, when continuing to exclude certain migrant citizens from being part of integrating Europe, and hence from equal recognition and entitlements in the polity, the indigenous majorities do not only extrapolate otherness over generations but likewise spoil chances of living with and possibly overcoming differences. After all, the fact that people develop their sense of belonging in the social routines of daily life means that the role of state institutions like schools is limited anyway to promoting a normative frame for personal (inter)agency.

References

Abu-Lughod, Lila 1991: Writing against culture. In: Fox, Richard (ed.): *Recapturing Anthropology: Working in the Present.* Santa Fé, New Mexico: School of American Research Press: 137–162.
Al-Azmeh, Aziz 1993: *Islams and Modernities.* London: Verso.
Anderson, Benedict 1991: *Imagined Communities: Reflections on the Origin and Spread of Nationalism.* London: Verso.
Appadurai, Arjun 1991: Global ethnoscapes: Notes and queries for a transnational anthropology. In: Fox, Richard (ed.): *Recapturing Anthropology: Working in the Present.* Santa Fé, New Mexico: School of American Research Press: 191–210.
Bade, Klaus 2000: *Europa in Bewegung.* München: Beck.
Barth, Fredrik 1994: Enduring and emerging issues in the analysis of ethnicity. In: Vermeulen, Hans & Cora Grovers (ed.): *The Anthropology of Ethnicity: Beyond 'Ethnic Groups and Boundaries.'* Amsterdam: Het Spinhuis: 11–32.
Basch, Linda, Nina Glick Schiller & Cristina Szanton Blanc 1994: *Nations Unbound: Transnational Projects, Postcolonial Predicaments and Deterritorialized Nation-States.* Amsterdam: Gordon and Breach.
Baumann, Gerd 1996: *Contesting Culture: Discourses of Identity in Multi-Ethnic London.* Cambridge: Cambridge University Press.
Baumann, Gerd 1999: *The Multicultural Riddle: Rethinking National, Ethnic, and Religious Identities.* New York & London: Routledge.
Baumann, Gerd 2004: Introduction: Nation-state, schools, and civil enculturation. In: Schiffauer, Werner et al. (eds.): *Civil Enculturation: Nation-State, School, and Ethnic Difference in Four European Countries.* Oxford & New York: Berghahn: 1–18.
Baumann, Gerd & Andre Gingrich (eds.) 2004: *Grammars of Identity and Alterity. A Structural Approach.* Oxford & New York: Berghahn.
Baumert, Jürgen et al. (eds.) 2001: *PIZA 2000.* Opladen: Leske & Budrich.
Bertilotti, Teresa, Sabine Mannitz & Yasemin Soysal 2004: Projections of identity in French and German History and Civics Textbooks. In: Schissler, Hanna & Yasemin Soysal (eds.): *The Nation, Europe, and the World: Textbooks and Curricula in Transition.* Oxford & New York: Berghahn: 25–63.
Billig, Michael 1995: *Banal Nationalism.* London: Sage.
Bommes, Michael 1996: Die Beobachtung von Kultur. Die Festschreibung von Ethnizität in der bundesdeutschen Migrationsforschung mit qualitativen Methoden. In: Klingemann, Carsten et al. (eds.): *Jahrbuch für Soziologiegeschichte.* Opladen: Leske & Budrich: 205–226
Bommes, Michael & Frank-Olaf Radtke 1996: Migration into big cities and small towns – An uneven process with limited need for multiculturalism. *Innovation* 9 (1): 75–86.

Boos-Nünning, Ursula, Manfred Hohmann & Hans H. Reich 1976: *Integration ausländischer Arbeitnehmer, Schulbildung ausländischer Kinder.* Bonn: Eichholz.

Bourdieu, Pierre & Jean-Claude Passeron 1977: *Reproduction in Education, Society and Culture.* London: Sage.

Brodengeier, Egbert et al. 1996: *Terra.* Erdkunde 9, Ausgabe für Berlin. Gotha & Stuttgart: Klett-Perthes.

Bründel, Heidrun & Klaus Hurrelmann 1995: Akkulturation und Minoritäten. Die psychosoziale Situation ausländischer Jugendlicher in Deutschland unter dem Gesichtspunkt des Belastungs-Bewältigungs-Paradigmas. In: Trommsdorf, Gisela (ed.): *Kindheit und Jugend in verschiedenen Kulturen. Entwicklung und Sozialization in kulturvergleichender Sicht.* Weinheim & München: Juventa: 293–313.

Bukow, Wolf-Dietrich 1996: *Feindbild Minderheit. Ethnisierung und ihre Ziele.* Opladen: Leske & Budrich.

Bukow, Wolf-Dietrich & Roberto Llaroya 1988: *Mitbürger aus der Fremde. Soziogenese ethnischer Minoritäten.* Opladen: Leske & Budrich.

Czock, Heidrun 1993: *Der Fall Ausländerpädagogik. Erziehungswissenschaftliche und bildungspolitische Codierung der Arbeitsmigration.* Frankfurt/Main: Cooperative Verlag.

Ebeling, Hans & Wolfgang Birkenfeld 1991: *Die Reise in die Vergangenheit, Vol. 6: Weltgeschichte seit 1945.* Braunschweig: Westermann.

Eriksen, Thomas Hylland 1993: *Ethnicity & Nationalism. Anthropological Perspectives.* London & Boulder, Col.: Pluto Press.

Finaldi, Daniela & Chris Shore 2000: *Crossing European Boundaries through Education: The European Schools and the Supersession of Nationalism.* Unpublished paper, presented at the 6th Biennial Conference of EASA in Krakow, July 2000.

Gellner, Ernest 1983: *Nations and Nationalism.* Oxford: Basil Blackwell.

Gemende, Marion, Wolfgang Schroer & Stephan Sting (eds.) 1999: *Zwischen den Kulturen. Pädagogische und sozialpädagogische Zugänge zur Interkulturalität.* München & Weinheim: Juventa.

Georgi, Viola B. 2003: *Entliehene Erinnerung. Geschichtsbilder junger Migranten in Deutschland.* Hamburg: Hamburger Edition.

Hall, Stuart 1990: Cultural identity and diaspora. In: Rutherford, Jonathan (ed.): *Identity, Community, Culture, Difference.* London: Lawrence & Wishart: 222–237.

Hamburger, Franz 1997: Kulturelle Produktivität durch komparative Kompetenz. In: Gogolin, Ingrid & Bernhard Nauck (eds.): *Folgen der Arbeitsmigration für Bildung und Erziehung.* Dokumentationsbroschüre der Fachtagung FABER vom 20.–22. März 1997 in Bonn: 151–161.

Hannerz, Ulf 1992: *Cultural Complexity. Studies in the Social Organization of Meaning.* New York: Columbia University Press.

Harker, Richard Kendall 1984: On reproduction, habitus and education. *British Journal of Sociology of Education* 5: 118–127.

Höhne, Thomas, Thomas Kunz & Frank-Olaf Radtke 2000: "Wir" und "sie." Bilder von Fremden im Schulbuch. *Forschung Frankfurt* 2: 16–25.

Höhne, Thomas, Thomas Kunz & Frank-Olaf Radtke 1999: Bilder von Fremden. Formen der Migrantendarstellung als der "anderen Kultur" in deutschen Schulbüchern von 1981–1997. *Frankfurter Beiträge zur Erziehungswissenschaft*, Forschungsberichte, Vol. 1. Frankfurt/Main: Universitätsdruck.

Hoffmann, Lutz 1996: Der Einfluss völkischer Integrationsvorstellungen auf die Identitätsentwürfe von Zuwanderern. In: Heitmeyer, Wilhelm & Rainer Dollase (eds.): *Die bedrängte Toleranz*. Frankfurt/Main: Suhrkamp: 241–260.

Hormel, Ulrike & Albert Scherr 2004: *Bildung für die Einwanderungsgesellschaft. Perspektiven der Auseinandersetzung mit struktureller, institutioneller und interaktioneller Diskriminierung*. Wiesbaden: VS Verlag für Sozialwissenschaften.

Jerusalem, Matthias 1992: Akkulturationsstress und psychosoziale Befindlichkeit jugendlicher Ausländer. *Report Psychologie*, February: 16–25.

Joppke, Christian 1998: *Challenge to the Nation-State: Immigration and Citizenship in Western Europe and the United States*. Oxford: Oxford University Press.

Kaschuba, Wolfgang 1995: Kulturalismus. Vom Verschwinden des Sozialen im gesellschaftlichen Diskurs. In: Kaschuba, Wolfgang (ed.): *Kulturen, Identitäten, Diskurse*. Berlin: Akademie-Verlag: 11–30.

Kastoryano, Riva 2002: *Negotiating Identities*. Princeton, NJ: Princeton University Press.

Koopmans, Ruud & Paul Statham 1999: Challenging the liberal nation-state? *American Journal of Sociology*, 105 (3): 652–697.

Krauter, Karl-Günther & Lothar Rother (eds.) 1988: *Terra*. Erdkunde, Berlin 8. Schuljahr. Stuttgart: Ernst Klett Schulbuchverlag.

Leclerq, Jean-Michel 1995: Die europäische Dimension im Geschichtsunterricht und in der staatsbürgerlichen Erziehung. In: Pingel, Falk (ed.): *Macht Europa Schule?* Frankfurt/Main: Diesterweg: 1–14.

Leggewie, Claus 1989: 'Multikulturelle Gesellschaft' oder: Die Naivität der Ausländerfreunde. *Arbeitshefte zur sozialistischen Theorie und Praxis* 84: 60–64.

Lütkes, Christina & Monika Klüter 1995: *Der Blick auf fremde Kulturen*. Münster & New York: Waxmann.

Mannitz, Sabine 2001: 'Why don't you just teach the Turks right from the start?!' Culturalization and conflict dynamics in teaching practices at a multi-ethnic comprehensive school in Berlin. *Zeitschrift für Ethnologie*, 126 (2): 293–312.

Mannitz, Sabine 2004: Pupils' negotiations of cultural difference: Identity management and discursive assimilation. In: Schiffauer, Werner et al. (eds.): *Civil Enculturation: Nation-State, School, and Ethnic Difference in Four European Countries*. Oxford & New York: Berghahn: 242–303.

Mannitz, Sabine & Werner Schiffauer 2004: Taxonomies of cultural difference: constructions of otherness. In: Schiffauer, Werner et al. (eds.): *Civil Enculturation: Nation-State, School, and Ethnic Difference in Four European Countries*. Oxford & New York: Berghahn: 60–87.

Mertens, Gabriele 1980: Türkische Mädchen und Frauen. Rollenkonflikte – nicht erst in der Bundesrepublik. *Westermanns Pädagogische Beiträge* 32 (2): 62–63.

Mills, Sara 1997: *Discourse*. London: Routledge.

Münch, Richard 1998: *Globale Dynamik, lokale Lebenswelten*. Frankfurt/Main: Suhrkamp.
Münz, Rainer, Wolfgang Seifert & Ralf Ulrich 1997: *Zuwanderung nach Deutschland*. Frankfurt/Main & New York: Campus.
Pingel, Falk 1995: Europa im Schulbuch – Einleitung. In: Pingel, Falk (ed.): *Macht Europa Schule?* Frankfurt/Main: Diesterweg: vii–xxv.
Pingel, Falk 2001: *National Perspectives on Europe*. Unpublished paper, presented at the conference "Teaching Europe" at the Robert Schuman Centre and European University Institute Florence, Department of History, 15–16 June 2001 in San Domenico, FI.
Prengel, Annedore 1993: *Pädagogik der Vielfalt: Verschiedenheit und Gleichberechtigung in interkultureller, feministischer und integrativer Pädagogik*. Opladen: Leske & Budrich.
Radtke, Frank-Olaf 1995: *Multikulturalismus: Regression in die Moderne?* Wien: Institut für Soziologie.
Radtke, Frank-Olaf 1996: *Multikulturell. Die Konstruktion eines sozialen Problems und ihre Folgen*. Opladen: Leske & Budrich.
Rahmenplan Erdkunde 7, 2001: Curriculum document of Senatsverwaltung für Schule, Berufsbildung und Sport, Berlin: Verwaltungsdruckerei.
Rahmenplan Weltkunde 9–10, 2001: Curriculum document of Senatsverwaltung für Schule, Berufsbildung und Sport, Berlin: Verwaltungsdruckerei.
Rogers, Alisdair & Steven Vertovec (eds.) 1995: *The Urban Context: Ethnicity, Social Networks, and Situational Analysis*. Oxford: Berg.
Rossteutscher, Sigrid 1997: Between normality and particularity – National identity in West Germany. *Nations and Nationalism*, 3 (4): 607–630.
Said, Edward 1978: *Orientalism*. London: Routledge & Kegan Paul.
Sassen, Saskia 1996: *Losing Control: The Decline of Sovereignty in an Age of Globalization*. New York: Columbia University Press.
Schepker, Renate & Angela Eberding 1996: Der Mädchenmythos im Spiegel der pädagogischen Diskussion. Ein empirisch fundierter Diskussionsbeitrag zu Stereotypien über Mädchen türkischer Herkunft. *Zeitschrift für Pädagogik* 42: 111–126.
Schiffauer, Werner et al. (eds.) 2004: *Civil Enculturation: Nation-State, School, and Ethnic Difference in Four European Countries*. Oxford & New York: Berghahn.
Schiffauer, Werner 1993: Die civil society und der Fremde. In: Balke, Friedrich et al. (eds.): *Schwierige Fremdheit. Über Integration und Ausgrenzung in Einwanderungsländern*. Frankfurt/Main: Fischer: 185–199. (English version available at: http://viadrina.euv-frankfurt-o.de/~anthro/veronli_s.html.)
Schiffauer, Werner 1991: *Die Migranten aus Subay. Türken in Deutschland: eine Ethnographie*. Stuttgart: Klett-Cotta.
Schrader, Achim, Bruno Nikles & Hartmut M. Griese 1979: *Die Zweite Generation: Sozialization und Akkulturation ausländischer Kinder in der Bundesrepublik*. Bodenheim: Athenäum.
Soysal, Yasemin 1994: *Limits of Citizenship: Migrants and Postnational Membership in Europe*. Chicago: Chicago University Press.

Stöber, Georg (ed.) 2001: *'Fremde Kulturen' im Geographieunterricht*. Hannover: Hahn.

Thränhardt, Dietrich 2000: Conflict, consensus, and policy outcomes: Immigration and integration in Germany and The Netherlands. In: Koopmans, Ruud & Paul Statham (eds.): *Challenging Immigration and Ethnic Relation Politics*. Oxford: Oxford University Press: 162–186.

Treibel, Annette 2003: *Migration in modernen Gesellschaften. Soziale Folgen von Einwanderung, Gastarbeit und Flucht*. Weinheim & München: Juventa.

Zur Zielsetzung und Praxis Politscher Bildung in der Berliner Schule, 2001: Curriculum document of Senatsverwaltung für Schule, Berufsbildung und Sport, Berlin: Verwaltungsdruckerei.

WHEN GERMAN CHILDREN COME "HOME."
EXPERIENCES OF (RE-)MIGRATION TO GERMANY – AND SOME REMARKS ABOUT THE "TCK"-ISSUE

Jacqueline Knörr

Foreword: On proceeding from experience to agency without knowing it (right away)

I was not sure whether to write this paper. It is based on randomly collected material I have gathered during the past 12 years while concentrating on other issues. It also draws a link to my M.A. thesis, which was published 15 years ago.[1] It is based on material I gathered in personal encounters and conversations, on notes, which I penned down – piling them in a tray labelled "Misc." – and on recollections of conversations stored only in my memory.

In my M.A. thesis I dealt with the upbringing of mainly German and Swiss children and youths in Ghana and with the experiences they made upon their "return" to Germany and Switzerland. I spent many years of my childhood in Ghana myself and the description and analysis of my own experience is part of my M.A. thesis. After that, I decided not to ever include any of that "personal stuff" in academic writing again. Not because this had been an awkward experience (although it was, to some extent), but somehow, I felt, that now that I had restored and analyzed my own past and that of my (re-)migrant peers anthropologically, I could proceed to becoming a "real," a more "professional" anthropologist and – as such – could do what "real" and "professional" anthropologists should do, namely study and explore the "real" others' existence. I knew about the dialectics of "self" and "other" then, and in anthropological endeavours and writing, it seemed, the "self" – situated in a relativistic frame of mind – should serve the better understanding of the "other." Apart from that, whenever I had told people I studied anthropology *and* had lived in Ghana for many years as a child and young girl, I was greeted with a reaction of something like "Oh, that's why you study anthropology." I was sick of it.

For the past 15 years – since finishing my M.A. thesis – I have primarily been studying identity matters related to processes of creolization, migration, poli-

---

1 Knörr 1990. Cf. Lenzin (2000), who studied the social and historical background and context of the Swiss community in Ghana. His study includes an evaluation and analysis of some of the parts of Knörr's study.

ticization, and interethnic contact. The people I study mostly live in towns, they are settlers, migrants, members of creole societies and diaspora groups. They are culturally heterogeneous, live in multiethnic environments and are involved in interethnic relations. They live in West Africa (in Sierra Leone and other countries of the Upper Guinea Coast) and in Indonesia (Java).

Several years ago, I was invited by the late Professor Albert Wirz to present a paper at the Institute for African Studies at the Humboldt University in Berlin. It was about Freetown, about my Ph.D. thesis, which had then just been published.[2] In the discussion that followed, someone asked me why I had chosen this topic after having written an M.A. thesis about German and Swiss children in Ghana. I said something about new theoretical interests, open research questions and that anthropology needed to deal with contemporary issues and the like, and that all this had nothing to do with my M.A. thesis. Professor Wirz frowned, and asked me, what had gotten me interested in that part of the world, in creole societies, and processes of creolization. (He had been quite positive about my M.A. thesis and I had been quite flattered when he considered it a good example of how personal experiences could be analyzed for the development of anthropological theory. He was not so impressed now, obviously.) I shrugged my shoulders and said something like: "Well, of course, originally there are always personal reasons for choosing specific themes and approaches as well as research regions, but..." He then made me summarize (almost) all of them. I ended up with the impression I was studying creole societies because I was somehow a creole myself. Now, I do not think I am, but I will never claim again that my interests in specific matters and regions are not (still) also related to my childhood and youth experience.

By "othering" myself in the process of writing my M.A. thesis – in putting my own childhood and youth experience within a comparative framework of analysis – I had put myself in a position that enabled me to examine and analyze anthropologically a topic that included my personal experience. By examining and analyzing a topic that included my personal experience, the process of "othering" the latter was enhanced and put in (a comparative) perspective. Whereas this did not free me of my childhood and youth – you are never free of that anyway – and whereas I had not proceeded from being a "not so real" to being a "real" anthropologist – I had proceeded from experience to agency by choosing to deal with my own childhood and youth experiences and with those of others "like myself" by means of anthropological research and writing – without being fully aware of it. So I might just as well write another contribution about something that is simply more directly related to personal experience than most other topics I deal with.

---

2   Knörr 1995.

Who and what this paper is (not) about

In this paper I will highlight some aspects concerning the experiences of German children and youths coming to live in Germany after having spent many years or almost their whole lives in Africa. I will deal with their reception by their new social environment in Germany and with their perception of and reaction to it. I will focus on white children because their experience is a special case that differs considerably from that of children with a mixed African-German background.

I deal with an issue that is hardly ever mentioned in migration studies, namely children of a Western – in my case German – background, who are brought up in a non-Western environment before "returning" to a "home," which in many cases has never been or is no longer home to them. These children are usually not considered (re-)migrants by their German teachers, peers, and relatives.[3] They are considered "homecomers" – and they are expected to behave accordingly.[4] I will come back to that.

There are several publications on what has for some time now been labelled "TCK" and "ATCK" – "Third Culture Kids" and "Adult Third Culture Kids." It was John and Ruth Useem who coined the term in the 1950s when they studied Americans living and working in India.[5] They defined the home culture of the parents as the first culture and the host culture where the expatriate family lived as the second culture. The "Third Culture" to them was the culture of the expatriate community, which they understood as a "culture between cultures" integrating cultural features of home and host societies. More recently the definition was broadened to include all children who move into another society with their parents. With regard to cultural identity, a TCK is defined as a person "who has spent a significant part of his or her developmental years outside the parents' culture. The TCK builds relationships to all of the cultures, while not having full ownership of any. Although elements from each culture are assimilated into the TCK's life experience, the sense of belonging is in relationship to others of similar background."[6]

---

3 Some of the more recent works on returning migration include: Allen 1994; Arowolo 2000; Firat 1991; Hammond 2004; Martin 2005; Paraschou 2001; Wolbert 1995. There are also studies on (and accounts of) Namibian children and youths who were brought up in the German Democratic Republic and returned to Namibia later on. They give an impression of childhood and youth re-migration "the other way round" – from Germany to Africa; see Engombe 2004; Kenna 1999.
4 Wolbert (1995) describes similar experiences of Turkish children and youths re-migrating to Turkey after having spent many years in Germany. Cf. Stenzel, Homfeld & Fenner 1989.
5 Useem & Useem 1955; 1993.
6 Pollock & van Reken 2004: 19. The authors adopt this definition from "The TCK Profile" seminar material, Interaction, Inc., 1989: 1. See also: http://www.tckworld.com/tckdefine.html. This website is a forum for TCKs.

This broadening of the term – while being inclusive, not making a difference between a Sierra Leonean refugee in the United States and an American son of an ambassador somewhere in Africa – is in danger of covering up some of the specific concepts and ideologies connected to the TCK approach. It stresses that the term TCK is not restricted to Western children – particularly not to Western children brought up in the so-called Third World – but it is nevertheless mostly connected to the latter and not to immigrant children in the USA or Germany. Most of the literature dealing with the topic – scientifically and/or (auto)biographically – is written by Western (mostly American) authors who deal with experiences of Western children living abroad and with the challenges they meet upon repatriation. Some of their most common experiences and emotional problems have been described and analyzed in Pollock's and van Reken's book on "Third Culture Kids," which also deals mainly with Western expatriate children.[7] Whereas it is stressed in current writing that a Turkish child growing up in Germany is a TCK as well, the simple fact that authors feel they need to point this out shows that a distinction is usually made, even if it is made implicitly. Turkish – and other – immigrant children are generally not perceived or treated as TCKs in academic research and writing. They are usually not studied with regard to the "Third Culture" they are producing, but with regard to their being "caught between different cultures," their integration problems, problems in learning the host country's language or with regard to the problems they are causing for their host society. To put it very simply, whereas the upper class of young, mostly Western migrants to – mainly – Third World countries are likely to be considered "Third Culture Kids," producing creatively a culture for themselves, the lower classes of young migrants – those from Third World or poorer countries migrating or fleeing to mostly Western countries – are likely to be considered immigrants with a cultural background, which does not fit their new environment and thus produce problems for themselves and their host society. There is an implicit – and qualifying – distinction made between TCKs on the one hand and other young (im)migrants on the other. With regard to the former, (appropriate) cultural creativity is emphasized; with regard to the latter (inappropriate) cultural conservatism. Academic approaches thereby largely and mostly implicitly reflect the – usually not so implicit – qualifying distinctions made in society at large.

With regard to the production of "Third Culture," however, these distinctions seem inadequate in real social life. Most of those, who are "classical" TCKs – Western expatriate children and youths, for whom the term TCK was invented in the first place – often do not produce much of a culture of their own located somewhere "in between" home and host society.[8] Many of them,

---

7   Pollock & van Reken 2004 (English edition); Pollock, van Reken & Pflüger 2003 (German edition). Other contribution on this group of migrants include: Roth 2001; Smith 1996; Storti 2001.
8   There are, of course, also many children who mix with the local population, especially children of missionaries and of parents who work in development pro-

I claim, are brought up largely within the boundaries of an expatriate culture, which is often socially and culturally isolated from its local environment, and which does not integrate much or any of the local culture. On the contrary, more often than not, expatriate communities – especially the Western ones – screen themselves off from local influences. Thus, in real life, a German child in Africa may survive quite well within the boundaries of a German or Western expatriate world, whereas a Turkish child in Germany is forced to deal with both its parents' Turkish and its host country's German culture in order to manage life in Germany. The definition of the TCK's "Third Culture" as a blend of one's parents' home and of one's host country's culture therefore does not apply to many contemporary expatriate children living in expatriate environments. Their social lives and cultural worlds, especially if located in places whose culture is experienced as very different from one's own, are rarely made up of such home-and-host composites. Many children of expatriates do not even experience much local culture because they largely share their parents' social lives and cultural worlds. These are, in many cases, expatriate forms of one's own home culture that have been adapted to the local social, cultural, and physical environment – a process, which under the condition of temporary – and sometimes even long term – stays abroad, rarely includes much incorporation of the culture prevalent in one's host culture, even less so, when the latter is not just experienced merely as different but as inferior as well. Thus, in many cases, expatriate worlds are not worlds that integrate fruitfully and creatively one's own and one's host culture; they remain apart from the latter while being far away from the former. The "Third Culture" that such TCKs produce – at least while abroad – is therefore in many cases nothing more than a children's and youths' version of the adults' (parents') expatriate culture containing little local input.

However, expatriate cultures may very well be unique for different reasons, even if they do not involve much mixing with the local culture. An expatriate culture may be unique in its ways of avoiding contact with the host country's culture or in its ways of avoiding the incorporation of the latter. It may be unique in its finding ways to maintain as much of one's own culture of origin while living abroad. It may be unique in its preservation of a colonial lifestyle unthinkable back home. It may indeed be unique in interconnecting and mixing different expatriate communities' cultures and ways of life, thereby producing a "Third Culture," but not one which involves home and host culture; it is this former sort of mixing which may often be confused with a mixing of the latter sort.

Despite these observations – and reservations with regard to the definition of "Third Culture" in the context of expatriate childrens' lives – I do believe and know from my own experience that expatriate culture, expatriates' social lives and lifestyles may indeed be very different from those of their compatri-

---

jects in locations far away from where the majority of contemporary expatriates live.

ots "back home." These expatriate worlds in many cases are the only ones they are familiar with, the only ones they consider home. Children of expatriates, even if they have not experienced much of the local culture of their host country, have a different cultural and social identity than those who they will meet upon repatriation in their parents' home countries, which in many cases is not home to them.

Whereas I agree that the term "Third Culture Kids" is not to be reserved for Western expatriates alone, I think one should not simply hide the, mostly implicit, ideologies of difference that often occur in its usage. Many children for whom the term "Third Culture Kids" was originally coined – children who are brought up in expatriate communities – are often not TCKs in the sense of creating an identity based on both home and host culture,[9] whereas others, who are still only rarely considered TCKs – like Turkish children in Germany and Sierra Leonean refugee children in the United States – usually are. "Third Cultures" may be different in content and structure and they may or may not be produced by (re-)migrant children of all sorts. Such differences, however, should not be ignored; neither should the differences in the experiences and treatment of (re-)migrant or repatriating children depending on social status and origin, differences, which affect the process of integration as well as the production of "Third Culture."

There are certainly similarities among TCKs all over the world – probably as a result of the similarities and interconnectedness of (many) expatriate communities and of sharing the experience of being brought up "elsewhere." But there are also differences between expatriate communities as such and their treatment of their child members in particular as well as differences between different "home" countries with regard to their treatment of repatriating children and youths.

I will focus on the experiences and agencies of the German species in this paper, on children and youths who have spent large parts of their lives in Africa before (re-)migrating to Germany.

Although Germany as an export country also "exports" a lot of manpower and "experts" to foreign countries, who become expatriates abroad and repatriates upon their return, and despite the fact that many German children are therefore brought up elsewhere before (re-)migrating to Germany, there is hardly any research on that topic and hardly any awareness of this phenomenon, neither in public nor in academia.

Who are the people whose information this papers is based on?
They are a rather mixed crowd. Since publishing my M.A. thesis I on occasion met some of the people I had interviewed back in the late 1980s in the framework of my fieldwork. We talked about their experiences since we met last,

---

9 They might be "Today's Colonial Kids" – which is a rather unique way of life and experience as well.

about changes that had occurred in their lives and attitudes. Some of the people I interviewed in Ghana and Germany as children and youths in the late 1980s were adults when we met and talked again. Others, who I interviewed about their (past) experience of having been brought up in Ghana and integrating in Germany were already young adults then and somewhat less young adults when we encountered each other later on.

Apart from those I already knew, I met others who had come from different African countries to live in Germany at different times in the past. There were children, youths, and adults among them.

Thus, the time span the experience of (re-)migration in childhood and youth relates to is around 30 years (1973–2003), the people were between seven and 50 years at the time of the interviews/conversations. They had experienced (re-)migration between a few months and 30 years ago. Thus, it is "new" and "old" experiences that I am dealing with. With regard to issues that are strongly influenced by the receiving social environment in Germany, the analysis will be able to show some of the changes that have occurred in Germany during the past 30 years – and point out, where continuities seem to dominate in the reception of (re-)migrant German children and youths. In some of the cases I can also point out some of the developments related to growing up and getting older.

The material gathered will be presented and analyzed in the form of "highlights." These highlights are in no way intended to give a complete picture encompassing all that can be experienced in the process of (re-)integration in Germany. They are meant to shed light on some of the experiences shared by many and on some of the major social dynamics involved in the process of (re-)integration in Germany and in the interaction of experience and agency.

Where is home and why?

As mentioned above, German children moving to Germany after having spent many years in Africa are usually not considered (re-)migrants but homecomers. Thus, their families, peers, and teachers do not expect them to have a lot of problems adjusting to their German environment. They are considered to be returning to their "real" home and in many cases they are supposed to feel to be "home at last." Frank,[10] who is 44 today and returned to Germany 25 years ago, said: "The first day I attended school in Germany, my teacher asked me 'how does it feel to be back home after so many years in Africa?' But I did not really understand. I felt like being in a strange country and I felt that I had left my home behind."

---

10 For the sake of confidentiality all names have been changed and specific African countries mentioned in the conversations/interviews have been "translated" to "Africa."

To feel at home is not something that comes with being where one's ethnic or national roots are according to one's parents' descent. It is something that comes with personal and emotional attachment. German "homecomers" have often had little opportunity to develop such an attachment before they are "repatriated" into what in many cases is only their parents', but not their own home country. Instead, they leave what they consider home behind. They leave behind what they feel attached to – their friends, their school, the place they used to live – and in many cases their parents, brothers, sisters, cats, and dogs. Their social environment changes as well as their way of life – and at the same time they are expected to feel at home "at last." Christina, 28 in 1995, after 12 years of living in Germany, said:

When I came to Germany to live with my uncle and aunt, it was okay for them that I missed my parents and my sister. They could understand that. But they didn't understand that I missed Africa. They thought I should be glad to be back in the civilized world or something like that. But I didn't like this kind of civilization. I wanted my home back where I felt free to do the things I liked.

In many cases children "coming home" only know Germany from summer vacations. Germany thus is a more or less strange place and not home at all. Judy (12) who had just returned to Germany at the time of our conversation felt that "[...] everything is different here and I feel homesick a lot. I miss my friends and my school and our garden. And I hate this weather... it's all so grey and depressing here." Conny, who is now 44, showed me an entry in her diary at the age of 15, several months after she had come to live with relatives in Germany. All across two pages, written in red capital letters, it said: "I want to go home!!! I want to go home!!! That's all I want, I just want to go home!!!" I asked her what it was that she had missed so much then and whether it was mainly her family, who had stayed behind. She replied: "I missed my parents, too, but most of all I missed... I don't know, I missed my home. Everything. I felt lost in Germany. Like a stranger. And there was nobody to relate to, who shared my experience, my attachment to Africa. Nobody."

This seems to be the worse part in many cases. Whereas "real" migrants in most cases have other "real" migrants with whom they can share their experience, who know the place back home and who go through similar experiences and feelings in their host country, German children and youths – especially 30 years ago – hardly met anyone like that. There were no other children and young people around at one's school who knew what they were talking about when talking about "home." Germans who grew up in Africa are still few and it is unlikely they will meet at the same school somewhere in Germany. Raul, who was 12 when I talked to him in 1996, after he had been living in a small Bavarian village for a year, said: "The other children think it is interesting to have someone like me around, someone from Africa. But of course they asked all sorts of silly questions like 'Are they really all black there?' or 'Did you live in a little straw hut?', 'Did you eat snakes?' Lots of things like that. When

I told them we lived in a big house, they could hardly believe it. I thought they were stupid."

Thus, children and especially youths – who often come to Germany as teenagers, at an age which is problematic anyway – tend to feel lonely and alone in Germany. They are expected to feel at home – at least to find it easy to integrate and adapt. They look the same as everyone else, they speak the same language, but they often have no one who shares their experience, no one who could make them feel at home "at home."

Of course there are other – and opposite – cases as well. Especially children who came to Africa at a later stage in their childhood and only stayed there for a short period of time, may feel the other way round – to them Africa sometimes remained the strange place, the place they did not feel at home. These children are, in fact, the real re-migrants. They are coming back home, feeling relieved – like Giselher, who was 11 when his family took him along to Africa and 13 when they all returned to Germany: "Gosh, I was so happy to be back here," he told me, "I hated it there. And I do not think, I will ever want to return."

It largely depends on the social environment, whether children and youths manage to feel at least a little bit at home upon their "return" to Germany. It is usually easier for those who come to Germany with their parents – and all the more so for those who have siblings to share their experiences with. It seems hardest – in most cases – for those coming back on their own, for those who move to small towns, who live in conservative settings where people are less familiar with dealing with difference and with people who have not shared their social and cultural world.

Some children, especially those whose families stay behind in Africa, often experience Africa as their first and "real" home, while Germany may become something like a second home, the place, where they go to school. After several years – with more and closer contacts in Germany, and with time – this might change and Germany might very well become their first, Africa their second home.

Many children leave Africa once and for all when their parents decide to leave and take their children along. While leaving Africa might also cause adults and parents some heartache after living there for many years, the situation for children is different, especially for those who have lived there for large parts or all of their lives. Whether their life happened to be integrated into the local context or isolated from it – it is often the only life they know and which they are familiar with. Doris, 13, who came to Germany to live with her grandmother six months ago, told me: "It is not because I think Germany is terrible. But everything is different here. It doesn't fit me. I'm different. It's because I don't feel I belong here. I belong to Africa. That's where my heart is, and home is where the heart is, they say. My heart longs for Africa all the time, and it hurts a lot." Doris got so homesick some months later, that, apart from the emotional "heartache" she developed physical disorders to a point where she was virtually unable to move because of "pain in my heart" at the age of 13.

On being a white child in Africa and how this affects re-migration

Although I will be concentrating on the experience of re-migration and (re-) integration in Germany there are some particularities concerning the social life of German (and other Western) expatriates in Africa that have a major impact on the process of integration in Germany and need to be addressed to understand what will follow.

Children and youths coming to Germany from Africa have experienced social lives and forms of sociability that differ from those in Germany. This is true especially for those who lived in Africa some 20 or more years ago. The "intra-ethnic" cohesion among Germans (and other groups of expatriates) was rather close then since there were not many of them and they tended to stay for longer periods of time than today.[11] In many African countries there was no television, much less video available, so people socialized by visiting each other in their leisure time, by spending weekends together etc. There was no internet in those days either, which would allow closer contact with "back home."[12] Apart from that, most German expatriates had little close personal contacts to Africans. But even today, whites largely stay among themselves with a few exceptions, consisting mainly of African spouses. Thus, most German children and youths in Africa experience a pronounced gap between blacks and whites, between the local population and themselves, that is.

Being white in Sub-Saharan Africa usually goes along with being part of the upper class in economic terms. Whereas there might be considerable variation in the income structure of whites in Africa, compared to the overwhelming part of the local population, most of them were and are rich. As well, being white – from the point of view of most whites, but many Africans as well – is associated with being more advanced, civilized, and educated than the local African population.

Despite internal hierarchies even within small expatriate communities, its members often cannot afford to cultivate too much of an internal bias with regard to class and income since they are too few. Thus, "otherness" is attrib-

---

11 This is true for all Sub-Saharan countries where my informants lived. Things are different in South Africa and Namibia and – to some extent – Zimbabwe, but none of my informants had lived there.
12 Many Germans who lived in Africa then and still live there today consider the introduction of videos and the internet the worst that could happen to the expatriate community because social life suffered immensely because "newcomers don't integrate [into the local expatriate community] but just sit at home and watch a video or sit in front of their computer to chat with their family or friends in Germany through the internet."

uted first and foremost to the local Africans with varying degrees of "otherness" in between them and one's own group – which correlate with shades of colours as well as with social and cultural differences. The message the majority of white children growing up in "black" Africa get is that being white goes along with being rich and superior. While blacks may also (be)come rich and advance economically for different reasons, being rich appears to be an innate and natural feature of being white, a feature of social class, which in most cases goes along with a feeling of cultural superiority. Whereas white parents in most cases have experienced that being white does not have such implications everywhere, many white children lack this experience altogether – and many of their parents prefer forgetting it while in Africa.

Coming to Germany, being white suddenly does not mean anything at all. Additionally, most children and youths experience a social decline when coming to Germany – not because their parents suddenly become poor but because they suddenly shift from being members of a small upper class in Africa to being members of a large middle class in Germany. To some children and youths this is a rather traumatic experience, to others it is at least surprising. Janet, aged 24 now, and Max, 25, told me about the experiences they had after their arrival in Germany.

I once saw a beggar in the street. A young African man who was just walking by stopped to put some money into the old man's hat, which was lying in front of him. I could not believe my eyes. A black man giving money to a white beggar! I felt this could not be true (Janet, 13 then).[13]

When I came to Germany nine years ago, I had an African boy in my class. He was from Guinea, really black. I went to a school in Africa where they were mostly whites, except some children with African mothers and then there were some Africans, too, but we didn't have much contact. The Africans I had contacts with most were servants. Now, this boy was a really bright student and he was also very nice. That really made me think. In a way I was surprised. We became good friends after a while. Now, don't you think it's funny that the first time I made friends with an African was after I had come to Germany? After having lived in Africa most of my childhood? (Max, 16 then).

When I myself went to Abidjan from Accra as a young girl, we went to a restaurant, where white waiters were serving African customers. I was truly puzzled since I had never seen anything like that before.

For children and youths who are brought up in families with pronounced racist attitudes and condescending ways of behaviour towards Africans, it often seems quite natural to give orders to African "boys," nannies, drivers, gardeners, and watchmen at an early stage in life. Upon their return to Germany, they often experience that their behaviour toward "the locals" is perceived as

---

13 Many Africans coming to Germany have similar feelings and thoughts when seeing beggars in Germany for the first time – and realizing that Africans are not always and everywhere poorer than Europeans.

inadequate, to say the least. Jonathan, now 34, told me what happened to him shortly after he had come to Germany at the age of 16.

> When I came to Germany, I was taking a ride on a moped which belonged to someone I had met. I was used to driving a car before so I didn't think about it. I was stopped by the police. When the policeman asked me for my licence and said something about legal consequences, I took out five Marks and handed the money to him casually, saying something like 'this should be enough, ey?' Of course, he did not take it and asked me, whether I also wanted to be fined for trying to bribe the police. I was puzzled and said something like: 'You don't want money, ey? The police in Africa are not as fussy." And he said: 'Young man, this is not Africa, this is Germany.'

It is not surprising that children and youths behave in this way if that is what they have learned to be adequate behaviour. Of course, there are many expatriate children who are brought up in less racist environments and whose parents do not act like colonialists. Children, whose parents do not cultivate racist attitudes, who socialize with Africans, who do not "protect" their children from local influence, may in fact experience Germans "at home" as racist and xenophobic. Lukas, 29, who was raised as a son of missionary parents, explained: "I was always among both white and black children. This seemed normal to me. In Germany many of my new friends thought of this as strange. They hardly communicated with their Turkish peers at school, for instance, whereas for me, this was perfectly natural. In fact, I enjoyed their company more because at least they knew what it was like to be different from the rest."

The experience of "being superior by nature" can also have negative effects when children start attending school in Germany. First of all, it is usually difficult anyhow to change schools and it is more so when everything else changes as well. Secondly, in many cases the schools the children attended in Africa do not meet the standards of schools in Germany. Schools in Africa are often modelled on different educational systems than the German one (British or French in most cases).[14] Thirdly, for many children it is the first time they experience something like "serious competition" and serious stress. This may be the case simply because it is difficult to catch up, but also that many (former) expatriate children are not used to having to do much for school, either because the standards were a lot lower and/or because "muddling through somehow" was common practice at the schools they attended. Tina, 12, who had attended school in Germany for only four months at the time of our conversation three years ago, said: "Oh God, school is so much more difficult here. It was so much easier before and you could talk to the teachers if you didn't understand something and then they would explain it to you again until you would understand and pass somehow. But here it's just take it or leave it, pass or fail, nobody cares."

---

14 German schools can only be attended where they exist, like in Nigeria, where the German community is quite large.

In some cases, schools and classes attended by expatriates in Africa were small; students know each other well and spend their time at school as well as most of their leisure time together. Teachers were often part of the expatriate community and if it is a small one, letting a child fail was a much more personal matter than in a setting where teachers are not parents' friends at the same time. The latter, of course, can also be the case in a small village in Germany. But the "way out" – for teachers, parents, and students – may have been even more limited in a small expatriate community. In many such communities, inter-personal relations were close and loyalty within them was expected to be high. Thus, in many cases, competition is also limited because "they would never not let us pass in the end." I am not saying all expatriate children were – and even less are – situated in school environments of that sort. Neither am I saying that such environments are necessarily bad, but in Germany things are different.

As white expatriates in Africa, even children who perform weakly at school often do not experience this to be a threat to their future because of their "naturally" superior status as whites and as members of the upper class. Sarah, 24 at the time of the interview, told me about her attitude when she came to Germany eight years ago: "In Africa, I did not care so much about the marks I got. It seemed to me that I would always be rich enough to live a comfortable life. I was white after all. But then in Germany I realized that not performing well at school may lead to a life in misery. And after a while I started working harder in order to get better marks."

Being white is normal in Germany – and competition is stronger. Most children returning from Africa are no longer members of the upper class in Germany. For many, it is the first time they experience not being "naturally" superior to most others around them. And to many this experience is a highly frustrating one. Kevin said, at the age of 17, after having come to Germany six months ago: "Everything is much smaller, our house, our garden, my room. And my freedom to move about." In fact, the potential mobility in Germany is usually larger, but would involve taking a bus. For children and youths who are used to being driven around or to drive themselves, this may very well feel like a limitation of their personal freedom. Kevin: "I could drive in Africa, why should I take a bus here." Household chores, unheard of before, may also lead to frustration. Kevin: "We had a boy to do these things before, and here I am expected to make up my room myself. I hate it, it's boring." Many children and youths who have been brought up "colonial style" think of the latter as the only style appropriate (to them). They feel de-privileged, punished, or humiliated by having to do such "boring" duties themselves.

Soon after Janet had come to Germany, she was invited to some of her classmates' homes. She experienced most of them as "poor, because they lived in flats. I knew that most people in Germany live in flats, but in a way I thought that most people in Germany are... well, not as poor as most people in Africa were poor... but a little bit poor." Most children know from vacations in Germany that housing conditions for most people are not as spacious as they are in Africa – it is just that they do not see themselves as or expect to be one of "most people" when coming to Germany. They see themselves and expect to be superior to the majority of the "locals" – to those in Germany now as to those in Africa before.

On the other hand, there are also many expatriate children who are highly flexible and adaptable – both in attitudes and behaviour – due to the many different conditions of life they have already experienced at an early age. Like Laura, 13, who said, a few months after moving to Germany in 1997:

Well, I knew things were to be changing again. We had always moved every two or three years, so I was used to moving and to things being different everywhere. In Africa white people were usually rich and we had a big house. In Brazil a lot of white people are poor and many are just so la la... and we had a nice place, but not so big. In Germany now, we have a nice place too. But not like in Africa. I don't mind that. But the weather, I really hate the weather.

There are also many children who had lived in Germany long enough before moving to Africa to remember more clearly that being white does not automatically correlate with being rich and superior. They usually have a more realistic image of life in Germany and what they are returning to.

How to continue feeling naturally superior "at home" – "Expatriate Germans are superior to Germans here"

How do you manage to continue feeling superior as a white person when suddenly everyone else is white too? One option is to turn to "culture" as a source of (superior) identification. You forget about being white and take on a different identity based on "being" or "having been an expatriate," or, more fashionably, on being a "Third Culture Kid" and – later on – an "Adult Third Culture Kid."

Strategies as such, in many cases, remain the same in Germany as in Africa. In Africa it was "the Africans" – the locals that is – who were looked down upon, who were considered and treated as different and – more often than not – as inferior. In Germany it is the locals as well, who are looked down upon, and who are considered and treated as inferior. An adult (and parent) "returnee" told me that there is "an enormous difference between those Germans, who have never lived anywhere else in the world, and us. They may go somewhere on holiday but that's not the same. They don't know what life in Africa – or elsewhere – is really like. They just know their way of life in Germany. Not like us who have lived abroad, who have seen the world."

It is often the parents who foster such attitudes in their children as well, especially when they try to comfort them when having problems integrating in Germany, when feeling lonely and rejected – at school and elsewhere. And parents often suffer as well when being "downgraded" to the middle class upon their return to Germany. Although many will have prospered economically – having earned well and saved while in Africa – fewer of them will manage to retain their membership in the upper class upon return. They often transform their superiority based on race and class to a superiority based on having lived abroad, on having been an *Auslandsdeutscher* (literally: a German from abroad). Even on vacations in Germany, while still living in Africa, many such *Auslandsdeutsche* – both adults and children alike – brag about their servants, houses, positions etc. in Africa. They thereby also try to maintain at least some sort of superiority to all those whites in Germany "who have never lived abroad." Despite the different environments, the cultivation of superiority, in both cases, is based on "being different from" – and "being better than" – the local population.

Feeling different

The (re-)migrant children under study here look the same and (usually) speak the same language as their counterparts in Germany. The repatriated children, however, are different because 1) they have no or only limited experience of life in Germany and 2) because they have lived in Africa for a long time and therefore have been exposed to social lives and lifestyles different from German ones in Germany. They have been influenced – to varying degrees – by African and/or by expatriate culture.

With regard to "sameness versus difference" most children and youths I have talked to experience themselves as being different from the children they encounter in Germany, all the more so, the greater the part of their childhood and youth spent in Africa.

For one, they often experience the lives of children in Germany – and of youths in particular – as "not as free as in Africa." They feel they had more liberties in Africa than in Germany – which in many cases they have indeed had due to their status and due to less rigid rules related to age. As well, weather can make a real difference in "feeling free" and less restricted in one's activities, especially to children and youths. One popular and common theme is the "party issue." Ask a 14-year old German boy or girl who has lived in Africa before about the things they miss most "about Africa" and a large percentage of them will tell you it is "the parties we had." It seems that due to a somewhat restricted field of potential other activities – or to a lack of interest in such – partying is a major sport at an early age among expatriate youths. One such boy explained to me:

You know you don't have neighbours the way you do here [Germany]. Seeing your friends means driving there. And of course, our parents had to drive us – or our drivers – unless you were 16 and could drive yourself. And there isn't much else to do at night, anyway. So usually we had a party every Friday. And, of course, our parents left the house or stayed upstairs then. Now, here, I can't believe it. I mean, we are 14 – 14! – and parents tell their children they have to be home at 10 or 11. They actually sit there with their children at the party – they hang around! There is no hiding.

We used to have boyfriends and girlfriends and I tell you, we didn't just kiss! But here, I mean, at 14, they are like children! We were really different, much more mature.

There are other differences as well. Whereas many children have been more or less isolated from their African environment in terms of social contacts, they have usually experienced a more international life than in Germany. They often had friends from all over the world. Expatriate culture might be isolated from its local environment, but internally it may be very varied with regard to nationalities, social and cultural backgrounds. In Germany, many children therefore find life rather "German." Uta, 15, said to me recently: "It's boring sometimes. All these Germans. In Africa I had friends from everywhere. From Italy, England, America... but here, only Germans." And Frank, 13, complained:

In Africa my friends were more interesting because they came from all parts of the world. And we had more fun because everybody was more open-minded. And you know, my friends' fathers were diplomats and... well, they had good professions, they came from good families. It's more mixed here when it comes to that... I mean, in my class there are children whose fathers are politicians and children whose fathers are just simple workers... it wasn't like that in Africa. And it was international... more international and... well, more people with better professions.

Many children and youths experience themselves as different because they have mixed more with children from around the world and because they are used to a different group of people. Whereas they often only had little social contact with their local environment, they were often exposed to different lifestyles of different (other) expatriate individuals and communities. In Germany, most children do not share that experience. Being exposed to different lifestyles in childhood – even if the local African lifestyle remains excluded – may very well result in being more open towards other cultures than one's own – even if such experiences are made within the boundaries of expatriate communities. Many expatriates – children as well as adults – may not get to know much about Africa, they may not socialize much with Africans while living in Africa – but they may very well get to know Italians, French, British, Americans etc. Expatriate environments may be rather exclusively expatriate, but they may nevertheless be rather international. Many expatriates therefore live a very international life indeed and get to know a lot about all sorts of different cultures existing outside of Africa.

There are also German children in Africa who live a more locally integrated life. They associate mainly with members of the local community, go to local schools etc. They will incorporate more African "ways," they will know a lot more about Africans and African life – but all this does not usually make them feel "more different" or "more disconcerted" in Germany than those children who have lived a less African lifestyle. It seems, living in an expatriate environment in Africa is experienced as being just as different from living in Germany as living in an African environment – not with regard to the "cultural stuff" but with regard to way of life, to the "feel" of life. Thus, "Germanizing" Germans in Africa might have a (more or less) German Christmas tree for Christmas, they might sing German Christmas songs and eat a goose. All this, nevertheless, feels completely different from celebrating Christmas in Germany. It is differently different than the difference experienced when joining an African Christmas celebration, but it does not necessarily feel less different in retrospect. Petra told me some years ago about her first Christmas in Germany at the age of 14: "I know, we had a German Christmas tree and all that – and we more or less did the same things that we do here now, but it was still all different there, it all feels completely different now. It is just not the same, no way." And a young woman told me about her family's experience in a rather remote African environment: "We used to celebrate Christmas with our African neighbours and friends. And with some of our German colleagues who lived just a few miles away. We joined the Africans in their celebration of Christmas. It was all very different from the German way. And now that we are back in Germany, our own ways of celebrating Christmas feel quite strange." More "Africanized" Germans – children and adults alike – will relate their feeling and being different more to having been influenced by African ways, whereas more "expatriatized" Germans will relate it more to having been influenced by expatriate ways.

Experiencing school: Why German teachers don't like German re-migrants (either)

Listening to experiences of migrant children in general, one thing seems to be quite clear – the majority of German teachers are ill-prepared to deal with culturally heterogeneous groups of students. Many seem to experience other cultural backgrounds than their own first and foremost as problems and nuisances, which need to be overcome. The backgrounds and motivations for their attitudes and approaches may very well differ – and are not my major concern here.[15] Those rooted in more conservative political thought often consider integration a success only if it results in a student feeling and acting like a real German. Anything that does not seem familiar – wearing a headscarf, speaking one's mother tongue, not eating pork, going to mosque, eating with sticks – makes them feel uncomfortable and is in many cases interpreted as a sign of unwillingness on the part of the migrant student to integrate properly. Germans tend to expect being disliked for being German and therefore tend to take migrants' desires and efforts to maintain (some of) their own culture as a sign of the latter's rejection of German culture and German people – because,

---

15 When criticizing teachers, one is often referred to the difficult situation they work in. Much has been written dealing with teachers' difficult situation. I do not deny that it is indeed difficult, but I am dealing here not with teachers' but with students' problems.

why would they want to maintain their own culture if they liked the German one? As well as that, a concept of identity that connects "culture" and "race" as closely as the German concept does, leaves little room for (internal) variety based on social or cultural influence. In very simplified terms – such influence may make a difference, but it cannot change the major essence of being German.[16] And, more importantly here, due to this interconnection of "culture" and "race" in German thought, it is also difficult to conceptualize "being German" as an identity that can be connected to "being something else" at the same time.

Those who have a more liberal or progressive outlook on the world – especially (former) members of the '68-movement and those influenced by it – often have strong feelings about the ideals and ideologies that many of them seemingly fear will not survive them. There is a strong notion of being a very special generation among many of them – especially in Germany, where they cultivate a belief of being the ones who unmasked and exposed the Nazi-generation. But despite their proclaimed anti-authoritarianism and their criticism of German nationalism, many of them tend to have rather dogmatic views when it comes to accepting those who do not concur with their understanding of the world, sometimes reacting in rather authoritarian ways in defence of their concepts of anti-authoritarianism. Mannitz describes in her contribution in this volume how this affects "the Orientals," but, as I will show, it affects (re-)migrating German children and youths as well.

Many German children and youths have problems catching up after having attended school in Africa. Their experiences at school have a major impact on the process of integration and play a substantial role with regard to developing a sense of being at home.

As mentioned before, the fact that they look the same and speak the same language as everyone else can make integration easier for them than for migrants who look different and speak a different language. On the other hand, there is often no one around who shares their experiences and their background. There are of course teachers, who understand that a child who has attended a school in Africa or elsewhere will have problems catching up and adjusting. But on the whole, German re-migrants – "homecomers" – are expected to function well in Germany.

From what I have been told and from what I have seen, it is not usually all that simple for re-migrant Germans to feel at home at school. Many teachers are experienced as friendly and helpful by repatriating children and youths, others as narrow-minded, ideology-ridden and nasty – and seemingly it takes only a few teachers to make life at school – and beyond – a rather unpleasant experience.

---

16 On German ideology about being German, see, e.g.: Dumont 1994; Bornemann 1991, 1993; Forsythe 1989.

Thomas, now 32, 13 at the time he came to Germany, told me : "One day I was late for school. When I entered the classroom the teacher said 'Thomas, you are not in Africa any more. This is Germany. This means you have to be on time." Now, one would think, this could happen to an African child as well – and it probably could. Yet, I am sure it is less likely, because it is a statement that could easily be regarded as racist if directed at an African child. Thomas told me that he was very angry and that he replied that he had to be on time in Africa as well.

When Susanne, 14 then, had problems in catching up in some of her classes, one of her teachers told her it would be better if she left the *Gymnasium* (German high school leading to *Abitur*/A-levels) to attend the Realschule (German high school, leading to *Realschulabschluss*/B-levels) instead, because "you cannot advance from an African bush school to a German *Gymnasium* just like that. I really don't understand how this could happen." Again, an African child might evoke the same kind of thoughts in a teacher, but I suppose he or she would be more careful when it comes to actually putting them into words and directing them at a child.

Peter, 29 at the time of the interview eight years ago, was 14 when he came to Germany and he spoke English fluently. He told me his English teacher – a German – could not deal with that fact. Once Peter – according to his teacher – made a mistake and the teacher remarked: "Maybe this is correct Pidgin English, but we learn Standard English here." This was not the only time such comments occurred, said Peter: "she told me that my English sounded like Bush English to her. And that with that kind of English I might get ahead in Africa, but not in Germany or elsewhere in the civilized world."

Karin, 14 when coming to Germany 14 years ago, described a scene from a geography lesson where at the time they were dealing with the "developing world," taking the example of the African country where Karin had lived. The teacher asked her what languages were spoken there and she named several. Apparently the teacher knew only one or two of the ones she mentioned, saying: "I have never heard about some of these languages you mention. They're probably just dialects." The teacher then asked her about the different ethnic groups living in that country and again Karin named several, of whom the teacher knew only some, saying: "Well, some of those tribes you mention... I don't know whether they still exist... they are not mentioned in my book."

From my own experience I remember that a teacher told us that it rained in Ghana every evening. I said that this is only the case in the rainy season and he reacted promptly: "Of course, it rains in Ghana every evening – Ghana is in the tropics, so you were probably already asleep or just didn't pay attention."

Instead of integrating the specific knowledge of children coming (back) from Africa, letting other students share it, some teachers seem to reject it altogether. Ideologically motivated reactions against German (re-)migrants were also not uncommon.

When Karl misbehaved in class at the age of 12, punching his (white and German) neighbour, his teachers said: "Hey, you are not to play the colonial master here. I know how these whites behave in Africa, but you are not going to do this here." And when Karl replied that he had not done what he was being accused of, the teacher said: "I am just telling you to make sure you know where you are now."

In many cases such accusations are not made as directly as in these examples, but in the framework of dealing with specific topics. One teacher mentioned that a lot of whites in Africa are like "modern slave-holders," without pointing out Hubert explicitly, who was 11 at the time (1983) and had just come back from Africa some months previous. Soon afterwards he was teased, children pointed at him, shouting "slave-holder, slave-holder!" Such accusations – whether expressed implicitly or explicitly – can have a variety of effects, depending on the character of the child and on other factors related to the respective social environment. Many children react by refusing to integrate, to comply with the rules, to go to school etc. I know of several cases where children ended up not eating. Hubert's mother told me: "He wouldn't eat. He wouldn't go to school. He said he would only eat if we would all go back to Africa." He finally started to eat again when his parents found a school in a nearby city where the setting was more multicultural and teachers more open-minded.

In general, children and youths attending a boarding school or an international school in Germany are less likely to suffer discrimination and isolation. They are more likely to meet people who share their experiences and teachers who are used to dealing with the different backgrounds of their students. Young children attending boarding school tend to miss their families though, and, depending on the boarding school, may miss the freedom they are used to.

The more openly discriminating reactions of German teachers towards German repatriates seem to have become a lot less during the past decade or so. But even today, even those teachers who are experienced as friendly and helpful usually make little effort to integrate (re-)migrant children's knowledge and experience into their classes. Michael, who is now 28 told me: "I think this is really strange. Our teacher took us to the Museum for Ethnology [*Museum für Völkerkunde*] once and showed us a replica of an African village they had put up there. He read out some information and all that... but he never ever asked me to tell the class something about what I knew about Africa. I think this is very strange." I think so too. Interestingly enough, even teachers who show some awareness of the impact of cultural differences when it comes to "real" migrant children – from Turkey for example – show little interest in German repatriates' cultural background. The latter rarely experience any genuine interest in their past lives, in their experience and knowledge. With no peers to share their experience – a serious disadvantage compared to most "real" migrant children and youths – this lack of understanding and receptiveness encountered at school may very well deepen their feeling of being alone and isolated in what is supposed to be their home country.

Many (German) teachers clearly have little interest in what children and youths have to tell them about social and cultural worlds beyond their own. However, learning about different ways of life and different ways of looking at things – not only elsewhere in the world, but within Germany as well – takes teachers who value and integrate diversity in a class instead of disregarding and suppressing it by ignoring their students' experience and knowledge.

"One day I will go back" – and then they hardly ever do: The African experience in retrospect

Especially children and youths whose experiences of re-migration to Germany are unpleasant tend to idealize their former home. They paint their former lives in Africa in bright colours, a life in stark contrast to the "grey life in Germany" (Tom, 11).

In some cases the idealization of "Africa" or "life abroad" goes along with a condemnation of life in Germany and with withdrawal from social life which – if pursued for long – can hinder children in their development and adolescents from growing up. It makes (re-)integration a painful and sometimes endless experience, which may end up in experiences of failure at different levels of life.

This problem in its more destructive form seems to affect boys and male adolescents more than their female counterparts. I know of several who have lived in Germany for more than 20 years, who are in their mid-thirties to early forties now and still fantasize about "going back" or "going to live abroad one day." Some of them have been back for short periods of time, but most of them have never made any serious attempt to actually establish an adult life "back in Africa." Why have they not done so? The reasons are quite simple, I think. It is not an image of adult life in Africa that these adult men are adhering and clinging to. It is an image of "Africa," of "life in Africa," of "life abroad" connected to childhood and youth. It is an image that would not survive a serious and adult "reality check." It seems, in fact, that the fantasies of going back on the one hand and not making any serious attempt at putting them into practice on the other are connected to the fear of destroying one's bright, but little realistic images. Adult life in Africa – even if it takes place in a white, upper class context – is a life, which involves doing adult stuff – like work, maintaining a house, struggling with shortcomings etc. It is not just beach, parties, servants, swimming, sailing, and having fun. I am not saying that white childhood in Africa is all about that – but it is what these nostalgic images of life in Africa and life abroad in many cases largely consist of. By maintaining such an image and connecting it to (potential) adulthood in Africa – or rather, by not realizing its childhood and youth connotations – it may very well keep a person from growing up and leading a fulfilled adult life in Germany. Why does this problem seem to affect mainly males?

I think the "superiority issue" described above affects men more seriously than women. Boys and young men in particular suffer more when they lose their upper class status and have fewer options for compensating that loss. To (re-)gain an equivalent status, they need to change both their attitudes and their lifestyle. Many expatriate children growing up in an expatriate environment (in Africa) do not get a chance to learn what society will expect from them later on in Germany. Boys learn it even less and boys would need to learn it even more. They are expected to work (themselves) to make things work out for them. As well as that, it is more socially accepted for a woman to share her husband's than for a man to share his wife's status, so getting married to a high-ranking spouse to secure or regain one's high status is an alternative strategy for women more than it is for men. To be successful, to be socially accepted, to achieve something – you are expected to work for it in Germany, especially as a man and especially when not belonging to the upper classes. This is the lesson many expatriates have not learned while growing up in Africa. Boys seem to suffer more when losing social status in Germany, probably because boys – especially adolescent ones – are more status-oriented, they depend on status more to impress their peers, girls, teachers etc. They feel more humiliated by "suddenly" having to work for a higher status that had seemed perfectly natural to them before. At the same time, they are – even more than girls – expected to be successful and tough. As a result, especially male adolescents tend to suffer more seriously and more self-destructively – often carrying their problems with them well into adulthood.

With regard to the bright images, which are maintained or constructed of Africa in Germany – often to compensate for the "grey life here" – I would like to point out that in many such cases of retrospective idealization the images are not so much related to Africa as such but to the kind of life one has lived – or retrospectively imagines having lived – there as a child and youth. It is not necessarily Africa as such that is missed, but particular lifestyles and ways of socializing. As well, due to the lack of peers who share their experience, many just want to escape their social and emotional isolation in Germany. I asked Roger, 17, after having lived in Germany for a year, whether he wanted to go back to the African country where he had lived before. He answered: "I don't care, as long as it is like it was before. I want the sun to shine, I want to go to the beach, I want to be free again. I want to have people around me who are like me. So I think, any Third World country would be fine with me."

"Going back" is important at least as a potential option – as a "way out" – for many. "If things don't work out here, I'll go back as soon as I can. I'll manage there for sure," said Karola (16) to me. Children, who got into closer contact with the cultural environment in Africa, sometimes also feel that liking Germany is somewhat disloyal towards their former home.[17] They feel they need to defend Africa, especially because many people have a rather dis-

---

17 This has also been found by Pollock & van Reken 2004: 249.

torted picture of it. Anja, 12, said to me a year ago: "I mean, if I say, I like it here, they will think, well, of course, everyone would like Germany better than Africa. Because they think it's all poverty, snakes, hunger, and dirt in Africa. That's why sometimes I say I like Africa better, so that they will ask me why and then I can tell them good things about Africa."

Ways in and ways out

Many children who have lived large parts of their lives within expatriate environments have problems feeling at home and feeling integrated in Germany. Especially in cases where there is no opportunity to return now and then to "check reality" as life goes on, they often idealize what they have left behind and construct a black-and-white image with Germany on the dark and Africa on the bright side. Some of these children tend to isolate themselves from their potential peers in Germany.

Children and youths often simply perpetuate the arguments of their parents. But, whereas they might be saying the same things, in many cases they suffer more. Whereas most parents have lived in Germany before, knowing life there will be different than in Africa, children are often not (as) aware of this. Whereas most parents have maintained some social or family ties to Germany, which they can build on upon their return, many children have not.

As a result of feeling lonely and "different," some children become loners. Others try to make friends but are rejected as arrogant and snobbish by others. Sabine, who came to live with her aunt in Germany at the age of 15, told me (at the age of 31):

I think during my first two years after coming back, I must have been quite a snob. I told everyone about the servants we used to have, about our big house and all. Only when I was gradually made aware by some of the people I really liked about the reasons for all this luxury, did I start being more sceptical. That's when I changed – and that's when my problems with my parents started.

This happens quite a lot as well. Some children and youths brought up in expatriate environments turn against their parents once they become – and are made – aware of the injustices involved in some of their (past) privileges. At an age where young people are prone to be critical of their parents anyway, the process of (re-)integration in Germany in combination with feelings of frustration and rejection can also trigger conflicts between parents and children. Sandra, now 32, said: "After having lived in Germany for a year or so, at the age of 14, I virtually told my parents, they are to blame for the injustices in Africa, for the racism in Africa, and for me having been involved in all that." On the other hand, the reaction might be quite different. A child or young person might defend his or her parents when being attacked by others, like Karl did at the age of 12: "When my teacher told the class that whites in Africa exploit blacks, I told him he is a communist and that it is the white people in Africa who civilize Africa and that Africans needed whites to develop the place. Well, I defended my parents and myself. I did not want to be a child of racists and exploiters." But setting oneself apart from one's parents often serves as a (first) step towards integration.

A lot of so-called "Third Culture Kids" in fact only become real "Third Culture Kids" in Germany. They turn to self-exotization – but they do so as a "way in." In fact, some of them try to "turn black" somehow, they "Africanize" themselves in Germany, thereby finding a place for themselves in German society. From what I have heard and experienced, this is one of the most creative and promising ways of integration, because it combines "being different" with "being here." Instead of cultivating difference by remaining an "ex-patriate" – someone who is really "*out*-of"-Germany, they turn – at least a little bit – African IN Germany. Christian, now 29, told me that he started wearing his hair Rastafarian style at the age of 17, two year after he had returned from Africa:[18]

I felt different but I looked the same. I wanted to show I am different. So I got dreadlocks to make me look African or... well, in a way, I suppose I wanted to show my African part. I had a friend who was half Ghanaian, half German. He had never been to Ghana, but he was always considered an exotic person somehow, whereas I, having spent 15 years in Africa, was considered the same as everyone else. I felt I was far more different than him. So I got myself dreadlocks and a Rasta cap. I also became an expert in Reggae and Highlife Music. In fact, that's when I started to feel at home somehow. After turning my African part inside out... Yes, I turned my African part inside out.

Turning the African part inside out" instead of carrying it "inside" enabled Christian to position himself culturally – and socially. He had found a way to integrate his African part by externalizing it, thus making others aware of it. Several years later he cut his dreadlocks off. "I didn't need them any more. They had lost their importance. I could now do without them. I had somehow found my place in Germany without having lost my African part.

In many cases, children and youths only discover – or (re-)invent – their African identity in Germany. Some convert their expatriate identity into an African identity, because this is a more promising strategy for integrating "being different" with "being here." Many children (initially) go into hiding in the process of being integrated – and disintegrate as a result, often going unnoticed until things get really bad. Disintegrating may end up in a vicious cir-

---

18 One of the more popular German TCKs – never labelled as such – is Momo (he has a brother as well, but he is not much of a TCK). He was and still is one of the main figures in the Lindenstraße, a popular series on German TV, which has been running for more than 20 years. Momo had lived in Ethiopia between the age of eight and 18 before returning to Munich with his family. Momo has always worn his hair Rastafarian style.

cle, it leads to the deepening of a child's or youth' desperation, it confirms its feeling of being alone and of being separated from the outside, German, world – which then leads to further disintegration. This can lead to complete emotional isolation, which in some cases can have devastating psychological and physical effects. Some of the people I know have suffered from anorexia or bulimia at some stage in their life. I know of two suicide attempts and of one suicide. There are many ways out of such vicious circles – and ways not to get into them in the first place. Getting out of hiding, externalizing one's experiences and feelings – turning one's self inside out – seems to be a first promising step.

It is usually children and youths who had a chance to learn how to deal with cultural differences and who were not secluded from their (African) environment that manage to integrate best in Germany. It is not those who were brought up in an exclusive – and seclusive – expatriate environment. They may find integration difficult – because things are all so different – but they will not fall into despair. They may rebel, but they will not disintegrate. The more secluded the social life children are part of while living abroad, the more difficult integration is in Germany. German children who have been a part of their local environment in Africa, will not only have become more "Africanised" and know more about Africa and Africans, they usually have less – and less serious – emotional problems when integrating in Germany. They are better able to adjust, to integrate and to make the best of a situation.

It is important for (re-)integrating children and youths to know that they are not the only ones. Therefore finding others sharing one's experience is important. Nevertheless, creating a "TCK" world and ideology of difference as a result of having been brought up in an expatriate environment may well not be primarily a sign of actual third-culturedness, but of a transformation of an expatriate ideology of "natural superiority" over the local African population to a "TCK" ideology of "cultural superiority" over the "ordinary" local German population – a transformation, which neither supports a child's (re-)integration nor its further personal development.

References

Allen, Tim (ed.) 1994: *When Refugees Go Home: African Experiences*. Trenton, N.J.: Africa World Press.

Arowolo, Olalele O. 2000: Return Migration and the Problem of Reintegration. In: *International Migration* 38 (5): 59–82.

Bornemann, John 1991: Uniting the German Nation: Law, Narrative, and Historicity. *American Ethnologist* 20: 288–311.

Dumont, Louis 1994: *German Ideology*. Chicago: The University of Chicago Press.

Engombe, Lucia 2004: *Kind Nr. 95: meine deutsch-afrikanische Odyssee*. Berlin: Ullstein.

Firat, Ibrahim 1991: *Nirgends zu Hause!? Türkische Schüler zwischen Integration in der BRD und Remigration in der Türkei; eine sozialpsychologisch-empirische Untersuchung*. Frankfurt am Main: Verlag für Interkulturelle Kommunikation.

Forsythe, Diana 1989: German Identity and the Problems of History. In: Tonkin, Elizabeth, Maryon McDonald & Malcolm Chapman (eds.): *History and Ethnicity*, London and New York: Routledge (ASA Monographs 27).

Hamilton, Hugo 2004: The loneliness of being German. In: *Guardian*, 7.9.2004.

Hammond, Laura 2004: *This place will become home: refugee repatriation to Ethiopia*. Ithaca: Cornell University Press.

Kenna, Constance (ed.) 1999: *Die "DDR-Kinder" von Namibia: Heimkehrer in ein fremdes Land*. Göttingen etc.: Hess.

Knörr, Jacqueline 1990: *Zwischen goldenem Ghetto und Integration. Ethnologische Autobiographie und Untersuchung über das Aufwachsen deutscher und Schweizer Kinder und Jugendlicher in der Dritten Welt am Beispiel Ghanas und ihre anschließende Eingliederung in Europa*. Frankfurt & New York: Verlag Peter Lang.

Knörr, Jacqueline 1995: *Kreolisierung versus Pidginisierung als Kategorien kultureller Differenzierung. Varianten neoafrikanischer Identität und Interethnik in Freetown, Sierra Leone*. Münster & Hamburg: Lit.-Verlag.

Lenzin, René 2000[2]: *Afrika macht oder bricht einen Mann. Soziales Verhalten und politische Einschätzung einer Kolonialgesellschaft am Beispiel der Schweizer in Ghana (1945-1966)*. Bern: Basler Afrika Bibliographien.

Martin, Jeannette 2005: *Been-To, Burger, Transmigranten? Zur Bildungsmigration von Ghanaern und ihrer Rückkehr aus der Bundesrepublik Deutschland*. Münster: Lit.-Verlag.

Paraschou, Athina 2001: *Remigration in die Heimat oder Emigration in die Fremde? Beiträge zur europäischen Migrationsforschung am Beispiel remigrierter griechischer Jugendlicher*. Frankfurt am Main etc.: Verlag Peter Lang.

Pollock, David C. & Ruth E. van Reken 2004[4]: *Third Culture Kids. The Experience of Growing Up Among Worlds*. Boston & London: Nicholas Brealey Publishing.

Pollock, David C., Ruth E. van Reken & Georg Pflüger 2003. *Third Culture Kids. Aufwachsen in mehreren Kulturen*. Marburg: Francke.

Smith, Carolyn D. (ed.) 1996: *Strangers at Home: Essays on the Effects of Living Overseas and Coming "Home" to a Strange Land*. Bayside, NY: Aletheia Publications.

Stenzel, Arnold, Hans G. Homfeldt & Günter Fenner 1989: *Auszug in ein fremdes Land? : türkische Jugendliche und ihre Rückkehr in die Türkei*. Weinheim: Dt. Studien Verlag.

Storti, Craig 2001: *The Art of Coming Home*. London: Brealey.

Useem, John & Ruth H. Useem, R.H. 1955: *The Western-educated man in India: Study of social roles*. New York: Dryden Press.

Wolbert, Barbara 1995: *Der getötete Paß : Rückkehr in die Türkei; eine ethnologische Migrationsstudie*. Berlin: Akademie-Verlag.

LEAVING THE *SHTETL* BEHIND.
CHILDREN'S LITERATURE ON JEWISH MIGRATION FROM EASTERN EUROPE

Jana Pohl

> Whoever has eyes that see and ears that hear
> absorbs enough stories to last a lifetime
> and to tell his children and grandchildren
> (Singer 1991: 172).

This well-known quotation from Isaac Bashevis Singer's children's story "Naftali the Storyteller & His Horse, Sus" exhibits how universal and pervasive stories are and what a pivotal role they can play in passing on memories from generation to generation. According to Singer, stories for children are not just important as entertainment. It is their content and their function of keeping the past with us that makes stories an essential part not only of children's but also adults' lives. Singer, who emigrated from Poland to the USA, dedicated much of his work to the memory of his country of origin and of *shtetl* life; his Nobel-Prize-winning work is highly imbued with the culture of the Eastern European Jewry. Alida Allison observes that "[...] his writing has uniquely contributed to keeping the memory of Eastern European Yiddish culture alive" (Allison 1996: 20). Children's literature as a means of remembering the *shtetl*, a particular form of predominantly Jewish settlement in past Eastern Europe, will be the subject of the second part of the article in which I will look at native U.S.-American authors and their children's literature[1] of the past 20 years and its depiction of the *shtetl*. My argument is that the depiction of the *shtetl* has been connected to the issue of migration[2] – a fact that can be explained with historical and cultural circumstances which differ from Singer's times. This analysis necessitates some general remarks on children's literature and migration to which the first part of my paper is dedicated.

---

1 "Children's literature" refers to literature for children as well as for young adults throughout this paper.
2 In children's literature the distinction between migrants, refugees and fugitives is not always easy to make. Therefore the term migration is used in a general sense.

Children's literature and migration

In answering questions about how children perceive migration and cultural differences, literature which is primarily addressed to children and is therefore adapted to their age, can serve as a key tool. Authors of children's literature tell migration stories for children and modify their topic and way of writing to the implicit child readers. Stories are often narrated through the "eyes of a child character," either from third or first person. These narrative strategies appear to give insights into the characters' minds and their perception of migration processes, as well as to the target audience of migration stories, the child readers. Certain genres, such as autobiography, diary or epistolary novel seem more inclined to take readers into a character's mind than others. Nevertheless, the reader has to keep in mind that it is in most cases the adult author who puts words into a character's head and mouth. The imagined child reader is one feature of children's literature which in narrating migration stories follows certain conventions. Two common traditions of children's literature are happy ending and the orphan child as a protagonist. Migration stories are set in either the country of origin or the target country – or both – or simply focus on the journey. In any case the happy ending is predicated on successful migration[3] which is indicated in the children's books by advancing assimilation to the target country, economic success, education, or by being joined by other family members. The orphan child as a protagonist[4] entails the message that children are capable of mastering the journey from one country to the other on their own.[5] These conventions have an important effect on the commercial success of a children's book.

Migration has been a prospering topic of children's literature. In accommodating the migration issue, children's literature interlinks with aspects of multiculturalism, discrimination, tolerance, and cultural plurality for informational, educational[6] and/or aesthetic purposes. Migration stories, depicting the movement from one place to another, immanently revolve around people, countries, and cultures that differ from the reader's background.

Migration has also been referred to as object, i.e. topic, and subject at the same time because it serves as the autobiographical background for the au-

---

3   Return migration is rarely a topic in children's literature, except for the depiction of flight during war and returning home.
4   Many famous hero(in)es of children's literature are orphans, for example Johanna Spyri's Heidi, Lucy M. Montgomery's Anne of Green Gables, Peter Barrie's Peter Pan, and Joanne K. Rowling's Harry Potter.
5   See for example Amy Hest's picture book When Jessie came across the sea (1997) which tells the story of the orphan Jessie and her emigration from Russia to America or Lillian Hammer Ross's story Sarah, also known as Hannah (1994) about 12-year-old fatherless Sarah who masters the journey to America on her own.
6   See Ruth McKoy Lowery's (2001) sociological analysis of migration stories in children's literature.

thors, thus implying a strong notion of subjectivity. Authors, who migrated as children, tell of their own experiences and memories or fictionalize their ancestors' life stories in children's literature. Due to their personal connection to the topic, they attribute a strong sense of authenticity to their writing.

No matter if object or subject, the depiction of migration usually takes place in the (former) target country. It is often the country of immigration and not the country of emigration where migration stories for children are generated and within which they are situated. This perspective entails the questions of "who writes the story?" and "who writes whose story?" Writers with a migration background are themselves successful immigrants or their descendants. Descendants of former migrants write the story of their own people, in contrast to authors who fictionalize the stories of ethnic groups other than their own. This question of perspective has important consequences for the stories and their claim for authenticity which shall be discussed later in the paper.

When looking at migration stories and their reflection of the children's perception of the migration process, one automatically touches upon matters of representation. Representation is closely connected to narrative patterns. One particularly interesting narrative form of "looking into a character's mind" is the first person narration which many migration stories use. First person narration is a typical feature of autobiography. The following chart visualizes the migration story's entanglement with all three genres of life story writing: autobiography, biography and fiction. In a post-modern blurring of genre boundaries children's literature on migration (except non-fictional history books) may incorporate elements of all three genres (shown in the overlapping of the three grey circles in the illustration below); autobiographical inclusion is not obligatory, for not every author includes autobiographical references in the book's story or paratext[7] (therefore the grey line is dotted). Many authors of children's books on migration, as we shall see later on, choose to draw attention to their autobiographical tie to the subject for reasons of authenticity. Autobiography as one genre of life story writing recounts the author's life or parts of it in hovering between objectivity and subjectivity, including a retrospective account of a life's important events among which migration certainly counts. Autobiographical accounts necessitate a narrator who is close in time and space and right in the middle of the story, which entails an impression of psychological depth and physical closeness. The narrator therefore takes on an androgenic role between describing, observing, and engaging in the story. Nevertheless, all three genres capture a sense of historical and socio-cultural context of the past or present migration process for which the black inner lines stand.

---

7   Paratext, a term coined by Gérard Genette, embraces all the signals which accompany the text, such as title, preface, notes, and all signals mediated by the book, such as font, illustrations, jacket etc.

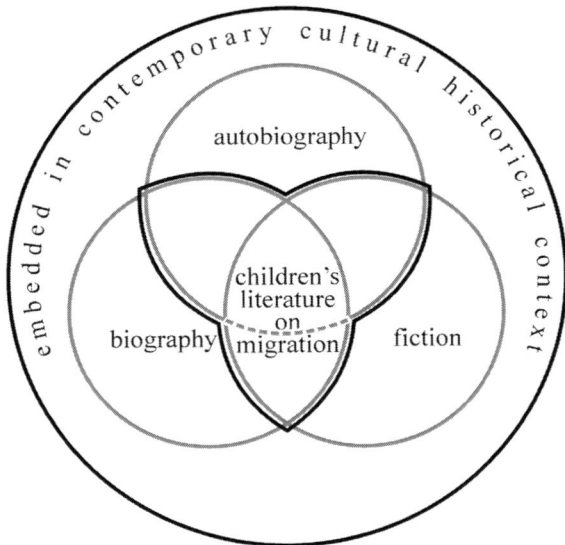

Illustration 1: Genres of life story writing

Contrasting with autobiography, a biography is a narrative account of someone else's life, describing the individual in the context of his/her life. Both biography and historical fiction recreate the past, mostly through chronologically narrating past events. In writing historical fiction authors assume the dual role of a storyteller and a historian at the same time. Migration stories therefore always contain elements of biography, because migration as an important life event is part of the plot. Proceeding from the premise that the line between true and fictional events in an autobiography or a biography can be blurred, we can conclude that text and protagonists of migration stories infiltrate the area of fiction in which the story is a product of the author's imagination. Many migration stories can be completely classified as fiction. Regardless of the genre, all migration stories are embedded in socio-cultural context and the literary system's traditions and conventions at their time of publication and reception (the latter can but need not coincide).

By describing migration from children's perspectives, children's literature not only represents certain migration waves. It documents the perception of cultural varieties and the assimilation to a new home. It informs about the historical period, in which migration took place, and the formation of an immigrant nation, such as the U.S.-American. At the same time children's literature recollects the life of a past culture and can thereby keep the heritage of an ethnic group alive, pass it on, and mediate it, from adult generations (grandparents or parents) to children. Migration stories, which I will focus on in the second part of the paper, stand for a generation of contemporary North American writers of children's literature on migration who narrate past migration stories for today's children. In blending life story genres, they all depict the migration of Jews from Eastern Europe to North America and remember the *shtetl* which stands for the country of origin of their protagonists'.

Remembering the *shtetl* in contemporary U.S.-American children's literature

Adult literature as well as children's literature has a long tradition of describing the *shtetl*s[8] (*shtetlekch*), "small market towns in Eastern Europe ranging in size from 1,000 to 20,000 people. Most *shtetlekch* had between 1,000 and 5,000 people, with the majority of the population being Jewish" (Eliach 1998: 782). Since the reign of Catherine II until the revolution in 1917, Jews in Russia were required to live in a special zone in the West of the empire which made up about four per cent of Russia and was called the *Pale of Settlement*.[9] Even within the *Pale*, Jews suffered discrimination. They had to pay double taxes, could not buy or lease land and were excluded from higher education.

*Shtetl*s existed both in the *Pale* and in Poland. Life in a *shtetl* often meant a life in poverty in a traditional Jewish community. Anti-Semitism, devastating pogroms, especially after the assassination of Czar Alexander II in 1881, restricted educational and economic opportunities as well as the threatening army service for Jewish boys pushed more than two million Jews out of the *shtetl*s to America. America, in particular the USA, radiated an image of the Golden Land, where the streets were paved with gold, and an image of the Promised Land, where Jews were free to exercise their religion. These images of America can be pointed out as major pull-factors. Eastern European Jews made up the vast majority of the Jewish immigrants in America in this migration wave around the turn of the last century. The Eastern European Jewry and this specific migration wave have been a reoccurring topic in adult literature and in children's literature. Despite the existing historical knowledge concerning life in the *shtetl*, it has often been described as an image, partly romanticized in literature, paintings[10] and in the children's literature of the 1970s and 1980s[11] as well.

In 1984, Barbara Mirel described the depiction of the *shtetl* in North American children's literature in her paper "Lost worlds of tradition: *Shtetl* stories for suburban children." According to her, *shtetl* life and its cultural setting are lost for modern young readers and *shtetl* stories by "classic" authors like Sholem Aleichem or Singer lack an audience. She draws attention to a group of books which give an introduction to Eastern European Jewish life

---

8 *Shtetl* (*shtetlekch* as one plural form) is a Yiddish word, derived from the Middle High German "*stetel*" which is a diminutive form of the German "*Stadt*" (town).
9 The Pale of Settlement included the territory of present-day Latvia, Lithuania, Ukraine and Belorussia.
10 Schoeps 2000: 160, see also Roskies 2000.
11 Mirel 1984.

because she considers these books important for the recreation of a past civilization and identity as well as for educational purposes. Mirel rightly points out that famous Jewish literature about the 19th century has a strong tradition of portraying the *shtetl* with its manifold cultural and religious facets. In terms of Yiddish children's literature Aleichem's *Motl Peysi dem Khazns* (first published in 1916) and Singer's *Stories for Children* (first published in 1984) are well-known examples. This illustrates that the *shtetl* as it represents history and cultural heritage of a long period of the Eastern European Jewry's past has a long tradition in literature in general as well as in children's literature. Literary narratives about the *shtetl* often focus on the time under Czar Nicholas II of Russia and particularly around the turn of the last century. When looking at the so-called classics of Eastern European Jewish literature (for example Yitskhok Leyb Peretz or Sholem Asch) and their depiction of the *shtetl*, specific essential features re-occur: stories display community life which existed in isolation from the Russian empire. They tell the reader about traditions and customs existing in the *shtetl*, including descriptions of various representations of Jewish religious culture such as synagogues, rabbis, and cheders[12]. In analyzing classic Eastern European Jewish literature such as Aleichem and Asch, Dan Miron delineates the fire metaphor, the unexpected visitor, and multiple scenes of departure as elements of the *shtetl* image, the latter of which is particularly important for contemporary North American children's literature (Miron 2000: 16–32).

However, contemporary and therefore retrospective children's literature about the *shtetl* especially in the time of the Russian empire differs in the depiction of past reality. Mirel outlined two major themes of American born authors in their treatment of the *shtetl* in children's fiction as "the response to anti-Semitism and the tensions arising from the infiltration of modern ideas into traditional patterns of Jewish life" (Mirel 1984: 7). She refers to U.S.-American authors and their works published in the 1970s and the beginning of the 1980s. Her examples – Chaya M. Burstein's two novels *Rifka bangs the Teakettle* (1970) and *Rifka grows up* (1976), Leonard Everett Fisher's *A Russian Farewell* (1980), Anita Heyman's *Exit from Home* (1977), and Marge Blaine's *Dvora's Journey* (1979) – are all completely set in Eastern Europe incorporating the atmosphere of the *shtetl* with its inherent reactions to anti-Semitism and its blend of modern ideas and traditional Jewish life. Scenes of departure are introduced only late in the plots. Hence, these examples from the 1970s focus on the *shtetl* and not on the experience of departure.

In the following part I will look at the development of the *shtetl* topic in U.S.-American children's literature during the past 20 years, i.e. since the publication of Mirel's article. Is the distinct culture of the *shtetl* still remembered in contemporary U.S.-American children's and young adult literature and if so, has its depiction changed over time? These questions can be answered with a clear yes. The high number of publications of children's fiction

---

12 Jewish school where children were instructed in Hebrew and read the Bible.

on Eastern European Jewry proves that Eastern Europe – although its depiction has changed – still is an important topic in U.S.-American Jewish children's literature. I will examine whether Barbara Mirel's assumptions regarding U.S.-American authors and their treatment of the *shtetl* are still applicable to the U.S.-American children's literature on the *shtetl* nowadays and will show how the depiction of the *shtetl* has been connected to the migration from it. Contemporary U.S.-American authors portray the *shtetl* differently due to deviant geographical, cultural, social, and historical circumstances.

The focus of today's U.S.-American children's literature differs from the classic Eastern European Jewish literature and from the U.S.-American children's literature 20 years ago. In remembering the *shtetl* in children's literature, the emphasis has been put more and more on the migration process. The "multiple scenes of departure," outlined by Dan Miron for the classic Eastern European Jewish adult literature about the *shtetl*, feature strongly in the U.S.-American children's literature of the past 20 years. Stories usually include descriptions of the *shtetl* and the living conditions in Eastern Europe as the country of departure, often from the perspective of a child narrator. But *shtetl* depiction and migration have been strongly linked. This corresponds to the historical reality in the *shtetl*s in which mass emigration to North America had been part of everyday life since the pogroms after the assassination of Czar Alexander II. The focus on migration is especially evident in picture books which shall be discussed first. The emphasis on the journey aspect becomes apparent not only in the stories as such but in their titles as well: *Escaping to America. A True Story* (Schanzer 2000), *Journey to Ellis Island. How my Father Came to America* (Bierman 1998), *When Jessie Came across the Sea* (Hest 1997), *Journey to the Golden Land* (Rosenblum 1992), *Leaving for America* (Bresnick-Perry 1992), and *Annushka's Voyage* (Tarbescu 1998).

The journey aspect underlines the autobiographical background of many children's books on the Eastern European Jewry and the *shtetl*. Many of the authors articulate such a background in their book's paratext. Edith Tarbescu, for example, dedicates her book "To the memory of my parents, Esther and Benjamin Roseman, whose names are inscribed on a wall at Ellis Island." She writes the book "For my mother, who has lived in many countries" and includes a picture showing her mother and aunt after their arrival in America. In her author's note she explains: "Ever since I was a child I heard the story of how my mother made that journey at the age of 13. This is her story." Rosalyn Schanzer bases her book on her father's and his family's story and dedicates it "To the memory of my family and to everyone who has travelled from another country to begin a new life on these shores." Roslyn Bresnick-Perry explains in the author's note that she was born in the *shtetl* Wysokie-Litewskie and later emigrated to America. Her picture book's opening lines are "We were leaving for America. My mother and I were leaving our *shtetl*, our little town of Wysokie, to join my father" (Bresnick-Perry 1992: 4). Carol Bierman's picture book is a biographical account of her father's migration to America, showing pictures of him in the book. She sets the story in a little village in

Russia called Pinsk; the setting is underpinned with material signifiers like a photograph showing Cyrillic letters and a samovar. Yiddish words, e.g. *"mentsch"* or *"tsuris"*[13] (1998: 14), and Jewish names such as Yehuda, the main character, indicate a Jewish context in *Journey to Ellis Island*. There is, however, no mentioning of a *shtetl* or Jewish religious life. As the title indicates the story is mainly about the journey to one's destination in exile. The turmoil of World War I in Russia is mentioned as a reason for emigration (16) as well as the family encountering a pogrom while fleeing – however, the focus is completely on the journey as such when the process of migration is described. First big brother Abe, whom the main character Yehuda didn't even get to know, migrates to America. He is followed by his father, then by Yehuda himself, his sister, and mother. The book charts various stages of their journey: the long march out of Russia, to Poland, to Rotterdam where they boarded the ship, the journey on board to America, the inspections on Ellis Island, and finally the arrival in New York. Thus, the journey and migration focus is so pronounced that the *shtetl* background is shunned by it.

The autobiographical background reveals that many writers are the descendants of successful immigrants, a fact that encourages a positive attitude towards the target country. An autobiographical connection appears to enhance authenticity. A paratext's revelation of an author's autobiographical tie to the subject seems to underscore the story's genuineness. An author who announces that a story is based on events in his/her own life presents him/herself as a reliable source and is therefore assumed to produce a reliable text, based on first-hand experience.

Books by descendants of immigrants tackle the question: why are we as the descendants of Eastern European Jewish immigrants here in America and how did we get here? This explains why migration from the *shtetl* is of central importance to the younger generation of U.S.-American writers and why they focus on migration from the *shtetl*. Many contemporary U.S.-American authors are the descendants of successful immigrants who came to America about a century ago. They often tell the stories of their families. Therefore their emphasis is on the push-factors that drove Jews out of the *shtetl* and across the ocean. Therefore anti-Semitism and pogroms often figure more prominently in their stories than Jewish religious life and *shtetl* culture. Therefore they focus on the "new country," which is at the same time the country of their implicit readers.

Barbara Cohen's picture book *Gooseberries to Oranges* (Cohen 1982), illustrated by Beverly Brodsky, for instance, is "a true story of a little girl who was born in Eastern Europe and came to live in America" according to the front flap. The illustrator dedicates the book "To my mother and the memory of my father whose stories of the old country inspired the creation of this

---

13 *Mentsch* and *tsuris* are explained by the author in the glossary in the end of the book. *Mentsch* is explained as "The Yiddish word for 'man.' *Mentsch* also means a decent, honorable person" and *tsuris* as "The Yiddish word for 'troubles'" (Bierman 1998: 48).

book" (imprint).[14] This is the story of the illustrator's mother. In an email Beverly Brodsky informed me that "This is certainly a story about my own mother" whom Barbara Cohen "interviewed to get information for her text." The first third of the book embraces scenes of the *shtetl*. Already on the second doublespread war and Russian soldiers terrorizing the Jews are introduced (see illustration 2). The text says:

But winter came, and war. We put feather pillows around the walls of the rooms so if bullets hit our house they wouldn't hurt us. Soldiers in steel helmets searched every corner, looking for boys to take away to the army. They tore the mezzuzah[15] off the door jamb because they thought gold was hidden inside. There was no gold inside the mezzuzah, only a little scroll inscribed with words from the Bible (Cohen 1982: n.p.[16]).

Illustration 2: from Barbara Cohen's Gooseberries to Oranges (1982, illustration by Beverly Brodsky)[17]

Cohen's little Eastern European village is characterized by anti-Semitism, poverty, and hunger. The book's focus is on the journey out of the *shtetl* and the new life in America, the latter making up about two thirds of the book. Cohen, as well as the authors of the above-mentioned picture books, all intro-

---

14 I am indebted to Beverly Brodsky for sharing this information on the creation of Gooseberries to Oranges.
15 A *mezzuzah* is a scroll of parchment with important words from the Torah, kept in a small container made from wood, plastic or metal and nailed to the doorpost of a Jewish home.
16 N.p. stands for no pagination.
17 The picture is reprinted with Beverly Brodsky's permission.

duce migration very early in the plot. That does not leave much room for lengthy *shtetl* descriptions. In the majority of the books the "village" is not even called a *shtetl*[18]. But the books do include various shibboleths for Jewish culture (e.g. *mezzuzah*s, Sabbath candles or Jewish names such as Avrom-Leyb or Feygl) and a setting in past Eastern Europe.

The autobiographical aspect can only serve as one possible explanation of the shift of focus. The growing remoteness of the *shtetl* experience is another. The time gap between the *shtetl* culture in the Russian empire as the (historical) background of the migration of the Eastern European Jews and the narrative accounts of it is constantly getting larger.

Classic Eastern European Jewish writers such as Aleichem, Peretz, and later on Singer still knew the *shtetl* life personally and had the chance to write from that personal experience. For modern U.S.-American authors – with or without autobiographical ties to the subject – the *shtetl* is a historical and fictional subject which is treated as such: sometimes authors treat the sujet with a lot of care, involving meticulous research; sometimes books are simply set in that time (at the turn of the last century) and place (a Jewish village, Jewish town or *shtetl*) without further explication of the *shtetl* as historical reality.

Elvira Woodruff's picture book *The Memory Coat* (1999) is one example of a fictitious account of the *shtetl* and migration to North America. It starts with the following introduction to the setting: "Long ago, a young girl named Rachel and her cousin, Grisha, lived with their family in a small town, far away in Russia. Such a town was called a *shtetl*. It was where many of the Jewish people lived. There they worked as cobblers, blacksmiths, tailors, and shopkeepers. Their little wooden houses and shops ran all along the cobblestone streets" (n.p.). The *shtetl* description includes many *shtetl* elements: Woodruff describes the community life in a *shtetl* and people's occupations; a synagogue is mentioned and so are prayers. The Yiddish language is displayed, and there is a pogrom which triggers the family's departure for America. Woodruff gives an impression of *shtetl* life and culture, and at the same time explains the need to leave, taking on the adventure story of migrating to a new country. The illustrations are not particularly *shtetl*-specific. The Russian setting cannot be deducted, but they show people in traditional clothing and men with long beards – as a sign of traditional Jewishness. *The Memory Coat* depicts *shtetl* life to some amount and adheres to parts of the common *shtetl* depiction. Woodruff's picture book, however, exceeds in its *shtetl* description many of the other picture books mentioned.

Mirel's statement (1984, see above) is still applicable insofar as "the response to anti-Semitism" features in the books. Anti-Semitism is mainly depicted in form of pogroms which have become an important component in the *shtetl* description. Along with the response to anti-Semitism comes the escape

---

18 The omission of the word "*shtetl*" can also be explained with the implicit readers of the picture books and the image of children; "*shtetl*" is after all of Yiddish origin and needs to be "translated" or explained to an American child reader.

from it. Emigration from the country in which pogroms take place is a logical conclusion. Young adult fiction, as we shall see, accommodates this component and at the same time exhibits in many cases the above-mentioned biographical factor of the literary *shtetl* depiction.

*Illustration 3: by Trina Schart Hyman,
in Kathryn Lasky's "The Night Journey" (1981)*[19]

Young adult books often exhibit an (auto)biographical link regarding the *shtetl* and the migration process. Kathryn Lasky's books are just one example. Her first (!) young adult novel, *The Night Journey* (1981), is based on her aunt's story of coming to America. Lasky herself notes: "My grandparents had all died by the time I was three, but that did not prevent me from asking my parents about their journeys to America. And still I had aunts and uncles who remembered" (as quoted in the paratext in Lasky 1998: 181).[20] Not surprisingly, her book is written for her aunt, "For Ann Lasky Smith, who remembers." The character great-grandmother Sashie, who is based on Lasky's aunt, describes her flight from the Russian empire to North America – an experience which is central to the novel. She passes on the story to her great-granddaughter Rachel before her own death. Lasky depicts her family's story about coming to the United States, and the way the *shtetl* is remembered bespeaks the "response to anti-Semitism:" the *shtetl* with its major elements is

---

19 Reprinted with the permission of Penguin Group: New York.
20 For the autobiographical background see also Brown (1998: 58f.) and Lasky Knight (1985: 28ff.).

subsumed under the flight process. It is associated with pogroms, violence, death, and the Russians as the originators of pogroms. During the flight Sashie's family passes through a *shtetl* where a pogrom had just taken place. The setting is described as such:

Sashie and Ghisa peeked between the slats of the wagon. And through the cracks and holes of the boards, the fragments of total destruction appeared like scraps from the apocalypse – a charred cart with a blackened hand reaching stiffly out; a cow bloated in death, its pointy hooves faintly absurd as they stuck straight up into the sky; burned-out cottages, their windows like blind eye sockets; a large star of David, once fastened to a prayerhouse door, lay scorched in a pile of rubble. The only sound was the soft hiss of the still-smoldering fires (Lasky 1981: 136).

Trina Schart Hyman's illustration (above) captures this gloomy image of the *shtetl*.

In *The Night Journey* Jewish religious life such as holidays, prayers, food, and a sense of Jewish community life are present in connection with the flight. The story's narration epitomizes hybrid remembering processes: the story is narrated in a blend of present and past in which passages shift between Rachel as a third person narrator in the present and Sashie as a young girl experiencing migration in the past. At the same time the author, Kathryn Lasky, remembers her aunt's migration story in writing an autobiographical young adult novel about it, herself standing for the generation remembering its cultural heritage.[21]

Margery Evernden's young adult book *The Dream Keeper* (1985) does not specifically express an autobiographical connection of author and subject but her book's dedication shows a personal biographical link: "In Memory of Mary Carbolofsky, Christian Gulbrandsen, and the uncounted brave children of many races and creeds who have followed their dreams across the seas to America." As Lasky's *The Night Journey* this book is also part of the so-called "grandmothers-fiction,"[22] meaning that the plot revolves around a grandmother, Bobe, and the granddaughter, Becka. Both assume central plot functions: the grandmother's life story, as the main part of the novel, is passed on to her granddaughter who is to keep the memory of her grandmother alive after her death. This narrative construction accommodates the migration process as an important historical event in the past. Bobe emigrated with part of her family to North America from a Polish *shtetl*. This story is embedded in a

---

21 See also Broken Song (2005), the sequel to The Night Journey.
22 The term "grandmothers-fiction" is taken from the Cataloging-in-Publication (CIP) Data from the Library of Congress which appears in brackets in the imprint of children's books. The library's staff compiles descriptions of the books and analyses the subjects. They determine subject headings of which grandmothers-fiction is one. It simply means that "a significant aspect of the book is about grandmothers, and it is a book of fiction." The quotation as well as the information about compiling CIP-Data are taken from an email from the Library of Congress (18.03.2004). I am indebted to the Library of Congress for answering my questions on grandmothers-fiction.

frame set in the present in which Becka gets to know about her grandmother's life in the Polish *shtetl* and life after her migration. The story's part which is set in the *shtetl* takes up most of the novel. Evernden gives a thorough account of life in the *shtetl* and of *shtetl* culture including its sense of isolation from the Polish and Russian surroundings: "Here in their higgledy-piggledy *shtetl*, like an island in the great sweep of Polish farmlands and forests, they had their own tiny home with its three, crowded rooms [...]" (Evernden 1985: 44). She weaves the historical frame of reference into the *shtetl* description: "That good life had been cruelly swept away by the Tsar's soldiers and by a *pogrom*, one of those terrible raids during which Jewish people were destroyed and their property seized. Jews had no right to own land and fine houses, the marauders had said. Mama could never bring herself to speak of the *pogrom*, only of the shimmering days of her youth" (Evernden 1985: 45f.). Evernden's *shtetl* exhibits a comprehensive spectrum of *shtetl* features: it includes the historical education system with its *cheder* and *yeshiva*[23] and its inherent differences for Jewish boys and girls, the community life, and a *shtetl*'s social hierarchies when it comes to marriage and marriage brokers (Evernden 1985: 57). But most importantly, it comprises various aspects of traditional Jewish religious life such as prayers, sitting *shiva*, keeping the Sabbath, going to *shul*[24], studying the Bible, and holidays such as Passover[25].

The past decade was reticent about *shtetl* fiction in young adult literature. Its young adult books with the Eastern European Jewry as a subject are mainly set in the new country, i.e. the USA and Canada. The migration tie is pursued to such an extent that the immigrants' fate is predominantly explored after the immigration to the new country. Eastern Europe and to some degree the *shtetl* serve as a backdrop for the characterization of protagonists and are therefore not of central importance to the narrative. Kathryn Lasky's young adult book *Dreams in the Golden Country: the Diary of Zipporah Feldman, a Jewish Immigrant Girl. New York City, 1903* (1998) is a diary of the immigrant girl Zippy set in New York City. This book is completely set in New York City in the first decade of the 20th century, right after the family's arrival on Ellis Island. The *shtetl* is depicted retrospectively in the book and only in minor passages, for example when the place of origin is given as background information: "we are from Zarichka, a little village in Minsk Gubernia" (Lasky 1998: 4). The past of the *shtetl* is narrated through the diary in form of side references which are often triggered by the Zippy's mother's old country ways. They are opposed to Zippy's rapid assimilation and therefore cause conflicts: "I hate Mama's old country ways. I hate her *shtetl*, village ways" (113). So the old country and the *shtetl* are deployed for comparative purposes: the old country and the *shtetl* are associated with traditionalism and old ways for

---

23 *Yeshiva*: traditional rabbinical school for the study of the Talmud.
24 *Shul*: Jewish house of worship, a congregation; used as a synonym for synagogue as well.
25 For information on the Jewish *shtetl* culture, its customs, traditions and holidays see Zborowski & Herzog 1967, Estraikh & Krutikov 2000, and Schoeps 2000.

which the mother stands. America, conversely, stands for change and modernism, hence for new ways.

The Eastern European Jewry still features strongly in contemporary young adult literature, but not necessarily the *shtetl*. It is here in young adult literature where the shift of focus is especially striking. There are a large number of books which simply delineate their protagonists' origin in Russia or a little village in Russia without exploring the *shtetl* itself because the books' focus is on the new country. Johanna Hurwitz, for example, describes the fate of her protagonist Dossi in New York City and Vermont in *Faraway Summer* (1998). She outlines her past in Russia in a few sentences (13f.) but the book's theme, Dossi's summer vacation with the Fresh Air Fund, takes on as a central theme. Hurwitz explains in the author's note of the book's sequel *Dear Emma* (Hurwitz 2002) that life in Russia was determined by "enforced inscription in the army, extreme poverty and starvation, and very limited chances for education and employment. Russian Jews also faced pogroms where hundreds of people were attacked and murdered for no reason other than their religion. And so people kept on coming" (146). Karen Hesse, who described an adventurous flight from imperial Russia to North America in her autobiographical book *Letters from Rifka* (Hesse 1993), explores the separation of children from their parents during the influenza epidemic in Boston in 1918 in her book *A Time of Angels* (Hesse 1995). The plot revolves around the Russian Jewish immigrant child Hannah whose mother "went to Russia to take care of Bubbe" (14) and who is now trapped in a "village in Russia" (51) due to World War I. But this information is mediated in the background. The novel centers on Hannah's and her sister's fate in the United States. Hazel Krantz pursues the story of the Jewish girl Sally Gottesman in Colorado in the 1880s and 1890s in her novel *Looking to the Hills* (Krantz 1995). Sally gets to know Daniel Rabinowitz, a Russian Jewish immigrant. A Russian Jewish background is imputed to him, but it remains only the background of the mass emigration of the Eastern European Jewry since the beginning of the 1880s in which "most were ordinary folk from the small *shtetl*s who refused to live under the painful restrictions of their native lands where good education was almost impossible, many occupations forbidden, and freedom to live wherever they wanted denied" (86).

The majority of the young adult novels of the past decade still features the history of the Eastern European Jewry, but not in the old country and not in the *shtetl*. Russia and the *shtetl* simply assume a characterizing function in order to outline a protagonist's background. The described development shows that the *shtetl* culture is less remembered in U.S.-American young adult literature of the past decade than it was 20 years ago, when Barbara Mirel drew attention to this fact. The focus of these young adult novels is not on the old country, but on the new country, the former target country of migration. This country coincides with the books' intended audience. By incorporating this topic, young adult literature takes up issues of forming teenage identities in an immigrant nation. Contemporary U.S.-American picture books with their graphic and visual opportunities are inclined to tell journey stories. They also focus on migration but still exhibit *shtetl* settings. Regardless of the focus, migration stories for children invoke the genealogical connection of migration and children's literature. Migration inscribes itself into the genealogy of people whose identity is defined by being first, second or third immigrant generation. Migration stories are one means of weaving collective memory in an immigrant nation together. They not only contribute to cultural heritage of ethnic groups, but at the same time show how the process of remembering can be embedded in the fiction itself as in the case of the before-mentioned grandmothers-fiction.

In hovering between autobiography, biography, and fiction migration stories for children can give an insight into a child's perception of the migration process. Stories transporting such cultural memory remain, however, in the genre's boundaries and evidence the remembering process of a generation as shown for the example of the *shtetl*. However, these narrations have been created by an adult retrospectively after the migration through an individual and historical lens.

In shifting the focus away from elaborate *shtetl* descriptions, as done in the 1970s and 1980s, to an emphasis on the journey to the target country and the increasing portrayal of life in the new country, the *shtetl* is on its way of receding into the background in contemporary children's literature on migration. With this increasing focus on migration and the target country of migration, contemporary U.S.-American children's literature on Eastern European Jewry, and especially the young adult book of the past decade, exhibit a tendency of decreasing depiction of culture of origin. Picture books and young adult books have turned their attention to the shaping of national, i.e. U.S.-American, history and national heritage. In taking up migration as a topic, children's literature not only documents and informs, but can also assume an important function in shaping cultural memory, especially where children's books with migration topics are used for teaching lessons on history and ethnic diversity. The above-mentioned picture book *Escaping to America*, for example, is included in a history unit on immigration for second grade[26] by the curriculum "Bringing History Home," which has been funded by U.S. Department of Education Teaching American History Grants.[27] Migration stories are often set in a historical context recounting the migration history of ancestors. By remembering past migration processes children's literature sets out to keep these (hi)stories in the consciousness of the younger generation and thereby tries to pass on cultural memory.

---

26 See http://www.bringinghistoryhome.org/g2-imm/lp/immigrationhistory.doc and http://www.bringinghistoryhome.org/g2-imm/biblio/g2-imm-Booklist.html (July 20, 2004).
27 See http://www.bringinghistoryhome.org (July 20, 2004).

References

Aleichem, Sholem 2002: *The Letters of Menakhem-Mendl and Sheyne-Sheyndl and Motl, the Cantor's Son*. Translated by Hillel Halkin. New Haven: Yale UP (Modern Yiddish Library).

Aleichem, Sholem 1996: *A Treasury of Sholom Aleichem's Children's Stories*. Selected and translated by Aliza Shevrin. Northvale, N.J.: Jason Aronson.

Allison, Alida 1996: *Isaac Bashevis Singer. Children's Stories and Childhood Memoirs*. New York: Twayne (Twayne's United States Authors Series 661).

Bierman, Carol (with Barbara Hehner) 1998: *Journey to Ellis Island. How My Father Came to America*. Illustrated by Laurie McGaw. New York: Hyperion, Madison Press.

Blaine, Marge 1979: *Dvora's Journey*. Illustrated by Gabriel Lisowski. New York: Holt, Rinehart and Winston.

Bresnick-Perry, Roslyn 1992: *Leaving for America*. Pictures by Mira Reisberg. San Francisco: Children's Book Press.

Brown, Joanne 1998: *Presenting Kathryn Lasky*. New York: Twayne Publishers (The United States Authors Series 708).

Burstein, Chaya M. 1970: *Rifka Bangs the Teakettle*. Illustrated by the author. New York: Harcourt, Brace & World.

Burstein, Chaya M. 1976: *Rifka Grows up*. Illustrated by the author. New York & London: Bonim.

Cohen, Barbara 1982: *Gooseberries to Oranges*. Pictures by Beverly Brodsky. New York: Lothrop, Lee & Shepard.

Eliach, Yaffa 1998: *There Was Once a World: A Nine-Hundred-Year-Old Chronicle of the Shtetl of Eishyshok*. Boston: Little, Brown.

Estraikh, Gennady & Mikhail Krutikov (eds.) 2000: *The Shtetl: Image and Reality. Papers of the Second Mendel Friedman International Conference of Yiddish*. Oxford: Legenda (European Humanities Research Centre. Studies in Yiddish 2).

Evernden, Margery 1985: *The Dream Keeper*. New York: Lothrop, Lee & Shepard Books.

Fisher, Leonard Everett 1980: *A Russian Farewell*. Illustrated by the author. New York: Four Winds.

Hesse, Karen 1993: *Letters from Rifka*. New York: Puffin.

Hesse, Karen 1997 [1995]: *A Time of Angels*. New York: Hyperion.

Hest, Amy 1997: *When Jessie Came across the Sea*. Illustrated by P.J. Lynch. London, Boston, Sydney: Walker Books [London: Walker Books, 1997].

Heyman, Anita 1977: *Exit from Home*. New York: Crown.

Hurwitz, Johanna 2002: *Dear Emma*. Illustrated by Barbara Garrison. New York: HarperCollins.

Hurwitz, Johanna 2000 [1998]: *Faraway Summer*. Illustrated by Mary Azarian. New York: HarperCollins.

Krantz, Hazel 1995: *Look to the Hills*. Philadelphia & Jerusalem: The Jewish Publication Society.

Lasky, Kathryn 1981: *The Night Journey.* With drawings by Trina Schart Hyman. New York: Puffin.
Lasky, Kathryn 1998: *Dreams in the Golden Country: The Diary of Zipporah Feldman, a Jewish Immigrant Girl. New York City, 1903.* New York: Scholastic (Dear America).
Lasky, Kathryn 2005: *Broken Song.* New York: Viking.
Lasky Knight, Kathryn 1985: *Atlantic Circle.* New York, London: Norton.
McKoy Lowery, Ruth 2001: *Immigrants in Children's Literature.* New York, Washington, D.C. etc.: Lang (Rethinking Childhood 13).
Mirel, Barbara 1984: Lost Worlds of Tradition: *Shtetl* Stories for Suburban Children. *Children's Literature Association Quarterly* 9 (1): 6–9.
Miron, Dan 2000: *The Image of the Shtetl and other Studies of Modern Jewish Literary Imagination.* Syracuse, New York: Syracuse University Press.
O'Sullivan, Emer 2005: *Comparative Children's Literature.* London: Routledge.
Rosenblum, Richard 1992: *Journey to the Golden Land.* Illustrated by the Author. Philadelphia & Jerusalem: The Jewish Publication Society.
Roskies, David G. 2000: The *Shtetl* as Imagined Community. In: Estraikh, Gennady & Mikhail Krutikov (eds.): *The Shtetl: Image and Reality. Papers of the Second Mendel Friedman International Conference of Yiddish.* Oxford: Legenda (European Humanities Research Centre. Studies in Yiddish 2): 4–22.
Ross, Lillian Hammer 1994: *Sarah, also Known as Hannah.* Illustrated by Helen Cogancherry. Morton Grove, Ill.: Albert Whitman.
Schanzer, Rosalyn 2000: *Escaping to America. A True Story.* New York: HarperCollins.
Schoeps, Julius H. 2000: Das osteuropäische 'Schtetl.' Lebensumstände, Bräuche und Befindlichkeiten. *Zeitschrift für Religions- und Geistesgeschichte* 52 (2): 160–167.
Singer, Isaac Bashevis 1991: Naftali the Storyteller & his Horse, Sus. In: Singer, Isaac Bashevis: *Stories for Children.* New York: Farrar, Straus and Giroux: 167–183.
Tarbescu, Edith 1998: *Annushka's Voyage.* Illustrated by Lydia Dabcovich. New York: Clarion Books.
Woodruff, Elvira 1999: *The Memory Coat.* Illustrated by Michael Dooling. New York: Scholastic.
Zborowski, Mark & Elizabeth Herzog 1967[5]: *Life is With the People: The Culture of the Shtetl.* New York: Schocken Books.

DISPLACEMENT AND IDENTITY.
THE MEMOIRS OF A JUVENILE DEPORTEE UNDER SOVIET OCCUPATION

Violeta Davoliute

In the introduction to a recent conference on the sociology of exile, displacement and belonging, Maggie O'Neil and Tony Spybey (2003) speak of how:

[...] war, ethnic cleansing, economic migration, natural disasters and environmental catastrophes have shaped the contours of what has come to be known as the 'refugee problem' or 'refugee crisis' (6). Indeed, the steady increase in population movements across the globe has drawn attention to the various types of migration, including the specific character of forced migration. For Stephen Castles, "forced migration – including refugee flows, asylum seekers, internal displacement and development-induced displacement – has increased considerably in volume and political significance since the end of the Cold War (13).

Of course, forced migration was not born with the collapse of the Soviet Union, and the study of earlier manifestations could prove instructive in addressing current concerns. The forcible displacement of entire populations that took place in the Soviet Union is an important historical case of forced migration, though it is not always recognized or remembered as such. Beginning with the forced exile of Poles in 1934 from their historic homelands in Belarus and Ukraine to Kazakhstan, the policy of forcibly transferring "disloyal" or "troublesome" ethnic populations intensified greatly with the transfer of Poles, Ukrainians, Jews, Lithuanians, Latvians, Estonians in 1940–1941, Germans in 1941, Chechens in 1945 and Crimean Tatars in 1945. Most of those displaced were settled into a system of work camps known as the Gulag (*Glavnoe upravlenie ispravitelno-trudovykh lagerei*), notorious in the West even during Soviet times thanks to the heroic efforts of such Russian writers such as Alexander Solzhenitsyn.

Russians suffered by the tens of millions in the Stalinist Gulag, but the ordeal of the non-Russian inmates was somewhat different, in that it took on many of the cross-cultural dimensions we now associate with the plight of the refugee. While it would be grossly inaccurate to call the victims of Stalinist population transfers "asylum seekers," their experience of forced migration is in many ways analogous, and thus a comparison of the two may be instructive. Individual and collective identity, cultural and moral values, and attitudes towards the homeland – all suffered profound changes as the displaced persons and communities struggled to adapt to the new host environment, to a different society and culture, under the most difficult of circumstances. The effects of migration upon identity became only more apparent as these displaced persons gradually made their way back to their respective homelands in the post-Stalin period; for some, like the Crimean Tatars, only after the collapse of the Soviet Union. The experience of exile and return, in most cases, fostered a strong and rather rigid sense of national identity. In the Baltic States of Estonia, Latvia and Lithuania, for example, the repatriated deportees were among the most resolute anti-Soviet dissidents who formed the core of the nationalist popular movements of the late 1980s.

Indeed, the publication of banned deportee memoirs, possible only under conditions of *glasnost'*, contributed to the resurgence of "collective memory" that fueled a genuinely popular movement that led to the collapse of the Soviet Union.[1] The mass recollection of trauma imbued Lithuanians and other non-Russian peoples with a sense of collective martyrdom, rallied them to reject Soviet rule and assert an independent voice. Ironically, such testimonies now appear to hold little interest to the broad public.[2] Given the tasks of modernization and integration into Europe, the affective power of traumatic testimony is thought to detract from the demands of "objective" historical research and pragmatic policy development. Invoked from time to time by marginalized politicians, the testimonies of recent suffering seem scarcely relevant to the current agenda of national consolidation.[3] Deportee memoirs are widely thought to express an irredentist, ethnocentric historical consciousness fundamentally at odds with the demands of modern, multicultural nationhood.

To make their work more responsive to current needs, scholars of deportee testimony in the Baltics have taken their cue from the more recent approaches to Holocaust testimony, especially those which try to differentiate how the historical trauma was experienced by different groups of people: the particularity of women's experience, or the manner in which different "generations"

---

1 My ascription of "memory" to a collective refers to the process by which questions of the past are made the focus of public discussion as an integral part of a political strategy that challenges an established political regime. The "counter-narrative" of "authentic" memory is presented as a challenge to the "official historiography" supporting the claims to legitimacy of the current regime. Similar processes played out in all of the former Soviet republics during the late eighties. Ana Douglas and Thomas Vogler (2003) provide an authoritative review of recent works in this field in the introduction to their edited volume Witness & Memory: The Discourse of Trauma.

2 Jūra Avižienis (2004) charts the sharp decline in publication runs of deportee memoirs in Lithuania since 1994. If a 100,000 copies of Valentinas Gustainis' Be kalties sold out almost immediately upon publication in 1989, the print-run of such memoirs after 1994 has rarely exceeded 2000 copies.

3 Avižienis notes how the International Congress and Public Tribunal to Assess the Crimes of Communism held in Vilnius on June 2000 had little public resonance, since "it was perceived as a political ploy by the conservatives to humiliate the President of Lithuania and disrupt friendly relations between Lithuania and its major trading partner, Russia."

of the Holocaust experienced and remember the trauma, and how they transmit the experience through memory from one generation to the next.[4] The focus on the particularity of children's and, by the same token, women's experience promises to re-invigorate and lend new relevance to the study of this literature by bringing to light stories and experiences that have yet to be fully incorporated into the received narrative of national oppression.[5] This paper continues along this path by focusing on the example of Dalia Grinkevičiūtė, who wrote what is perhaps the best-known Lithuanian testimony to the mass deportations of the Baltic peoples during WWII. As discussed below, her work retains an enduring significance because it represents the unique experience of a girl whose self-expression embodies the tension between particularist and universalist conceptions of community brought into play by the experience of migration.

Grinkevičiūtė's life and work

Born to a middle-class family in Kaunas, Dalia Grinkevičiūtė's (1927–1987) childhood was brought to an early end by war and deportation. The Nazi-Soviet Pact of 1939 gave the Baltic states to Stalin, who extinguished the short-lived political independence of Lithuania, Latvia, and Estonia. The Red Army occupied these states in the summer of 1940, while the NKVD (Soviet secret police, a precursor to the KGB) began to deport potential opposition leaders: politicians, trade unionists, intellectuals, teachers, and wealthy landowners. All businesses and all but the smallest landholdings were nationalized and a growing number of Russian officials and immigrants began to settle in the Baltics. A week before the German invasion, on the night of June 14–15, 1941, Grinkevičiūtė, her mother, and brother, along with tens of thousands of Lithuanians, Latvians, and Estonians, were arrested by the NKVD and loaded onto cattle-cars bound for Siberia. Her father, a member of the conservative party *Tautininkai* and a former high-ranking official in the independent Lithuanian government, was arrested the same night by the Soviet secret police and separated from the family.[6]

Grinkevičiūtė was destined for Trofimovsk, a virtually uninhabited "settlement" in northeastern Siberia. She and her fellow deportees, mostly Lithuanians, were shipped north by riverboat to the mouth of the Lena River where it flows into the Laptev Sea. With inadequate shelter, miserly rations, and a murderous work-regime, most inmates died during the first winter. Dalia and

---

4   The literature on this these topics is enormous and cannot be summarized here. For a short, insightful overview of the generational approach to Holocaust memoirs, see Suleiman. For a recent example of this new approach to the study of deportee memoirs see Kirss 2000.
5   Kirss 2004: 14.
6   Juozas Grinkevičius died of starvation in October of 1943 in a prison in the Ural Mountains.

her mother survived and managed to relocate further south. In 1949, Dalia's mother was close to death, and the two risked their relative security and returned illegally to Kaunas by plane from Yakutsk. They lived in hiding with friends and family, often changing location. Now on the verge of death, Dalia's mother asked to go to their former house, even though this increased the risk of discovery. They did, and when Dalia's mother died, she had no alternative but to bury her in the cellar of their home, again, to avoid detection and arrest. Shortly thereafter she was discovered, retried, sent to prison, and then back into exile.

After Stalin's death, Grinkevičiūtė was released but still forbidden to travel west of the Ural Mountains. In 1954 she started her medical education in Omsk, and after Khrushchev's amnesty of 1956 was allowed to return to Lithuania. She obtained a medical degree from Kaunas University, and took up a job in the hospital of the small provincial town of Laukuva. Grinkevičiūtė was bitter but not broken by the experience of exile and was outspoken in her criticism of the regime. She became an active participant in the Soviet dissident movement, which meant that she was subject to regular police surveillance and harassment by the authorities for the rest of her life.

When Dalia had first escaped to her homeland in 1949, she wrote a memoir of her ordeal. Shortly before she was caught and sent back into exile, she sealed the manuscript in a glass jar and buried it in the garden of her former home in Kaunas. When she returned to Lithuania in 1956, she was unable to retrieve her memoirs, and so wrote a second version in 1976. This text, written in Russian, was published in 1979 by the underground Moscow-based journal *Pamiat'*. It was further circulated through the underground dissident publishing network known as *samizdat*, and was eventually smuggled abroad and published in French and English. Some time in the early eighties, Grinkevičiūtė rewrote the 1976 version in Lithuanian.

Since she was prominent in the independence movement during the late eighties, Grinkevičiūtė's life and testimony made a sensation when her 1949–50 memoirs were discovered in 1991; shortly after her death and the year Lithuania regained its independence. The manuscript, composed of dozens of individual sheets of paper, had badly decomposed, and it took several researchers at the War Museum in Kaunas to restore the manuscript to a legible state and decipher the contents. This early testimony was first published in serial format from 1996–1997. Grinkevičiūtė's complete works, including her early and mature testimonies, fragments from several notebooks, dialogues, and sketches for short stories were published in a book entitled *Lietuviai prie Laptevų jūros* (Lithuanians at the Laptev Sea) in 1997.[7]

---

[7] For the sake of clarity, I will refer to the 1988 (1990 in English translation) publication as Grinkevičiūtė's "mature" testimony, and the 1997 (2002 in English translation) as the "early" testimony. Page numbers following citations in English refer to the 1990 and 2002 English translations of the "mature" and "early" testimony, respectively. Citations of the original Lithuanian are provided in foot-

Grinkevičiūtė's early testimony

Grinkevičiūtė's early testimony is focused on the traumatic experience of deportation and forced labor that provoked a premature "coming of age," a point made in the title given posthumously to the English translation of this work: *A Stolen Youth, a Stolen Homeland*. In her analysis of childhood testimonies to the Holocaust, Susan Suleiman says that cognitive psychology distinguishes three discrete groups of children who have suffered from a traumatic experience. First, there are those from infancy to around three years of age who were "too young to remember" the events; those from four to ten who are "old enough to remember but too young to understand;" and those from approximately age eleven to fourteen, who are "old enough to understand but too young to be responsible" (283). At 14 years of age, Dalia was at the cusp of adulthood, which Suleiman defines as the state "where one is both capable of naming one's predicament and responsible for acting on it in some considered way" (283). On the one hand, she possesses the capacity to think hypothetically, to employ abstract concepts to reason and the vocabulary to name her experience, and in this respect differs from pre-adolescent children. On the other hand, she is still far from fully formed as an individual, and her memoirs reflect an intensely thoughtful period of coming to terms with a truly bewildering experience.

Perhaps it is precisely because of the rudimentary nature of the concepts at Grinkevičiūtė's disposal that the early testimony contrasts so sharply with the standard hagiographic representations found in other deportee memoirs of the Lithuanian deportee as a "saint" devoid of "base" human characteristics, and disturbs the normative view of the deportees as a homogenous group of Lithuanians (Avižienis).[8] The majority of deportee testimonies draw a sharp line between the representation of deported non-Russian peoples, who are seen as the victims, and the Russian camp administrators, workers, and even prisoners who are explicitly or implicitly blamed for creating and supporting Stalin's system. In these works, the distinction between the victim and perpetrator is made along national lines. Instead, the young Grinkevičiūtė's emphasis is on conveying her personal experience in the greatest possible detail, and events are framed in a quasi-tragic narrative of personal development and coming of age under the direst circumstances. Events are narrated in the first-person singular in the present tense, lending the work an expressive immediacy that lets the reader "re-live" the main stages of the deportation: the journey from Lithuania through Russia to Trofimovsk, the terrible first winter, and work at the fish factory during the summer.

---

notes, with page numbers referring to the 1997 publication of Grinkevičiūtė's complete works.
8 Avižienis 2004.

As Dalia and her fellow deportees are taken away from Kaunas in a transport train, she writes of her impressions as she and her compatriots were taken by train from her home town Kaunas:

> "I feel I shall never see all of this again," said my mother. Her words were like a knife piercing my brain. A fight for life is beginning, Dalia. School, your childhood, fun, jokes, theatre and friends: all these things now belong to the past. You are a grown-up already. You are fourteen. You have to look after your mother and take the place of your father. The first part of your fight for life is starting (14).[9]

At the last stop before the train crosses Lithuania's border, Dalia saw another train full of men. She got out of the car and walked along the other train, asking if anyone had seen her father. After she returned to the car with her mother, she thinks: "I wanted to and could have run away, but I realized immediately that I had a helpless mother to take care of. I felt as if I were 20 years old" (15).

After several days of travel, the deportees arrived in eastern Siberia, where they spent some time before being shipped by riverboat down the Lena river to Trofimovsk in the Far North. Living conditions here were quite good, and at this time the Lithuanian deportees are seen united in their longing for their homeland, the memory of which remained very close. Here, Dalia draws upon their shared folklore and traditions to represent the strength of their community.

> Living in the forest, we used to gather wood to keep the fires going till the morning. Old and young people sat together around them. A huge area was covered with the dots of glimmering fires, around which thousands of Lithuanians tried to drown their sorrows in song. [...] The songs united us, gave us strength, and seemed to warn us that we would still have lots to endure; but the children of Lithuania had to survive. For a moment the songs brought us closer to our homeland, encouraging us not to lose hope of returning (22).

Although Grinkevičiūtė clearly identifies with her fellow Lithuanian deportees in terms of a common longing for home, she shows how precarious national solidarity can be once conditions become desperate. As their common ordeal continues, Grinkevičiūtė expresses her disillusionment in highly critical portraits that break down the categories of class and nation to which the deportee community still clings. She ridicules the attempt of some deportees to maintain bourgeois standards of culture and to maintain their former status in exile: "Madame Žukienė, dressed in long Japanese silk mantel, is swishing along the deck of the barge like some noblewoman. Even at the most critical times she does not forget her manicure and massage to preserve the skin on her face.

---

[9] "Prasideda gyvenimo kova, Dalia. Gimnazija, vaikystė, išdykavimai, fokusai, teatras ir draugės – praeityje. Tu jau suaugusi. Tau jau suėjo keturiolika metų. Tu turi globoti motiną, pavaduoti jai tėvą. Prasideda pirmas mano gyvenimo kovos aktas" (36–37).

She looks down upon everyone because she was the wife of a colonel."[10] Later, step-by-step, Grinkevičiūtė shows how Lithuanians begin to steal food from each other, how a pious Catholic steals and then prays, how a "devoted husband" urges his wife not to give up hope for survival and then eats her bread when she is not looking.

Given the extreme conditions suffered by the deportees, Grinkevičiūtė's harsh critique of her compatriots' behavior seems excessive; however, the real object of her contempt is not human weakness but hypocrisy and bad faith. This becomes clearer in passages describing sexual relations between Lithuanian women inmates and Russian administrators and workers. Although she herself was still a teenager and not yet in the "market," Dalia witnesses a range of sexual encounters, and is indirectly drawn into discussions. Grinkevičiūtė judges their "shameful" conduct as acceptable under the circumstances: "There's no cause to be indignant. Each of those women was saving her life the only way she could. They could not be accused of depravity because all their instincts had already atrophied from hunger. And even if they enjoyed what they were doing, there was nothing wrong with that. Human life is short, and it is only normal to do what nature demands."[11] Indeed, Dalia reserves her criticism for the hypocrisy of the moralists:

I am sitting on my bunk and pretending that I am sleeping because I am watching how Štarienė is flirting with a soldier. This woman is very pious or at least wants to create such an impression, a big patriot. If some child somewhere learns a Russian song and starts singing it, she smiles ironically and reproaches the parents. Meanwhile she is making out with Russians and Chekists [secret police agents who ran the Gulag] [...]. She smiles to a Russian and he pushes her down and makes out with her. When she talks about her husband Bronius who is in the camps, it seems that real tears are running from her blue eyes. The Jesuit![12]

Grinkevičiūtė's early testimony presents life in the north as a trial, a test of strength, will, and principle that all deportees must face. Her account is very judgmental, dividing deportees among the fallen, whom she despises, and the heroic, whom she strives to emulate. The primacy of ethical action is pre-

---

10 "Ponia Žukienė su japonišku, ilgu raudono šilko apsiaustu tarsi kilminga didikė šlama po baržos deni. Ji net kritiškiausiomis minutėmis nepamiršta manikiūro, masažo veido odai išlaikyti. Į visus žiūri iš aukšto, kadangi ji buvo pulkininko žmona" (52).
11 "Piktintis nėra ko. Kiekviena daro daro taip, kaip nori, gelbsti gyvybę kaip kas gali. Ištvirkimu apkaltinti negalima, nes temperamento liaukos nuo bado atrofavęsi. O jeigu ir taip, argi baisu, žmogaus gyvenimas trumpas, ir tai visai natūralu, jei pati gamta liepia" (99).
12 "Sėdžiu savo guolyje ir apsimetu, kad miegu, nes stebiu, kaip Štarienė flirtuoja su kareiviu. Tai labai pamaldi moteris, ar bent stengiasi tokia atrodyti, didelė patriotė. Jeigu kuris vaikas kur užgirdęs uždainuoja rusišką dainą, ji pajuokiamai šypsosi ir iškalba tėvams, o su čekistais ir rusais tai lardosi [...] Šypsosi rusui, o tas ją verčia ir glamonėja. Kai ji kalba apie savo Bronių, kuris lageriuose, tai, rodos, tikros ašaros rieda jai iš mėlynų akių. Jėzuitė" (51).

sented as a lesson which she has learned in the camps, and which forces a revision of the prejudices of her childhood. If the plight of the women has forced her to revise earlier notions of sexual morality, the heroism of the doctor Samodurov forces Grinkevičiūtė to rethink her concept of beauty. Grinkevičiūtė describes her initial impression of doctor Samodurov in racial stereotypes: she calls him "bowlegged" with a "typically Jewish nose." The young Grinkevičiūtė contrasts Samodurov to Borisas Charašas, a handsome Jewish boy who lost an arm to frostbite due to the cruel punishment for stealing some bread. However, when Dalia sees Borisas smiling and ingratiating himself with the man responsible for his punishment, she is repelled, and wonders how can he help but spit in the face of his oppressor: "Borisas did not look so handsome to me anymore. He's just a disgusting brownnoser, a human being who does not respect himself, who humiliates himself before the others, and deserves only pity and antipathy, in my opinion."[13] This extremely harsh criticism of Borisas is developed into a reflection on the relationship of beauty and goodness, in which the bowlegged Samodurov comes out looking much better: "The beauty of Apollo, devoid of any spiritual qualities, was repellent [...]. Borisas was a plain failure. Samodurov, who in the opinion of the majority was a monster because of his abnormally huge and distorted figure, seemed handsome to me because he was very humane."[14]

In her early testimony, Grinkevičiūtė romanticizes her own ethical strength in living to tell the truth, no matter what punishment is threatened. In a detailed narrative of how she was put on trial for stealing wood, she makes it clear that she stands apart from most prisoners. She, along with five Lithuanians, is on trial for stealing boards from the storehouse. Stealing firewood was the only way to heat their barracks, to dry out their clothing and bring a brief, inadequate respite from the deadly cold. All prisoners stole constantly as a matter of survival and the response from the authorities was harsh punishment. In line with the "camp mentality," all the defendants denied having stolen: "[...] the whole brigade lies. The Soviet Union lied and will lie forever. They stole, they steal, and they will steal. All four detainees protest their innocence. Behind me I hear an approving rumble from the crowd. Soon it will be my turn."[15] At this point the narrative flashes back, to when Grinkevičiūtė stole the boards, fired up the stove, and made some tea for her dying mother. When the guards entered the barracks and asked who stole the boards,

---

13 "Borisas man jau nėra gražus. Jis tik šlykštus padlaižys. Žmogus, kuris negerbia savęs, būdamas teisus žeminasi prieš niekšą, yra tik pasigailėjimo ir pasišlykštėjimo vertas" (114).

14 "[...] neįdvasintas, apoloniškas grožis man šlykštus. [...] Borisas Charašas man negražus, nevykęs jaunuolis. Samodurovas, kuris, daugumos nuomone, yra pabaisa dėl nenormaliai didelės kreivos figūros, man gražus, nes jis humaniškas"(114).

15 "[...] meluoja visa brigada, melavo ir meluos per amžius visa Tarybų Sąjunga, vogė, vagia ir vogs. Visi keturi užsigynė. Už savęs girdžiu pritariantį minios šurmulį. Tuoj mano eilė" (74).

Grinkevičiūtė immediately confessed. Now, facing the judge's questioning, Grinkevičiūtė again proclaims that she stole the boards. The climax of the scene is when the judge asks if she is not ashamed to be sitting on the bench of the accused: "I feel everyone's curious eyes boring into me. Is she ashamed? Ashamed? Because I gave water to my dying mother? [...] You want to see repentance in my eyes? Shame? You should be ashamed, you murderers, not me."[16] The four accused who denied their guilt are sentenced to two years, while Grinkevičiūtė is found not guilty on the basis of her age and confession. Grinkevičiūtė represents herself as having emerged with her dignity intact: she may have stolen to secure resources to survive, but she never debased herself by compromising her higher ideals.

The moral dilemmas involved in surviving under an unjust and murderous regime are expressed in an extreme form in Grinkevičiūtė's overall positive appraisal of two female tramps, Lidia Vorobyova and Yulia Yudina. These two Russian women were caught up in the Gulag by chance and are seen by Dalia as utterly degraded, and yet somehow fascinating: "They were creatures whose sex and age were very hard to determine. They were extremely shabby. Gorky's tramps would have looked like lords in comparison with those two women" (164). Vorobyova and Yudina represent an extreme form of Soviet mentality: stealing openly, procrastinating, and ignoring authority. Vorobyova refuses to work, dresses in rags, and sleeps all day. She responds to the threats of the administrator by emptying her bowels in front of his office. Expressing their philosophy of survival, Yudina claims: "Here, stealing is a matter of honor, nobility and heroism. And a necessity, if you don't want to croak."[17] For Grinkevičiūtė, these women embody the true principle upon which the Soviet system worked: "As I learned later, almost all Soviet citizens share this psychology, only their ways of stealing are different. They all steal, grab and use whoever gets a chance to get a hold of something."[18] The lack of shame demonstrated by the "tramps" seems to repulse and fascinate Grinkevičiūtė at the same time. On the whole, her portrayal of Yudina is sympathetic, if not positive, insofar as she is "living the truth" of the Soviet system. Dalia's mixed feeling towards their behavior reflects her process of adaptation and simultaneous resistance to the demands of living under the brutal Soviet system.

---

16 "Jaučiu, kad visi įsmeigė į mane smalsias akis, įdėmiai stebi. Ar man gėda? Gėda? Ar dėl to, kad mirštančiai motinai vandens padaviau? Jūs žiūrit į mane, sotūs Mavrinai, Sventickai ir Travkinai, norit pamatyti atgailą mano akyse? Gėda? Jums gėda, žmogžudžiai, o ne man! Girdžiu kartojant klausimą. 'Ne, man visiškai negėda'" (79).
17 "Vogimas pas mus yra garbės, šlovės ir herojiškumo reikalas [...]. Būtinybė, jei nenori dvėsti" (153).
18 "Kaip paskui įsitikinau, kone visų tarybinių žmonių šitokia psichologija, skiriasi tik glemžimo būdai. Vagia, džiauna, naudojasi visi, kas kur ir kaip prieina" (153).

The memoir ends shortly after a scene that could be interpreted as the enactment of Dalia's self-assertive adaptation to the demands of her environment. Dalia and Maryte, a 15-year-old girl, were working in a group of Finns and Lithuanians collecting logs from the riverbank and placing them into piles. They were paid by volume, so the crew as a whole was working at a pace that neither Dalia nor Maryte could sustain: "We were not old enough for such hard work. We did not want to eat, we felt sick, and we flopped down to our beds immediately. I started wondering what we should do to avoid the pain. Life and hard work made me think" (172).

Dalia assumes a leadership role, telling Maryte that she has figured out a way for them to survive, provided Maryte follows Dalia's orders: "I am the head of the team. It is my duty to deliver the work, and it will be I who decides when we have to work and when we can rest. If you want to work with me and not with them, be so kind, please, as to do what I say" (173). Here Dalia's actions reflect the influence of the Yudina and Vorobyova's philosophy. She explains to Maryte how and why they should cheat, building hollow piles of logs and deceiving their supervisor.

> I explained to her that we should not work too hard, that work never made anyone rich, it only made him grow a hump, that I did not want to give my youthful strength to the state as a present, that we were both still going to need our strength, and that the government had already robbed us of everything. They had robbed us of our youth and our homes, they had turned us into slaves, and had pushed us into the dirt. If we had to work, after all, it was better to work with the head and not with the hands. Shocked by the audacity of my reasoning, Maryte stared at me with her surprised, wide open eyes. Once during my long oration she even burst out crying (173).

Dalia's lecture to Maryte shows how she has adapted to the culture of the camps.

By the end of the memoir, under the sheer pressure of the brutal daily regime, Dalia's memory of her homeland had become extremely faint. After the brief reprieve of the polar summer, when "for two days we could even take off our quilted jackets" the winter winds again began to blow, signaling the onset of another brutal, deadly winter: "Our yurt was very close to the water's edge. Foaming waves would roll right up to our doorstep: the sound of the sea would send us to sleep, the sound of the sea would wake us up." With this evocation of her remote location in the wild north, Dalia comments: "Not even for a minute could we forget where we were. Lithuania seemed to be only a dream, created by our imaginations. We would talk about it as if we ourselves could not believe any more that the country existed and that we had ever lived there" (176). In such primitive conditions of survival existence, Dalia began to equate the notion of "homeland" with that of civilization and culture. In the very last scene of the book, the sound of "Swan Lake" playing on a radio was the first music that she had heard since the beginning of her ordeal. Just to hear this music provoked an outburst of emotion and memory of her homeland.

Grinkevičiūtė's mature testimony

Grinkevičiūtė's mature testimony reflects her development into a committed dissident. Unlike the early testimony, with its expressive and romanticized narrative, the mature testimony is focused on making concise judgments about the nature of the regime, marshalling historical events as evidence of its criminality. It is much shorter and less expressive than the early version: the same events are retold in summary, analytical form, with precise dates and political context. Grinkevičiūtė recounts her experience in the historical past this time, and dramatizes very little, only occasionally switching to narrating in the present tense to convey her immediate impressions of the time.[19]

This forensic style of Grinkevičiūtė's mature testimony may reflect her self-declared identification with the Decembrists and *Narodnaya vol'ya* (People's Will), a pre-revolutionary Russian terrorist organization. Šulskytė, Grinkevičiūtė's friend and roommate, writes that among Grinkevičiūtė's favorite books was *Sudebniye rechi russkikh yuristov (The Pleadings of Russian Barristers)*, and that she cherished the speeches of the pre-revolutionary Russian lawyers Kon', Plevak, and Aleksandrov as much as the classics of literature, if not more. She had memorized the summation of Aleksandrov's defense of Vera Zasulich, a People's Will terrorist, and was especially moved by its closing words: "she may leave this room convicted, but she will not leave it in shame."[20] The climax of the mature testimony occurs in the third part, in her reported dialogue with the interrogators at the time of her second arrest:

I refused to sign the verdict. When they asked me why, I answered that the verdict has no legal basis. Exile is a punishment. For committing a crime one can only be exiled by a court. I was exiled as a child without having committed any crime or having any trial, only because I was born into this family and not some other. Therefore, I do not consider my leaving Yakutsk either an escape or a crime. I do not recognize the verdict.[21]

---

[19] In this respect the manner in which the English version renders the early testimony in the historical past tense is completely unacceptable. It robs the work of its immediacy, and evens out the young Grinkevičiūtė's choppy, hard-hitting syntax. This editorial decision may reflect a certain anxiety with respect to the emotional impact of the work, particularly those sections which do not portray the deportees in heroic terms. The historical past tense de-fictionalizes the work in the sense of minimizing the dramatic mode. Intentional or not, it focuses the reader's attention on the events reported, rather than the perspective of the author.

[20] "ona mozet otsyuda viyti osuzhdyonnoju, no ona ne viydet opozorennoyu" (quoted in Šulskytė 1995: 125).

[21] "Po nuosprendžio pasirašyti atsisakiau. Į klausimą – kodėl? – atsakiau, kad šis nuosprendis neturi jokio juridinio pagrindo. Ištrėmimas yra bausmė. Ištremti gali tik teismas už nusikaltimą. Mane ištrėmė vaiką be jokios kaltės ir teismo, vien dėl to, kad gimiau toj, o ne kitoj šeimoj. Todėl ir išvykimo iš Jakutijos nelaikau nei pabėgimu, nei nusikaltimu. Nuosprendžio nepripažįstu" (187).

This passage expresses Grinkevičiūtė's self-identification as a dissident and outspoken critic of the regime. Given the limited sphere of criticism allowed by the more liberal regime in the sixties and seventies, the dissidents focused on questions of individual morality, honor and dignity, and resistance to the degradation of the Soviet citizen. Dissent was expressed in a legal vocabulary that sought to unmask the bad faith on which actual policy decisions were based. Written in the typical style of the dissident text, Grinkevičiūtė's mature testimony is ostentatiously directed as an accusation against the Soviet regime.

As noted above, Grinkevičiūtė's mature testimony was written in Russian and first published in Moscow for a Soviet-wide audience. It could be described as "politically correct": though devastating in her criticism of the camp regime and of the secret police, she carefully avoids any suggestion that "Russians" are to bear collective responsibility for the suffering of her compatriots. Indeed, "Russians" are not mentioned at all, only "Chekists" and the "NKVD." The only time someone is identified by ethnicity is when she again testifies to the heroism of Samodurov. Grinkevičiūtė does not explicitly identify him as a Jew, but takes care to mention his patronymic, Solomonovich, on two occasions, which clearly identifies him as Jewish. His courage and self-sacrifice are amplified, moreover, by a report that he was killed at the front during the war. Grinkevičiūtė's sense of community with the dissidents is expressed by her description of all the "wonderful intellectual people" she met in prison: "It seemed that Stalin had locked up the country's mind, its honor, and its conscience here. Scientists, film and theater actors, lecturers, doctors, students and others were jailed here."[22] Categorical in her condemnation of the Soviet system and specific individuals, Grinkevičiūtė shows how Russians too have suffered, and takes care to avoid any suggestion that Russians as a whole bear any form of collective guilt.

The mature testimony is also, at first glance, focused on events witnessed and experienced by Grinkevičiūtė the individual. However, unlike the early testimony, which tends at times to romanticize Grinkevičiūtė's *individual* conduct and experience, the mature testimony is focused on a *collective* narrative of deportation as a catastrophic exile threatening the Lithuanian nation as a whole. In her account of how Lithuanian teachers were singled out for punishment by the regime, Grinkevičiūtė calls them the "educators of the nation," and represents them as carriers of culture and of the nation's historical memory: "From them children learned about Lithuania's heroic past, about their forefathers who for hundreds of years protected Lithuania from conquerors from the East and from the West. They taught children to love their native tongue, one of the oldest languages in the world, which had been forbidden by the Tsar for four decades."[23] By referring to how Lithuanians suffered under

---

22 "Atrodė, kad Stalinas čia uždarė šalies protą, garbę ir sąžinę. Kalėjo moksliniankai, kino ir teatro aktoriai, dėstytojai, gydytojai, studentai ir kt (188).
23 "Iš jų vaikai sužinodavo apie didvyrišką Lietuvos praeitį, apie protėvius, kurie šimtmečiais gynė Tėvynę nuo užkariautojų iš Rytų ir iš Vakarų. Jie mokė vaikus

the Tsarist Empire, the time frame of Grinkevičiūtė's testimony suddenly stretches back for hundreds of years. By evoking the memory of past oppression, her narrative of modern oppression taps into the ancient, mythological history of the nation: "They were the first to tell children about the revolts of 1831 and 1863 which were brutally suppressed, after which entire villages were exiled to Siberia."[24] The commonality of fate between Grinkevičiūtė's generation and prior generations of Lithuanian exiles brings the collective dimension of the experience to the fore.

Moreover, the constant reference to graves and burial in Grinkevičiūtė's mature testimony evokes of her sense of kinship, nationhood, and territorial belonging. Katherine Verdery shows how the ideological vacuum left in the wake of the collapse of socialism has been filled by a renewed sense of community based on a religious association of kinship and territory, reinforced by what she calls the "politics of dead bodies." Throughout Eastern Europe, the remains of persons persecuted by the communist regimes have been disinterred and reburied with elaborate ceremony as a means of "giving new contours to the past through revising genealogies and rewriting history" (40). Classifying modern nationalism as a derivation of kinship and religion, she traces its origins to the practices of ancestor worship in traditional societies: "Ancestors were buried in the soil around the dwelling; their presence consecrated that soil, and continuous rituals connecting them with their heirs created a single community consisting of the dead, their heirs and the soil they shared" (104). For Verdery, the ancient notion of kinship as being rooted in particular soils is the basis for nationalist political movements. Likewise, in Grinkevičiūtė's mature testimony, the pervasive reference to and description of burials invoke an apocalyptic perspective on the deportation, establishing a spiritual bond between the nation and its territory.

Part One of this testimony is highly commemorative, elegiac and, for extended passages, the names of individuals and families who perished are simply listed with no narration or explanation, creating the sense that we are reading a series of epitaphs. Indeed, Grinkevičiūtė presents her testimony as the only gravestone that most victims of the deportation will ever have: "I breathe easier knowing that I – as much as my strength, intelligence and abilities allowed me – built a kind of monument for the victims of the North. The world learned about the thousands of nameless victims of torture buried in the icy graves. This cannot be destroyed or erased. It is now history. It is also a monument for my parents."[25] The presentation of her testimony as a monu-

---

mylėti gimtąją kalbą, vieną seniausių pasaulio kalbų, kuri keturis dešimtmečius buvo caro draudžiama" (177).
24 "Jie pirmieji pasakojo vaikams apie žiauriai numalšintus 1831 ir 1863 metų sukilimus, po kurių ištisi kaimai buvo ištremti į Sibirą" (177).
25 "Man labai lengva kvėpuoti nuo minties, kad aš, kiek leido mano jėgos, protas, sugebėjimai, pastačiau šiokį tokį paminklą Šiaurės aukoms, pasaulis sužinojo apie tūkstančius bevardžių kankinių broliškuose lediniuose kapuose. To

ment is no mere rhetorical flourish. It literally stands in for the lack of a proper burial for her compatriots, who died in Trofimovsk without a trace: "In 1949, when they took the last of the exiles to other places to fish, the waves had already begun to destroy the edge of the common grave and it had started to crumble. It is absolutely certain that the waves have long since washed away all the corpses."[26] Siberia is a land of forgetting, because even those cemeteries created are destroyed by the shifting course of the river Lena.

At times, the testimony reads like an ethnographic account of burial practices in the Gulag, detailed yet concise, and objective in tone:

The corpse bearers themselves were starved and weak; therefore they would tie a rope to the corpse's feet and together drag it out of the barrack. They would then put the dead on sleds, and harnessing themselves into the ropes pull them several hundred meters beyond the barracks. There they would unload the corpses into a common pile. The dead people's hair would remain frozen to the barrack walls.[27]

Improper burial is presented not only as undignified for the dead, but as a tortuous and harmful process for the living as well.

The extensive description of improper burials is juxtaposed to the principal event of Part Two, namely the burial of Grinkevičiūtė's mother in the cellar of their former home in Kaunas. The contrast between the brutal, anonymous deaths in the Gulag and this different death is conveyed in detail: "She lies laid out among flowers. Her face is peaceful and blissful. The end of her suffering has come. I open the window so the soft Lithuanian breeze can stroke her face for the last time [...]. Your greatest final wish has been fulfilled. You died in Lithuania, and your native land will shelter you."[28] Part One ends with Grinkevičiūtė's evocation of the ghosts of Trofimovsk that wander endlessly searching for the road to their homeland. In Part Two, Grinkevičiūtė shows us a proper burial, the main characteristic of which is the territory in which it takes place. By burying her mother, not only in her homeland, but in the cellar of her former home, Grinkevičiūtė evokes powerful associations between death, burial, kinship, and territorial belonging. She entrenches her individual and collective sense of belonging to the territory of

---

nebegalima nei sunaikinti, nei ištrinti. Tai istorija. Tai paminklas ir mano Tėvams" (5).

26 "Kai 1949 m. paskutinius tremtinius išvežė žvejoti į kitas vietas, bangos jau pradėjo griauti broliško kapo kraštą, ir jis ėmė irti. Nėra jokios abejonės, kad visus lavonus bangos seniai išplovė" (178).

27 "Patys vežiotojai buvo labai išbadėję ir nusilpę, todėl pririšdavo pie lavonų kojų virvę ir bendromis jėgomis traukdavo iš barako. Paskui mirusiuosiu dėdavo ant rogių ir, įsikinkę į virves, veždavo keletą šimtų metrų toliau nuo barako. Ten lavonus išversdavo į bendrą krūvą. Sienų leduose likdavo prišalę mirusiųjų plaukai" (170).

28 "Guli ji lovoje pašarvota tarp gėlių. O veide – palaima ir ramybė. Galas kančioms. Atidarau langą. Tegul Lietuvos vėjelis paskutinį kartą paglosto jos veidą. [...] Išsipildė tavo didžiausias paskutinis noras. Tu numirei Lietuvoj. Tave priglaus gimtoji žemė" (183).

Lithuania through the burial of her mother in Kaunas, and contrasts this proper burial with the improper burials of her compatriots in a foreign, inhospitable land. The spiritual dimension of this contrast is apparent in that those who died in Trofimovsk are represented as ghosts, cursed to wander forever in search of their homeland.

From this perspective, the deportation as a whole is portrayed as a catastrophe. The collective loss of homeland is dramatized by this improper burial of the deportees in a foreign land where they leave no trace or tangible presence for their descendants to see and remember. The travesty of the senseless suffering and death is compounded by the fact that nobody will commemorate their death. Grinkevičiūtė's discourse of collective memory seeks to commemorate the dead and thus resist the tide of forgetting. In burying her mother, Grinkevičiūtė enacts a ritual of profound significance on a biographical, national, and religious level. Burial is a core ritual of kinship, expressive of community based on common descent. The sense of what constitutes a proper burial is profoundly communal, and touches the core of what makes for a community in a traditional sense.

In view of Verdery's argument, the focus on burial, commemoration, and kinship in Grinkevičiūtė's mature work could support a nationalist interpretation of her testimony. However, having witnessed the perversion of socialist ideals and the collapse of ethnic solidarity in the face of extreme oppression and deprivation, Grinkevičiūtė's testimony also reflects a cautious, anti-heroic stance towards notions of collective identity and belonging. In this respect, Grinkevičiūtė's testimony supports the argument of Edith Wyschogrod, for whom the cataclysms of the twentieth century have resulted in a displacement, not the reinforcement, of territoriality as the foundation of identity in the myth of autochthony, whereby the nation is understood to have been born from the earth. Wyschogrod (1998: 220) writes: "the idea of place persists, but locales have become sites of mourning, not of life but of death. Burial places are the fragments of vast memory palaces, reminders less of the events awaiting historical remembering, than of the historian's responsibility to remember". She argues that this displacement of autochthony establishes the possibility of narratives of collective memory that are not *exclusive*, but *inclusive* of otherness, based on claims of *ethical citizenship*, rather than *kinship* and *territoriality*. While the narrative of autochthony "must be heroic history [...] an incessant remythologization of the divine origin [of the community from the land]," she insists that the "reverse autochthony of burial places cannot generate such a recalling [...]. To speak from the burial place is to inhabit a terrain that is not a terrain, an exteriority that is the non-place of ethics, the 'space' of authorization of historical narrative" (225).

Even in death, Grinkevičiūtė's sense of ethical community transcends national boundaries. A third cemetery appears in Part Three, as Grinkevičiūtė commemorates the death of prisoners summarily executed in a prison in the Gorky (now Nizhny Novgorod) region:

One of my favorite places in the prison zone was a corner where beautiful luxuriant grass grew like nowhere else. Here it was quiet and peaceful and birds alighted sometimes. I was amazed at why the grass was so lovely here. Then an old prisoner explained to me that between 1941 and 1945 this plot had not yet been prison territory, and prisoners who had been shot or killed were buried here.[29]

Her reverence for this territory ("This place – each blade of grass, each flower – appeared holy to me [...].")[30] is set in the context of her discovery of the "wonderful community" of dissidents of all nationalities, and follows a hagiographic description of the Muscovite Boris Vorobjov, a dissident who lost his eye during his brutal interrogation but nevertheless refused to bear false witness to incriminate his colleagues, an act of martyrdom that testifies, among other things, to the fact that Russians too were victims of the Soviet regime.

Conclusion

In the early testimony, the young Grinkevičiūtė struggles to make sense of a bewildering experience that forces to accept responsibility and act in a role beyond her years. Not surprisingly, the narrative is structured on a "coming of age" motif and highlights the difficult choices involved in adapting to the demands of an exceptionally harsh regime. Her preconceptions concerning nation and class are steadily broken down by her analysis of everyday events. The harsh conditions of life in the camps is portrayed as a trial which levels all differences except for moral rectitude.

In the mature testimony, the politically mature dissident writer still highlights the importance of moral integrity, but takes care to articulate the heroism of others more than her own. In addressing questions of ethnic and cultural difference, she now has the tools to articulate a dialectical internationalist perspective: she shows how people who stand up to the Soviet system are honorable, but does not fail to testify passionately to the specific, collective claims of the Lithuanian nation. Grinkevičiūtė's work offers enough material to support a wide variety of interpretations: as the testimony of ethnic community, based on ties of kinship, and as the testimony of an ethical community, founded on ties of citizenship. While the first envisages common descent as the basis for belonging, the second envisages community as the reciprocity of legal and ethical obligation. The continuities between the early with the mature testimonies show the evolution of Grinkevičiūtė's ethical develop-

---

29 "Lagerio zonos pakraštyje buvo viena mano labai mėgstama vieta – nedidelis plotelis, kuriame kaip niekur kitur augo nepaprastai vešli ir graži žolė. Čia ir paukščių kartais atskrisdavo, buvo tylu ir ramu. Mane stebino, kodėl čia tokia graži žolė. Vienas senas kalinys kartą man paaiškino, kad 1941–1945 m. čia buvo dar ne lagerio teritorija ir toje vietoje buvo laidojami mirę, sušaudyti ir nušauti kaliniai" (188).
30 "Ši vieta – kiekviena žolytė, kiekviena gėlytė – man atrodė šventa [...]"

ment, and yet the differences in accent and form reveal the particularity of a child's experience.

Referencies

Avižienis, Jūra 2004: *Performing Identity: Lithuanian Memoirs of Siberian Deportation and Exile*. Manuscript.
Bumblauskas, Alfredas 2002: The heritage of the Grand Duchy of Lithuania: Perspectives of historical consciousness. In: Potašenko, Grigorijus (ed.): *The Peoples of the Grand Duchy of Lithuania*. Vilnius: Aidai: 7–44.
Castles, Stephen 2003: Towards a sociology of forced migration and social transformation. *Sociology* 37 (1): 13–34.
Douglas, Ana & Thomas A. Vogler 2003: *Witness and Memory: The Discourse of Trauma*. New York & London: Routledge.
Grinkevičiūtė, Dalia 1988: Lietuviai prie Laptevų jūros. *Pergale* 8: 151–165.
Grinkevičiūtė, Dalia 1990: Lithuanians by the Laptev Sea. The Siberian memoirs of Dalia Grinkevičiūtė. *Lituanus* 36 (4): 37–67.
Grinkevičiūtė, Dalia 1997: *Lietuviai prie Laptevų jūros*. Vilnius: Lietuvos Rašytojų Sajungos Leidykla.
Grinkevičiūtė, Dalia 2002: *A Stolen Youth, a Stolen Homeland*. Translated by Izolda Geniušienė. Vilnius: Lithuanian Writers' Union Publishers.
Kirss, Tina, Ene Kõresaar & Marju Lauristin (eds.) 2004: *She Who Remembers, Survives: Interpreting Estonian Women's Post-Soviet Life Stories*. Tartu: Tartu UP.
O'Neil, Maggie & Tony Spybey 2003: Global refugees, exile, displacement and belonging. *Sociology* 37 (1): 7–12.
O'Neill, Maggie & Bea Tobolewska 2002: Renewing methodologies for socio-cultural research: Global refugees, ethno-mimesis and the transformative role of art. In: Rugg, Judith & David Hinchcliffe (eds.): *Recoveries and Reclamations: Advances in Art and Urban Futures*, vol. 2. Bristol & Portland: Intellect Books: 141–55.
Suleiman, Susan 2002: The 1.5 generation: Thinking about child survivors and the Holocaust. *American Imago: Studies in Psychoanalysis and Culture* 59 (3): 277–95.
Šulskytė, Aldona 1995: Daktarė Dalytė. *Metai* 95 (May): 212–240.
Verdery, Katherine 1999: *The Political Lives of Dead Bodies: Reburial and Postsocialist Change*. New York: Columbia UP.
Wyschogrod, Edith 1998: *An Ethics of Remembering: History, Heterology, and the Nameless Others*. Chicago: University of Chicago Press.

CHILDREN MAKING MEDIA. CONSTRUCTIONS OF HOME AND BELONGING

Nadina Christopoulou and Sonja de Leeuw

What breaks first in the process of migration is the family, nuclear or extended. How children see themselves positioned within family relationships is a key theme in the lives of children in the process of migration and settlement. This has been one of the central themes of a European research project on Children in Communication about Migration (CHICAM).[1] The project aimed to explore and develop the potential uses of media and communication technologies as means of empowering these children and enabling them to realize their potential. The research was carried out in six European countries: Germany, Great Britain, Greece, Italy, Sweden, and the Netherlands. CHICAM was conceived as a form of action research, combining ethnography and analysis based upon social and cultural theory. Media clubs were established in each country accommodating children in making visual representations of their lives and their experiences in their new locations over a long period of time (one school year) using photography, digital video and internet.[2] The research centred on the children and prioritized the children's view of their lives, families and migration experiences. The children came from very different countries and continents: Africa (Congo, Somalia, Ethiopia, Angola, Morocco), Latin-America (Colombia, Ecuador, Peru), Asia (Iraq, Syria, Turkey Afghanistan) and Europe (Kosovo Albanians). Most families came as refugees or asylum seekers, some other as immigrants under labour migration law.

---

1 CHICAM was a three year European research project funded by the European Commission. Theme: Improving Human Resource Potential and the Socio-economic Knowledge Base: New Perspectives for Learning (Framework 5). It was coordinated by the Institute of Education, Centre for the Study of Children, Youth and Media, University of London. The project began in November 2001; it ended October 2004. See Application to the European Commission, Institute of Education, London, 2000. Also: Project Deliverable nr 1, London, April 2002 and CHICAM web site www.chicam.net.
2 Also see Kolar-Panov (1997) on the use of technology and the media (video in particular) in creating links between separated communities and places. The British and German partner had previous experience in enabling and researching self-made media production. See Buckingham, Graham & Sefton-Green (1995) and Buckingham (2001) as well as Niesyto (2003).

What the children said, how they acted and how they negotiated and challenged their places with each other and within social institutions were the foci of the research. The project was designed as ethnographic research and involved the production process, audience reception and the productions themselves. It has generated a range of original data that will be presented in this article. They provide new insights into the experiences and perspectives of migrant and refugee children. In this article we would like to discuss these insights, drawing out the wider implications for practice and policy that the results of this project highlight.

In our attention for the child and its environment we follow Bronfenbrenner (1979) who, in his view on ecological psychology, suggests that interactions with others and the environment are key to the development of children, and that we all experience more than one type of environment. The types of environment that apply in particular to our research are the "microsystem" (referring to factors located in the immediate environment of the child: family, friends and school) and the "mesosystem" (describing the way in which factors in two or more microsystems interact such as the connection between a child's home and school).[3]

The experience of migration is what first and foremost informed these contexts. Living in the Diaspora, the children participating in the project and their families in the project all had experienced some degree of disruption and discontinuity. In the new country new bonds were created that allowed for establishing new forms of continuity and for a redefinition of the notion of "home." In cases of Diaspora and disruption the family is the only mediator between the past and present that people can hold to. In the new country precisely the family becomes the site of negotiating identities for the children as they deal with the obvious cultural tensions between the "old" and the "new" world that they are bringing into the home. Vansina in his study of oral culture (1985) refers to "double portraits" and draws a distinction between private and public image. According to his analysis, the public facade is formed according to roles, social status, values and principles, while the private image often contains contradictory memories and reveals hints of fear and doubt. In the media club productions, the children often created small counter-histories that contained both worlds and expressed things previously untold.

In terms of constructing the notion of family and belonging as well as in terms of references to the past we consider instrumental the analysis of Bourdieu's *habitus* (1977), as the non-static, but rather subject to change set of predispositions which in turn affect actions and evaluations as a second, hidden nature or a "forgotten history." Strategies of survival of refugee children, as well as the paths of their memory are often rooted both in their current situation of uprootedness, as well as in their pre-migration *habitus*. Both the new and the old *habitus* form and reform, informing one another, the con-

---

3   Bronfenbrenner further distinguishes the "exosystem" (the wider social environment such as the neighbourhood) and the "macrosystem" (the larger social cultural context).

text within which new actions and reactions could be invented. A lot of this information revealing pre-existing structures as well as new strategies was revealed not through the formal research roots, but rather through shared informal social instances.

Children are active agents in making meaning in their lives and in negotiating their identities through their social interactions. In the context of migration, ideas of family and friends often differ from the mainstream culture or transform to fulfill new social and emotional needs. How these processes of change in family and friendship are understood and negotiated within school are then of crucial importance and were reflected in the work done by the children of CHICAM in the clubs. As family is a key issue here, we will be primarily drawing on the family theme.[4] With the help of some illustrative examples from the media work done by the children we will discuss the interrelations of conceptions of home and cultural identity as perceived by refugee and migrant children as they are being re-established in the new country.

Concepts of identity

There are different dimensions of identity that are intertwined in children's life; they concern both the need for identification[5] and a growing consciousness about their role in social life. Social identity articulates the relationship between the individual and his or her social environment. It has become popular among academics since the end of the 1980s and early 1990s, a period referred to as the late modern era[6] that places identity, more specifically ethnic identity, in the forefront. As Giddens (1991) points out, the need for identity has increased and the process of identity construction has become more difficult and complex. One set of factors in this respect is the experience of migration and globalization. People encounter others with different histories, ambitions and needs and as a consequence they are getting involved in a continuous process of redefining themselves in relation with others. This process of identity building and of "finding oneself" is one of active intervention and transformation (12). The world of modernity enables the creation of space for more and more intimate personal expression. According to Giddens "modes of behaviour and feeling associated with sexual life have become mobile, unsettled and open."[7] Hall & Du Gay (1996) convincingly argue how identity not only becomes an understanding of being, but also of becoming. If this also applies to individuals, the main focus here is on cultural identity as a

---

4   The authors Christopoulou (Greece) and De Leeuw (the Netherlands) were responsible for the family theme in the project. See: Christopoulou & De Leeuw 2004.
5   The work of Erikson (1969, 1974) on this is leading.
6   Giddens 1991.
7   See Giddens 1991: 12. Giddens refers to the research work of Wallerstein & Blakeslee 1989.

complex of collectively experienced values and standards that allow for a group or community to imagine itself or to be imagined by others. All groups and communities are imagined and they tend to be quite different in their style of imagining.[8] As there is no such thing as the objectivity of differences, the process of identity construction concerns the production of meaning that is given to differences between groups. Hall, a leading scholar in the field of cultural theory and identity politics, distinguishes between an essentialist approach (the one true self) and a non-essentialist (dynamic) approach, based on differences. In his view cultural identity primarily is organized around points of difference as it speaks to "the different ways we are positioned by and position ourselves within the narratives of the past."[9] This means that our identity changes when our history will be told in a different way.[10] The manner of telling is as important as what is being told.

In giving voice to underprivileged minorities we can at the same time bring recognition to spoken cultures, such as those of immigrants in societies dominated by the written word. As soon as we recognise the value of the subjective in individual testimonies, we challenge the accepted categories of history. We reintroduce the emotionality, the fears and fantasies carried out by the metaphors of memory.[11]

Identity can not be reduced to a fixed and finished object, rather it is a continuously shifting position. In post-modern debates the key word here is "hybridization", which we prefer to use over "creolization" and "syncretism" as it refers to a shifting within and between structural and cultural discourses.[12] What they share is a recognition of difference and a belief in the production of something new.

There is however another side of the picture. Hybridization of cultures also undermines old certainties and the fundamentals of identity. This is especially true for families living in the Diaspora for whom these fundamentals are crucial. To put it differently, people may have problems with the dynamics involved in the process of identity construction and they may feel the need to look for foundations. Especially in the context of migration this position needs further discussing, as the encounters between different groups of people are no longer just temporary. This is the main reason why Baumann considers cultural identity a dual discursive construction: "all having of culture is a making of culture, yet all making of culture will be portrayed as an act of reconfirming an already existing potential."[13] In order to understand the new migratory societies all over the world both the essentialist and non-essentialist ap-

---

8   Anderson (1983) offers a fundamental text as to what he considers "imagined communities."
9   Hall 1990: 225.
10 Also see Tonkin (1992) in her analysis of the construction of identity through the reconstruction of the past.
11 Raphael & Thompson 1990: 2.
12 Barker 1997: 192 and further.
13 Baumann 1999: 2.

proaches are relevant. Where you are and where you belong to are not by definition synonymous. However, the awareness of the "old place" (of origin) might be heightened in the context of moving from one such (familiar) place to a new place in the new society (one that is unfamiliar).

In the context of migration people are confronted with several degrees of discontinuity. As their notion of identity is undermined they apparently start looking for continuity in order to feel "at home" again. In the new space people feel the need to relate themselves somehow to the past. Identity thus is a question of memory and of memories of home in particular.[14] In the context of migration identity construction is informed by both past memory and current experience in the new place. The notion of home is being articulated in particular in the concept of family, yet imagined.

The very definition of family came into question all through the research, as it was often both things: the family *here,* as well as the family *there.* In the course of the research the children (and ourselves) used different definitions of family at different times ranging from nuclear family to extended family. In order to accommodate different conceptions of family and to incorporate the current domestic circumstances of the children, we have used the concept "domestic group" interchangeably with that of "family" in reference to the current situation of each child, meaning the significant bonds between people living under the same roof and sharing daily routines and events. We have noticed that domestic groups were of crucial importance and were often created in order to secure basic necessities and to provide an otherwise lacking framework.

Constructing family narratives

As the children were reluctant to share their memories and to reveal information related to their roots and their past in the club, most clubs used the format of the family tree to bring the past into the club smoothly, to accommodate Diaspora experiences and to construct a family narrative. Drawing a family tree gave a lot of information, not only about the family members and the family history, but even more so about how the format of the tree, allowing for the representation of dynamics and emotions involved in migratory history, was used by the children to construct a family narrative. Their concept of family consisted of different generations, of people here and there, of people dead and alive, of people whose names they could not sometimes recall as well as of friends. As examples from different countries may illustrate the actual shape of a tree provided a shelter to their own "imagined community." Different colours and shapes, the use of graphics, photographic portraits as well as print in various languages offered us glimpses into their private lives and their living memories.

---

14 Morley & Robins 1995: 91.

Stivan, a 13-year-old boy from Iraq, who came to Greece as an unaccompanied minor in order to escape the army, leaving all his family behind, draws a tree with thick brunches with the names of his four siblings under his own, and the names of his parents beside those of his dead grandparents. "When I say mum or dad, I feel that they are all I have," he writes. All of a sudden, in the printed form, there is an outburst of emotion that spoken words – the very obstacle that we had been trying to surpass – did not allow. Stivan does not know yet how to read and write in Greek, as, instead of joining school he works double shifts in order to support himself and his family in Iraq. He asks his cousin who is fluent in Greek to write for him. He puts her picture as well as those of his other relatives who are currently living in Greece in his family tree page. He then qualifies his choice: "[...] because they are like my family."

For Stivan, as well as for many migrant children the difference between "my family" and "like my family" represents a fundamental break in their private lives. "My family" is what they have known as such since they were born, it is what they remember from their country of origin. Furthermore, it is most likely what they are now missing, the unit that broke because of or along the journey of migration. Even if they are fortunate enough to live in the new place with part of their family or even with their whole nuclear family, they are almost always separated from parts of the wider structure that they have learned to recognize as "my family." All migrant families in a sense are broken families.

"Like my family" on the other hand, is what they have come to recognize as family in the new place, out of choice or out of necessity. Distant relatives, friends, party comrades, companions in the journey or in the camp, neighbours can all be part of the new family structure, as they are the ones to whom they may turn when in need, and their lives are often intertwined.

This division informs identity formation from the early stages of childhood. Bourdieu, treating kinship relations as "something that people *make*, and with which they *do* something" (Bourdieu 1977: 33–35), distinguishes between *official kinship* and *practical kinship*. He characterizes the relations practical because they are "continuously practiced, kept up and cultivated, in the same way as the geometrical space of a map, an imaginary representation of all theoretically possible roads and routes is opposed to the network of beaten tracks, of paths made even more practicable by constant use" (37–38). In the same sense, for refugee children, their notion of family is defined upon these beaten tracks, either with those who are far away or with those who are right beside them, sharing the difficulties of building a life in a new country.

In another page of the family tree book of the Greek club, Semset, an 11-year-old girl from Turkey, uses the photo of her mother holding her best friend, standing beside a satellite antenna (the latter representing the constant link with the country of origin, hence fortifying the memory and sustaining the connections). Above it, there is another photo of the mother with a boy (Semset's friend) and two adult men whom she calls her uncles although they are not related by blood but rather by friendship and solidarity through a mutual affiliation to an outlaw political party. The use of family terms in addressing members of a wider social network is a common practice in such circumstances. It further denotes the importance of the concept of family as an "umbrella" under which one feels protected and secure at times of exposure and insecurity. When the family itself does not exist either at all or in the way it used to do, one has to re-create it with whatever means are available. This is comparable to van Boeschoten's point in her study of exiled children and their separation from their parents in the aftermath of the civil war in Greece (2000), about identification with their peer group instead of their family and the re-invention of their identity through this affiliation[15]. For migrant children this is a common experience whereby something which is "remembered" but may no longer exist as such, becomes substituted, "re-membered" and reconstructed in a new context.

In the Swedish club Shpresa, a girl from Kosovo Albania, talked about her relatives all around the world, from the United States to Norway, something she seemed to be quite proud of. On one occasion, when the researcher was talking about the Greek project on family trees, Shpresa spontaneously started drawing a family tree on the blackboard, just as if she were a teacher. In a short space of time she had outlined her family history of at least 68 people: aunts, uncles and cousins, etc, all of whose names she knew. In the middle of the tree, she put down her own name as if she were the most central figure. She also mentioned with a smile that one uncle had two wives.

In most clubs information coming from drawing a family tree was more relevant to the children's interpretation of family than actual statistical data. In the same way the immediate family was conceptualized as people the children cared about and whose loss made a difference in their lives. Besides nuclear family members, these can also include grandparents, uncles, aunts, etc. Quotes from an interview in the Italian club where six children, which is half of the Italian club, were fatherless may illustrate children's considerations revolving around the concept of the domestic group.

Carmen: Why is it always the men who leave?
Antonio: Yea! So why do they have kids!?
Marisol: Before, they go 'Oh, you are so beautiful, etc, etc' and then...
Renato: I still have a mother and a father.

---

15 There is a whole body of literature regarding Greek refugee children in the Balkans in the aftermath of the civil war, referring to questions of identity and identification in the context of Diaspora. See: van Boeschoten 2000; Brown 2004; Ristovic 2002; Faubion 1993; Brown & Hamilakis 2003. In the Netherlands however research regarding migrant children so far focuses more on labour immigrants, not so much on refugees. Besides most of it is in Dutch. One of the exceptions is: Crul, Lindo & Pang 2002.

Antonio: My father gone when I was two years old I can't remember him, my brother can but I can't. One night I dream he was on a motorbike going around and then I discover that yes, he had a motorbike, but it was a bad dream because I was trying to see his face but couldn't.

Marisol: I'm not going to write my father's name because is not important. My mother wants to get married again.

A Somali boy, Kambooye, in the Dutch club seemed very well aware of his roots. Though he had never seen either his great grandfather, or his grandfather, he knew stories about his ancestors and it was through these stories that his ancestors remained present in his memory. It was very obvious that his ancestors appeared in his family tree. Also for Sarah in the German club, drawing a family tree provided a way of (re)defining her own relationship to her German and American relatives. She told the researcher that she dreams in German and that in her dreams her American father from whom she lives apart also speaks German, which he is not able to do!

In some clubs also photographs proved to be useful media to help to construct a family narrative in cases of disruption. Ibish was the only member of the Swedish club who showed family photos from Kosovo. On one occasion after a couple of months in CHICAM he brought in a set of pictures, which were well thumbed. They were taken during a trip to Kosovo when the whole family visited the village they used to live in. Several pictures were focused on the remains of their house, which was burnt down during the civil war. It was originally a farm surrounded by buildings. Then there were pictures showing how his father was building a new house. One picture featured a small cottage in woods. It looked new. It was a cottage that they had been given as aid after the war and were supposed to live in during the restoration of the farm. Ibish said that the house was of poor quality and that the roof leaked. Other pictures were very beautiful; a lake or parts of a bay. Though the village was not on a map, Ibish pointed out the spot. He also noticed that the text on the map was in Serbo-Croatian language. During the club activities, Ibish returned to his memories from the village more than once. He also made a drawing of the village and the graveyard, where his grandfather is buried.

These experiences tell us a great deal about the "economy of memories" that migrant children adopt. In most family narratives, there was a definite emphasis on positive rather than negative recollections. There was often an observable need to leave out what was perceived or experienced as negative, painful and destructive, either by suppressing it or by alternatively shifting the focus to reverse feelings, some of which were constructed in retrospect. We experienced how the CHICAM club could offer a space to reconstruct family history with the help of audiovisual media. What is kept in the memory, is what can free the imagination and the projection into the future: the strength, the courage, the persistence, the lack of fear. All these past things could be utilized in the present. What is kept is what can be used. The rest is discarded, forgotten, repressed, or left unspoken. Almost all children showed this "economy of memories" at very specific moments during club work, and it was clearly in operation in their families as well. Family history was thus a defining factor in this kind of memory work. It is not only where one comes from, that defines one's identity in the present; the stories that are told about one's origin, and the (big) picture created by these stories, also contribute to the notion of "who I am" at a certain moment in one's personal history.

Negotiating memory

Negotiating memory is a complex activity. On the one hand, the reconstruction of past life serves to keep one in touch with the "positive" aspects of life in the country of origin. On the other hand, it also brings forth "negative" experiences, which are not always easy to deal with. Memory has to keep one's origins alive. At the same time it has to provide explanations and justifications. This implies a constant and determining conflict. As a result, the memory of the family is often strictly kept within the household borders and the private sphere. CHICAM club work helped to bring these memories into the public sphere and to bridge the gap between private and public. Many a time, CHICAM became the space where things that would not be easily brought up at home or at school, were expressed and discussed.

Memory negotiation is also a very sensitive area and plays an important role in the process of identity building. At the same time it makes it difficult to comprehend the past of the family. Remembering relatives, places and friends in fact always added a melancholy mood to the children's narration, along with feelings of loneliness and loss. For example Eritria from Ethiopia in the Italian club said: "I arrived here two years ago, with my mom, my father and my brothers [...]. I'm so lonely; poor me! All of my stuff is still over there. They weren't able to bring it here, pictures, dresses [...]." Even though her nuclear family was in Italy, she felt alone. Besides this melancholy, there was also a will, even necessity, to present the country of origin as a pleasant place – a space of harmony, joy and freedom: memories were filled with romantic notions of the home country, focusing on positive aspects.

Photographs seem the most concrete proof of a family living "there." The children in several clubs confirmed their importance. Kambooye from Somalia in the Dutch club: "you should only know how often we look at them!" This was also true for Beaugarçon from Congo. Both their families seemed to use photos to keep memories of the family "there" alive and to tell stories. Most children in the Dutch club had their own photo album, some even had their own photos. Hakan in the German CHICAM club kept photographs from Turkey in a metal box, which revived in him positive memories of a harmonious family life. Though some children pretended there were no photographs to be taken to the club (as with the Syrian Kurdish kids in the Greek club), their existence and importance became clear when the researcher visited the family: actually there were a lot!

How families dealt with photographs may illustrate the very different ways of negotiating memories both by the children and their families. These are partly due to different experiences of Diaspora. We will discuss several cases. The first case illustrates how even absent pictures can be an incentive and a tool for recollection. Mozde in the Greek club remembered her journey from Afghanistan to Greece, one evening during an informal interview at her parents' kiosk where she occasionally works. She had not mentioned anything about it before and had evaded the question. This time, after briefly claiming not to remember, she began by contrasting there to here in terms of friends and explained how the pictures of the family got lost on the journey:

"We knew too many people there, we had friends and relatives, cousins, uncles, aunts, but mostly uncles. They have now spread everywhere. I do not remember them any more, not even their names."
'Do you have pictures of them?'
"No... they got lost."
'How did they get lost?'
"On the journey."

She explains how she was walking along with her parents while they were carrying her younger siblings. The journey companions were helping them carry their luggage.

We did [manage to get here], but the others didn't. They were following but they could not keep up with our pace. They were left behind. We kept going. We went on. They stayed behind. We don't know what happened to them. That's how the photos got lost. They were helping us carry our stuff. When they stayed behind all that got lost. We were the only ones who managed. Just us. Our family.

Mozde narrates in a structured way: from there to here, "us" versus "the others," "me" as opposed to the "rest of the family." Mozde in her mind associated the loss of the journey companions with the loss of their photos and the disappearance of her past. As she thrust forward, her past withdrew. The faces on the photos (along with the faces of all those left behind) were fading away. The past for Mozde was another country.

In the Dutch club children made a family video using existing photographs. Two Iraqi brothers, Elias and Simon, only brought a few pictures from home. Both boys had great difficulties in remembering who the people were. Their struggle is reflected in the silent intervals in the story, told by Elias, to go with the pictures in the video. The obvious lack of memories had a reason that became clear when the researchers visited the family. Their mother clearly stated that she did not show the pictures to the children, because she did not want them to form a picture of life and family there: "I really don't know if I am right not showing them the pictures. But for the moment we want to focus on the Netherlands and try to build up a new life here and leave life in Iraq behind. I am reluctant to tell much about Iraq, because I don't want the children to long for a certain image of Iraq that they possibly will never experience. That is not realistic." The family was strongly living in the here and now. To some extent they hid a part of their history from the next generation, while expressing a parallel anxiety about adapting to a new reality and leaving the old world behind.

The reworking of pictures, absent or present, also helped to (re)define their own relationship with the past. Not only photographs, but also other "media" (drawings) and less obvious activities, such as travelling, helped to trigger memories about journeys and places where the children had lived. When the Swedish researcher was driving Hana, a girl from Kosovo Albania home, she started to talk about a journey to Kosovo, when the whole family was assembled. That was a happy moment in her life. The best thing was the car trip itself and that they had stopped and slept over on three different occasions. But when they arrived in Yugoslavia, they had to drive across the mountains, and then her father was afraid. When drawing a childhood memory, Hana was composing a picture of a couple seen from behind, sitting on a sofa and watching a blue-green sea or ocean. It was her family on a visit to Kosovo. A year later, in a series of photos from her summer holiday with her mother in Kosovo, she returned to a similar composition, where her mother is sitting on a stone in the sea or ocean. The scene with the parents at the lake seems a projection of a romantic dream about Kosovo, cultivated by the parents, a dream they wanted to preserve and which helped them to overcome all the horrible events that took place there: an idealized representation of "home."

In the German and UK clubs it turned out to be much harder to get to know how children had conceptualized the past, due to both the reluctance that the researchers displayed to deal with this and the fact that over the year family stories changed as in the UK club. Stories were told differently according to context. In the UK club Sahra from Somalia was very willing to speak about her family and their lives but it became clear that what she told was not the present reality but the stories now past, stories of happier times. She told these stories to maintain an image and to help herself through the present bad times. In a video made at the very beginning of the club she showed photos of her family (particularly her father who had died) and talked about Somalia. That film is very much based in the past.

David from Angola maintained his silence on his past throughout the year but even then his changing attitude to his present and future meant that in some ways he was reassessing his past or his relationship with it. Haamid took a long time to talk about the family he used to live with in Guinea and then he did it mainly through drawings representing the village and the house he had lived in with his family, and some family members. Being reunited with his father was a major factor in how he viewed past and present. However, he never spoke about his mother.

Meroe, a girl in the Italian club from Ethiopia who does not live with her parents in Italy, showed a drawing made for her grandparents with some greetings written in Italian. She had apparently lost her mother-tongue language, having arrived in Italy six years ago. When the researcher asked her if she was going to send the drawing on, she said no, due to both the language barrier and the great amount of time that had passed since the last time she communicated with her grandparents. She kept the drawing for herself on her bed, often touching it tenderly. As we see in the above situation, loving memories can also hurt. Silence is also very significant in this context.

What stands out from the experiences in all clubs is that an important aspect about memory negotiation is the family situation as such: children who have no family at all or have a really problematic one encountered more difficulties when elaborating ideas of past experiences abroad. Not only was the symbolic aspect of the connection complicated, but also the technical one was quite intricate. Children who had good relationships with parents enjoyed more occasions to keep in touch with relatives in their countries of origin, while the others did not. Some of the children in the Italian club had significantly poor relationships with their parents. Obviously in these cases they did not want the researcher to meet their family. The use of video, on the other hand, gave them a new chance to express the anger and frustration they lived with in a free manner. Some of them used the camera (and the CHICAM space in general) to "confess" bad ideas and difficult feelings about parents and relatives. The CHICAM Club became a space to free these emotions, while being a space well separated and protected from the family. Although some of these issues would be raised for children from any background, how family history is viewed and experienced by migrant children in particular is above all formed through the experiences of family distance, separation and reunification.

Memory and (questions of) identity

The negotiation of memory shapes identity. Self-definition in the new country is often characterized by referring to what is left behind. The roots may stand as a source of inspiration for the current life as well as a source of strength. On the other hand, the past may be re-invented and accommodated into the present, in order to create mechanisms of survival and new, hybrid identities, articulating positions drawn from a variety of discourses and sites.

Beaugarçon in the Dutch club had no autobiographical memories of the Democratic Republic of the Congo. In order to create a family history, he invented stories that mixed the stories that were being told within his family and the ones he might have heard or read for example on TV or in the newspaper. He used these stories about the past repeatedly to develop his identity in the present: "I kept asking [my mother] when we finally could go there [Congo]. In the end we went for a vacation and to see some family. Everyone has a nice villa, but it is dangerous because of robbery. I have witnessed one myself." As it was impossible to go to Congo because of the political and military situation, the boy's mother confirmed that they indeed never went there. The difference between truth and fantasy did not seem to be relevant. Creating a fully formed picture was more important. Media helped him to fulfill this ambition:

in the club, he made a family video with the help of existing pictures from the family and a "new story" along with these told by Beaugarçon himself. This combination of pictures and commentary made it possible for him to tell his family history as a continuous story in which the "there" and "here" are linked. We also noticed this link on a different level. He represented himself as an average teenage boy (clothes) who does not hide his African background, using African icons in his drawings, wearing family jewellery: an African chain that his uncle gave his father and his father passed on to him. On one of his video diary tapes he played a sort of African king, putting on a curtain for a cloak, and dancing.

In Beaugarçon's case, there is first and foremost an observable need to establish continuity between past and present in order to surpass the discontinuity of migration. The construction of a family history serves as a tool in this pursuit, bringing together, on a shared and recognizable ground, things that have been standing apart. The memory of his past is filtered through the knowledge of the present. On the other hand, his current situation becomes connected to his past and his roots, as though the one stems from the other through a smooth continuity rather than a disruptive discontinuity. In pursuing this, he is mixing truth and fantasy in order to construct his personal history and place it within a context. History and the past are re-invested with meaning through imagination. When the real links are missing and the explanations do not always come handy, imagination serves as a way of building bridges and holding together tentative, fragile and fragmented realities.

On the other hand, the pressures of adaptation may challenge habits kept for the sake of nostalgia and in order to sustain the sense of belonging. This is not simply a matter of cultural confusion. Living between and within two worlds and two cultures (or more in some cases) the children build hybrid identities, pertaining to more than one frame. This became visible when the children brought to the club music from their countries they liked to listen to, and stories related to the journeys they made to their home countries.

In the Greek club, the children were asked to bring an object from their country of origin and speak about it in front of the camera. This request caused some confusion to the two Turkish girls, Odil and Emine, who were born in Greece, as to what exactly we meant by "their country": this one or the other? They seemed to find it difficult to locate and define the concept "our country".

Odil:	Which country?
Emine:	This is our country.
Odil:	We were born here!
Emine:	Where should we bring something from?

Some children did not bring anything, told a story or sung a song (which they heard or learned in their country, but which was not necessarily representative of their country). The choices, however, were not always charged with personal meaning. Often, they depicted what they thought others wanted to see or hear. Beyond this schematic representation however, a lot of culturally embodied knowledge was conveyed (dressing in traditional costume, dancing in a ceremonial way) that revealed the dynamics involved in continuously negotiating between different identities. Michelle, for example, sung a French song, which she learned, at her French Catholic school in Congo. Her choice of representative things or images was defined in reference to her French educational background as opposed to the Congolese or the Greek. This was the dominant culture to which she was exposed, and at the same time, her "passport" to both countries: French education and Catholicism would be acceptable in both contexts, if not considered superior to the local.

The negotiation of memory was filtered down to a "symbolic" item that involved questions of identity. Claiming the right to pertain to different contexts and identities, as well as selecting their own dynamic of when and how, proved to be the determining element in the clubs, where the children set their own rules and acted accordingly.

Family representations

How the children experienced family life in the new country and the living between two worlds and two cultures, how they built not only flexible but also hybrid identities became visible in their representations of family life as such. The children articulated their own conceptions of home in the new situation both in terms of success and in terms of a continuous mediation between the old and new which appeals to different dimensions of identity as they are being experienced in children's lives: to mention the need for identification in becoming an adolescent, the notion of self-representation in relation with their closest peer groups and their particular ethnic background that is informed by experiences of disruption.[16]

In her family video show a girl from Armenia in the Dutch club exclusively used photos of the family having fun, showing affection towards each other. The photos were all taken in the host country. One of them even shows the family celebrating Saint Nicholas, a truly Dutch feast. The representation of the happy family life indicates the family's ability to adapt as well as the family's successful attempts to start a new life in a new country. A Kosovo Albanian boy in the Swedish club in his video essay *Mohammed's Family*, focuses on status symbols, such as electrical appliances and technical equipment in the kitchen as well as the computer and the two parable antennas. Material assets and economic status often act as symbols of integration and of doing well. Mohammed's choice to focus on them, perhaps more than indicating that the material standard of living was important for him, was an attempt to affirm and confirm to himself and to others that his family had earned its place in the

---

16 See Erikson 1969, 1974; Giddens 1991; Hall & Du Gay 1996.

new country. In this particular cases identity was not so much a question of memories of the past, not so much a question of "becoming" rather in its emphasis on "economic success" it confirms identity in terms of "being," being well, being like anyone else.

Other video productions illustrate how "home" has become a site of negotiating identity. Sahra, the Somali girl in the UK club took the camera home to film in her house, at her local shop, on the way to school and with some friends at school.[17] She modelled the first section of her production on a show on MTV on which celebrities show the viewer round their homes. Her sister welcomes you at the door and says: "Come in, I'll show you my palace." Once we are in the house the girl guides the viewer through the living room (the TV is on and music is playing but no-one is there!), through the back of the house where the snooker table is. Then into the kitchen where food is ready on the cooker. There is also a stereo there "in case you get bored when you are cooking." As Sahra's sister goes round the house she lists all the objects in each room: bed, wardrobe, TV etc. Downstairs again and we are shown out of the house; "You've seen my palace now, so get your arse out here, go, go!" The video movies illustrates both Sahra's family oriented attitude and her orientation towards the new present. Also in interviews with the UK researcher the girl described herself mainly as "London-ish," while at the same time she pointed to her Somali identity in terms of food, however not in terms of religion or traditions connected with the past. On the contrary she rather stressed the fact that being in a new country for her meant the possibility of distancing herself from traditional rules especially as they apply to women. These decisions are closely linked to building new identities that help children to be part of their new lives. In Sahra's case this put her in conflict with some of her Somali community (if not directly with family members). She was building her own new future.

Often, under the pressure of their new peers and the influences of the new society as well as the media images which bombarded them with new cultural codes, there was a tendency on behalf of migrant children to dismiss what the family and the household symbolized.[18] The new role models in the country of residence as well as the children's exposure to other ways of family life, frequently led them to a questioning and a severe criticism of the family roles and rules. In addition to their passage to adolescence, this usually caused friction within the family. In the Italian club some of the children who were living in a convent even admitted that they were "ashamed of their parents." There were various reasons for this such as the cultural gaps, the language problems, but also psychological dimensions of identity formation can be observed here, such as the tensions in parent-child relationships especially on the verge of adolescence, their consequent need to keep a situation under their own control

---

17 Description from the national UK report on family relations.
18 This is a clear illustration of Bronfenbrenner's "mesosystem" pointing to the interaction between relevant factors in the immediate environment of children.

and to affirm their own perception of themselves without the mediation of their parents.

However, when requested to conceptualize the "home" in the CHICAM club, most children chose to focus on the emotional relations at home and not on the material standard. The "home" was rarely represented as a site of material objects within which one lives. Even when material objects were carefully placed in a "homey" mise-en-scene the purpose was to communicate a feeling: to convey the warmth of the domestic space. In *Clara's colours and sounds* a Lithuanian girl in the UK club discusses the ambivalence of being in the new country, pertaining to both the past and present. In her film she shows objects that are a mixture of those that have great emotional significance, have associations with the past and also with connecting her to the past.[19] Others are entirely connected to the present. Each one can be seen as significant. They go in this order: a red heart object (filmed after a red decorative heart that her grandfather had sent her and that hangs on her bedroom wall), the blue wallpaper from her bedroom, a map, a cooking pot, a green bag she had been given, a soft toy, a pencil, a Winnie the Pooh clock, a picture of a monkey she has hanging on her bedroom wall. She has kept the film very personal to her but also quite anonymous and unconnected to her family and everyday life. It was significant that she did not want to include her family or in a sense locate where they were. The warmth of the domestic space was filtered through the girl's ambivalence about being in the new country, as she understood why they had left Lithuania yet feeling tremendous homesickness for "there."

In the Greek club, when explaining the pictures that she shot at home, Rengin, a girl from Turkey, admitted that she re-arranged the objects in the kitchen in order to make it "look beautiful." Her mother was standing in the middle of most of her pictures and also in the family tree page that she made, nicely dressed and with make-up on. Rengin was very eager to emphasize her mother's importance in holding the household together and taking care of the whole family. In the Swedish club, in a documentary on her home, a girl focused on family relations, her parents, siblings, for example a visit to her brother's home, where she put emphasis on filming his little baby son. She here had the chance to focus on emotional moments as when her mother was hugging the cute little baby.

What is emphasized even then, is the role of, for example, the mother in creating and maintaining the „hearth," the familial bonds and the closeness, which keep a family together despite disruptions and displacements. That after all is what each one of the children had to learn well and constantly keep in mind: home is where the hearth is.

---

19 Description from the national UK report on family relations.

Notions of cultural belonging

Cultural identity is negotiated and redefined in the new place, even when the ties to the ethnic or religious background are strictly maintained. Cultural identity is a tentative concept, especially as it closely encounters a new world, new influences and new habits. The latter cannot but have a major effect upon the values and habits that were carried along, even in regard to day-to-day routines. The conflict between the old world and the new is one of the major issues that all migrant families or communities have to deal with. The role of the migrant child within the family and outside the family is crucial: cultural identities between different cultures, changing responsibilities, roles being sought and negotiated, all reflect upon the children even before the adults. The "hearth" was not a fixed place, rather became a site where cultural identity was negotiated and redefined in the new place allowing for the construction of flexible and hybrid identities, that enable the children to choose from the different cultural and social worlds they are part of. The "hearth" thus changes as the family encounters these different worlds. Family routines, events and celebrations are of vital importance in preserving the cultural identity of a migrant community and are often attended with more dedication than they would in the country of origin. The pace of life inside the household is kept with a remarkable similarity to that in the country of origin. When everything "outside" is changed, the "inside" of the household and the family life remain – or struggle to remain – the same. Clutching upon old habits and re-investing them with new significance is a vital process for people who have experienced major disruptions and discontinuities.

Many a time the children expressed the idea of food being central to their cultural identity. Eating is an important everyday ritual for most families, and a lot of time and energy is invested in this. The family table is the "hearth" around which the familial bonds are nurtured and sustained, and the time spent with family members and friends around eating is valuable for re-asserting the unity of the family, a unity often threatened by the shift in circumstances. Bodily memory sustains complex emotional ties. Although the children were exposed to local dietary habits (such as fast food), they often expressed their preference for the diet of the country of origin.

Eating routines in most families followed as in the country of origin. Every meal is a shared event and the fact that it is prepared with the material and emotional ingredients that it has always been maintains and re-affirms a sense of consistence, collective identity and belonging. Food is emotionally charged as a family ritual. Masja, an Armenian girl in the Netherlands, declared in a rather representative way that family life for her "means sitting and eating together." All the children in the UK club talked about family outings, parties, celebrations. These were mainly with the family members.

From the children's stories about how religious holidays and events are being celebrated at home and within the community as well as from our direct observations, we have noticed how family routines (i.e. fasting) and traditions are often structured by religion. Often religion plays the role of sustaining cultural identity and serves as a reminder and a fortifier of habits and traditions which were forcibly left behind. This becomes all the more important when "homelessness" is experienced in asylum seeker's centres where people wait for a (temporary) residence permit or to be expelled. For a Syrian girl in the Dutch club the experience of homelessness deeply influenced her perception of the world and her immediate future. She reworked her experiences in a drawn animation movie. In an interview she highlighted especially the rituals and religious holidays that were celebrated intensively and remembered vividly in the centre. These celebrations gave her something to hold on. The nuclear family was very close, besides she felt strongly related to other Syrian families. Here the notion of the (constructed) extended family comes to the fore, offering primarily a site of remembering the home country and of reconstructing an ethnic identity! She bonded both with children who shared the experience of living in an asylum seeker's centre and with children who shared the same ethnic background.

From this and other examples we noticed how cultural identity indeed was often experienced through religion; many of the children followed the standards and values connected to religion, at least to the family's way of practicing religious laws and rules. In some occasions where the parents declared to be atheist, the children may follow the religious traditions of their country of origin. Continuity in family life was also sustained through language. The children all spoke the local language in the public space, however nearly all spoke their mother tongue at home with their parents, most of who were not fluent in the new language. Language is a strong bearer of cultural identity; it contains the family stories and histories, it helps people to remain connected to a homeland. On the other hand, language is also a tool to develop a new sense of identity, to get connected to new communities. Concerning language, the children's role is crucial in respect to the rest of their family, as they are the ones who learn it first (mainly at school but also through the everyday use in the neighbourhood, playground or their other activities) and who in turn act as translators and mediators. The parents often have to rely on their children in coming to contact with the locals, something that affects the distribution and negotiation of roles within the family. For all families language seems to be an important tool in building the notion of continuity in family life as it is here and now, but also for some children language represents possible ways of being mobile, of finding their place in a global world; they preferred to speak English.

In all media clubs in the countries involved the representation of family life had two major aspects: on the one hand it was geared towards a constant attempt to sustain the family links that had been disrupted by the journey, while on the other hand it was directly related to the investment made in making a new start in the new country. These contrasting attitudes towards the family in terms of the family images that were projected by migrant children are significant in capturing the tension that they are experiencing. The conflict between the old world and the new is one of the major issues that all migrant families or communities have to deal with. Family life itself becomes affected seeking its place in terms of tradition and in terms of modernization in a global world. It could be argued, that often migrant children experience a split reality or learn to incorporate a dual discursive construction, caught between two very different worlds: that of the current country which is new and unexplored, and to some extent feared, and that of the country of origin which is often painfully left behind, yet mostly vigorously sustained within the family through both memory and desire. Private space is hence differentiated from public space. Different roles are allocated to different spaces. Family life in itself becomes a site of negotiating cultural identities.

Family as mediator between the private and the public

Inside the clubs, family life was not a constant reference, or an easily talked about subject. There were different reasons for this among which: traumatic experiences, being a teenager, having bad parent-child relationships, identity separation between family space and school space. Yet, how the children experienced family life and how they defined their role within the family, has become visible at many moments both implicitly and explicitly during our club work. It slowly became part of the ongoing discussions, but not before establishing a close relation of mutual trust. Even then, it was mostly discussed on an individual basis and not in the group. Access to family life for the CHICAM researchers was limited. The private space of family life was carefully kept separate. Besides we have noticed at some points a dialectical relationship between being a child or teenager and being a migrant. One way to deal with this seemed to clearly divide and segregate different roles into different spaces (outside and inside the family).

In defining their place as children within the family and outside the family, the children were challenged to negotiate between the demands of the family traditions and rules and the demands of the outside world. This also involves negotiation of new roles between the parents and the children. Parental intervention ranged from regulated freedom and autonomy to strict control. On the one hand, there is the fear of the unknown, which may lead parents to want to control all their children's activities in order to protect them and to avoid exposure to dangerous situations. On the other hand, having to survive with meagre means in a new country may require the participation of all the family members in subsistence activities. Family members have to rely on one another and show trust. Parental control may be direct and prescriptive or indirect and oriented. Instructions and advice were a common form of such control, as well as precautions or threats. Another equally effective way however is when the current situation is seen as much better than the alternative in the country of origin – thus cultivating a sense of obligation of the children towards their parents. The degree of openness and freedom that the parents allowed in the family relations depended also on the degree of integration and social involvement and the existence of a wider social network. Inevitably, the new rules and circumstances increased insecurity and the fear towards the unknown. Parental control and regulations were usually related to the expectations of the parents for the future of their children. Migrant parents invest in the future of their children and in offering them the best possible opportunities, mainly through education. This may also offer some security in terms of their long-term plans. Almost contradictory there was often a high level of expectation in terms of fulfilling duties within the family (i.e. looking after younger children), when parents had to be away for work and that kept the children away from school. Taking on more responsibilities at a young age inevitably makes the children more autonomous.

The video production that the girls in the Italian club made, *Rules of Life*, discusses the dialectical relationship between being a migrant and being a teenager as well as the different roles children take up in different spaces. The articulation of their wish not to be treated as kids and to set their own rules, and at the same time the realization of their responsibility to look after themselves and to behave as adults fending for themselves are communicated as the main messages of the film. This is but one aspect of growing up in a new country. It illustrates how different dimensions of identity (e.g. psychological and ethnic) become interwoven even when they are addressed at different moments.

However many a time the domestic space itself becomes a place to explore different sometimes even conflicting roles that the children are expected to play within the family. A Dutch animation movie, using liquorice of all-sorts, displays this as the maker, a boy from Congo, represents himself looking after his three baby sisters and brothers who disturb his favourite activity at home: watching music videos. He simultaneously points to the global youth culture that he enjoys and to his African background using African iconography in his animation drawings. Here the crossroad of different cultures is linked to family life as it manifests itself within the private space of the house. We have observed how for the children and their families "family" indeed was primarily a private, even domestic space in the literally sense that was kept separate from the public domain. In the CHICAM club the family became a subject matter that involved the interaction between the domestic and the public space. In this interaction the children were the main mediators linking the outside world to the inside space of the family.

From how media actually were used in structuring communication among family members and from the symbolic meanings that were attached to media within the family we noticed the function of the family as mediator between private and public. There is much to say about this as it involves parental control of media consumption of the children and the shift between different cultures as is expressed e.g. in renting video movies from the home country and watching the national news in the host country. More important turned out to be the role of satellite TV as a link between the "there" and "here." Often it played the role of the hearth: the focal point around which the family gathered. Tuned to programs in the country of origin, it stood as a constant reminder and a permanent link. It became a relentless carrier of the life there into the life here: the satellite brought the public space of the distant country of origin into the private space of the living room. All in all the wide range of media use within the private space of the family offered the children a platform through which they were able to experience a plurality of possible life styles parallel to a plurality of identities; this applies in a particular way to children growing up in the context of Diaspora.

Concluding remarks

The first thing that is affected in the lives of children in migration, is the family. Family relations are always disrupted, whether this affects an immediate or an extended network. The family being the main mediator between the past and present in the new situation becomes a site of negotiating identities. This is especially true for children as they are the first to bring the new world into the home. "Home" then accommodates the encounter of different worlds and images, both public and private, informed both by the pre-migration *habitus* and the Diaspora *habitus*. Notions of home and belonging shift, as they have to adapt to the new world that the children encounter. The outside world of the new country primarily interacts with the inside world of the home. In the context of migration family life replaces "home" as a pillar of identity, yet it is continuously negotiated in the migratory context where the family lives.

The family theme turned out to be the most difficult to deal with both with the children and the researchers. The research methodology uncovered aspects of children's lives that are hard to get at. The research project has made clear how media can be used as tools for different purposes, addressing key areas of children's lives, speaking to the different realities as they are being experienced by them. These experiences were articulated through media production processes without the researchers having to ask about these explicitly.

The CHICAM club first and foremost provided a productive space where the primary concern was to let the children's voice be heard and to let their own gaze be recorded. For children with limited or no access to such spaces, the club established a platform of communication with other children with similar experiences, as well as a platform upon which to step and articulate their own sense of who they are. By making media productions, the children created a particular media space for themselves in which they could explore the potential of media as means of communication and where they were able to represent themselves on their own terms and to speak about themselves in a free way.

The insights drawn from the research may inform practice and policy in several ways as the children's voices were central in the project. Media production helped children elaborate on their migratory experiences. Access to media production and expression appears to be an important means for negotiating memory and finding their place in the new society. Such activities could be made available as part of school curriculum or community activities. Media also provide migrant families with opportunities for expression of their own experiences and perspectives. Platforms that allow for exchange among different communities can be seen as vital instruments in intercultural communication. They in turn provide useful data for researching Diaspora experiences among families.

As may have become clear from the data that we presented "flexibility" is a key issue in addressing family relations in a migratory context. This applies to theoretical concepts of identity and children's experiences of discontinuity and disruption alike. The process of identity building is a continuous process that involves a permanent redefinition of oneself in relation to others. Finding "oneself" in a migratory context is informed by both past memory and current experience in the new world. We have observed how making media productions facilitates the process of identity building as it involves making "narratives" and representations of family life in which identities are being created and given meaning. Not only did the children articulate flexibility in their conceptions of family and home, also they seemed to have incorporated the changing power relationships that take place within families in transition. Children becoming the mediators with the new world often form hybrid identities between the family culture and the new society; however in the new context they also need safety and stability as pillars of a new house that could accommodate feelings of "belonging."

References

Anderson, Benedict 1983: *Imagined Communities: Reflections on the Origin and Spread of Nationalism.* London: Verso.
Barker, Chris 1997: *Global Television. An Introduction.* Oxford: Blackwell.
Baumann, Gerd 1999: *The Multicultural Riddle. Rethinking National, Ethnic and Religious Cultures.* London: Routledge.
Boeschoten, Riki van 2000: The impossible return: Coping with separation and the reconstruction of memory in the wake of the Civil War. In: Mazower, Mark (ed.): *After the War Was Over: Reconstructing the Family, Nation and State in Greece, 1943–1960.* Princeton: Princeton University Press.
Bourdieu, Pierre 1977: *Outline of a Theory of Practice.* Cambridge: Cambridge University Press.
Bronfenbrenner, Uri 1979: *The Ecology of Human Development.* Cambridge, MA: Harvard University Press.
Brown, Keith S. & Yannis Hamilakis (eds.) 2003: *The Usable Past: Greek Metahistories.* Lanham: MD.: Lexington Books.

Brown, Keith 2004: The 'children-grandparents' of Macedonia: Internationalist politics of memory, exile and return, 1948–1998. In: Gounaris, Vasilis & Iakovos Michailidis (eds): *Refugees in the Balkans: Memory and Integration*. Athens: Pataki Publications.

Buckingham, David (ed.) 2001: The video culture project. *Special issue Journal of Educational Media* 26 (3).

Buckingham, David, John Grahame & Julian Sefton-Green 1995: *Making Media: Practical Production in Media Education*. London: English and Media Centre.

Christopoulou, Nadina & Sonja De Leeuw 2004: *Home Is Where the Heart Is. Family Relations of Migrant Children in Media Clubs in six European Countries*. The European Commission, Community Research. Deliverables 11 and 12, February 2004.

Crul, Maurice, Flip Lindo & Chin Lin Pang 2002: *Culture, structure and beyond. Changing identities and social positions of immigrants and their children*. Amsterdam: Het Spinhuis.

Erikson, Erik 1969: *Childhood and Society*. Harmondsworth: Penguin Books.

Erikson, Erik 1974: *Identity: Youth and Crisis*. London: Faber and Faber.

Faubion, James D. 1993: *Modern Greek Lessons: A Primer in Historical Constructivism*. Princeton: NJ.: Princeton University Press.

Giddens, Anthony 1991: *Modernity and Self-Identity. Self and Society in Late Modern Age*. Cambridge: Polity Press.

Hall, Stuart 1990: Cultural identity and diaspora. In: Rutherford, Jonathan (ed.): *Identity, Community, Culture, Difference*. London: Lawrence and Wishart: 222–37.

Hall, Stuart & Paul du Gay 1996: *Questions of Cultural Identity*. London: Sage.

Kolar-Panov, Dona 1997: *Video, War and the Diasporic Imagination*. London: Routledge.

Morley, David & Kevin Robins 1995: *Spaces of Identity. Global Media, Electronic Landscapes and Cultural Boundaries*. London: Routledge.

Niesyto, Horst (ed.) 2003: *Video Culture: Video und Interkulturelle Kommunikation*. München: KoPäd Verlag.

Raphael, Samuel & Paul Thompson (eds.) 1990: *The Myths We Live by*. London: Routledge.

Ristovic, Milan 2002: *A Long Journey Home: Greek Refugee Children in Yugoslavia 1948–1960*. Thessaloniki: Institute for Balkan Studies.

Tonkin, Elisabeth 1992: *Narrating Our Pasts: The Social Construction of Oral History*. Cambridge: Cambridge University Press.

Vansina, Jan 1985: *Oral Tradition as History*. London: Currey.

Wallerstein, Judith S. & Sandra Blakeslee 1989: *Second Chances*. London: Bantham.

CHILDREN WRITING MIGRATION.
VIEWS FROM A SOUTHERN ITALIAN MOUNTAIN VILLAGE

Jan C. Oberg

One day a tourist came and asked me to describe my town. So I said to him that it was called Tramonti, that it is a very simple town but located very nicely between the mountains [*tra i monti*]. Here in Tramonti there is a lot of nature and the air is clean, but there are not so many people here since they all went away – to the north.

The community of Tramonti being described by 11-year-old Vittorio is located in the Southern Italian Campania region in the mountains of the Amalfitan peninsula only a few kilometres from the Costiera Amalfitana. With its breathtaking cliffs and attractions (Amalfi, Ravello, Positano etc.), this coastal region has been considered one of the "oldest and most famous tourist areas" in Italy and is called on annually by innumerable tourists from around the world (Richter 1998: 7).

Very few of these tourists stray in to the 13 small *frazione* (hamlets) of Tramonti.[1] Instead, this mountain town is "connected to the world," as its residents say, in another way, namely through its migrants. Or, as some pupils from the local secondary school revealed to me, "who goes on a holiday to Tramonti? Well, the emigrants from the north do!"

The periodical absence or presence of a significant part of the population does in fact influence life in the town significantly. When I first came trudging through the snow of the seemingly deserted town in the winter of 1996 working in a joint project of the universities of Bremen and Rome on "Children's spaces in a tourist region," I was met with a friendly yet puzzled shaking of heads when asking questions about the community's children.[2] There were other, more urgent problems, it seemed, principal among them the problem of emigration. There was only little industry, people told me, agriculture was deteriorating and thus no longer provided enough jobs. Most people from Tra-

---

1 Tramonti today is made up of 13 so-called *frazione* (larger hamlets), each with its own institutions including a church and a kindergarten. Around 50 smaller, formerly "independent" hamlets – often constituting only one or two households – have been incorporated into these frazione.
2 The research project at the University of Bremen took place in the winter of 1996 under the leadership of Maya Nadig and Dieter Richter in cooperation with the Universitá La Sapienza (Rome) and the Centro Universitario Per I Beni Culturali (Ravello). The results of the study were presented in the exhibit "Una geografia dell'infanzia" in Ravello and Bremen.

monti would emigrate sooner or later. This, they said, would be the major problem.[3] The number of residents has in fact shrunk by half to about 3900 since 1950 (CDT 1991). The unemployment rate in Tramonti averaged 32 per cent in the 1990s, youth unemployment was around 60 per cent.[4]

I would therefore, predicted one of my first informants, not find children in Tramonti anyway. Despite these gloomy prospects I managed to meet several children in the following weeks. Their knowledge about the local migration history was remarkable, as 13 year-old Marianna demonstrated:

At the beginning of the [20th] century, so many people emigrated from Tramonti to foreign places like North America, South America, Canada, Brazil and Argentina. These people left and they had to leave their fields, their family and their homeland behind. In the 1950s a lot of people emigrated to European countries like Germany, France, Switzerland and England. In the past 20 or 30 years many young people have left Tramonti for Northern Italy where they specialized in Pizza.

The children of Tramonti grow up in a social environment that extends well beyond local geographical limits and social relationships. Tramonti's migrants are an ideal example of migrant networks as described in the sociological and anthropological literature of the last decade.[5] Many of the network structures described there can be found in Tramonti. The migration pattern of the Tramontini, for example, reflects one of "impermanent movement", i.e. instead of true emigration, we are dealing with a circular movement between sending and receiving society.[6] The contours of the emerging "transnational social space" of children and their families can be traced geographically from Tramonti via the Italian North into Switzerland, Germany and America.[7]

---

3   The local economy in Tramonti is thus tied closely to the activities of their emigrants in the "north"; without their remittances and inter-family support structures (which also prepares the way for temporary emigration to the north by additional relatives), the situation of many families would be, according to local opinion, completely hopeless.
4   Beguinot 1994.
5   Ackermann 1997; Glick Schiller 1997; Kearney 1995, 1996; Morokvasic & Rudolph 1994; Pries 1997.
6   Salt 1987: 243.
7   Pries 1997. In Ludger Pries' understanding the term "transnational social space" means the everyday life-worlds that develop in the context of international migration processes. They are "spatially diffused" but at the same time "constitute more than a merely transitory social space, which serves as an important referential structure for social positions and for the structuring of people's everyday life, biographical (employment) projects and identities [...]" (Preis 1996: 23). This includes the affected children, one has to add. And all this is true for Tramonti. These impulses from migrations studies and transnational anthropology (Appadurai 1998) have found little echo in childhood studies so far. An exception is Dorle Drackl é (1996). In "Jung und wild" [Young and wild], she suggests to take into consideration the "interrelatedness of national with transnational processes" in future "studies of childhood and youth" (39).

Beside its geographical extension, this transnational children's space also includes an imaginary dimension, which by means of employing the term *il nord* is equipped with meanings including both fears and desires. "When I grow up, I want to go to the north," says 13-year-old Fortunato, "because there is lots of work and you can improve your life and you can have fun both at work and in your free time." Andrea, also 13, has a more concrete vision: "I've decided to one day go to work in my uncle's pizzeria in the north!"

Many children seemingly have no greater desire than to follow their brothers, uncles or cousins as pizza bakers to the north. To them, migration apparently bears a far more positive meaning than the general complaints heard in the town would suggest.

How then do the children deal with these contradicting implications of migration? What can their perceptions and interpretations reveal about Tramonti and its migrants? These are the focal questions I will be dealing with and I will do so by describing and analyzing a collection of over 200 short essays written by the children – interpreting them in connection to my observations, interviews and conversations.[8] By letting the children speak for themselves I am trying to meet the demands of a new anthropology of childhood which looks at children as active producers of culture rather than at childhood as an intermediary phase before adulthood.[9] Following Florence Weiss (1995) statements made by children themselves are the focus of my work on children.[10] The essays from which I will quote in the following are: "My favourite place to play" (I), "My house" (II), "My family" (III), "My most exciting adventure with my friends" (VII), "Describe your village" (VIII), "What do you want to do when you grow up" (X), "How do you spend your summer?" (XI), and "Once upon a time in Tramonti" (XII).

---

8 The latter topic is the only one suggested by the local authorities and the school, whereas all others I suggested myself. The Roman numerals indicate from which essay the citations were taken.
9 Cf. van de Loo & Reinhart 1993: 9; Hardmann 1993: 60; Weiss 1995; Dracklé 1996.
10 Authors of classical ethnographic childhood studies such as Margaret Mead (1970) have for some time now been accused of considering childhood as a phase, whose major value is to be overcome on the way to adulthood (Weiss 1995). Contemporary social scientific studies on childhood on the other hand are remarkable in their pessimistic predictions. Debates about modernization (e.g. du Bois Reymond 1994), commercialization (Glogauer 1993), the disappearance of childhood (Postman 1982) and critical discussions about isolation (Zeiher & Zeiher 1994), institutionalization and domestication of children's life-worlds (Zinnecker 1990; du Bois Raymond 1994) have been predominant in the past two decades.

Tramonti in narration

Migration, we can gather from the essays, offers an economic perspective, but is nevertheless a highly controversial issue. Migration as children's plan for the future is not just held in little esteem by adults in Tramonti but is regarded critically by children as well. Especially when the latter are asked "officially" to portray their town history they are unanimous in their negative evaluation of this "difficult phenomenon" (Iolanda, 13, XII).

"Emigration has greatly affected our Tramonti," writes Iolanda; it has become "a town populated largely by old people" laments 11-year-old Marco (XII). The children all experience over-ageing, depopulation and the disappearance of traditional fields oSf work and patterns of life as negative effects of migration, perceptions concurrent with official descriptions. Tizianan, 11, wrote: "A long time ago there were many peasants here. Today there are only a few left and they are old and not young [...] and many fields are no longer being tilled – all because of migration!" (XII).

The frequency of such phrases indicates that these arguments against migration are included in the school curriculum. In fact, before my first stay in Tramonti, an essay contest on local history titled "Once upon a time in Tramonti" was initiated in local schools by the county (1995/96). Bonaventura[11] reveals the point of the contest in his essay: "The children are to be made aware of the problem of emigration."

The fairy-tale-like title – "Once upon a time..." – implies a fairy-tale-like past, revealing the officials' intentions to encourage children to identify with the locality.[12] In dealing with the village's past, a local affinity was to be created in the present, thus combatting further migration. The local tourist organization *prolocco* supports such endeavours. It wants to invigorate local traditions to promote tourism and thus achieve independence from remittances sent by migrants.

Despite their positive image of the north the children meet these demands in their essays, describing highly imaginatively a (long lost) mythic period of flourishing prosperity: "The families were numerous and there was no lack of work force in the many booming sectors. Small industries, different trades and professions developed. Innumerable cows stood in the cowshed and each family earned enough to survive by selling the milk they produced" (Romina, 13, XII).

12-year-old Sylvia also traces the origin of the name *monti lattari* (Milk Mountains) – indicating the surrounding mountains – to this mythical period in which huge herds grazed on the slopes around Tramonti and "diligence" and "industriousness" were "the fundamental characteristics of the people of Tramonti" (XII). Similarly, Annalisa, 12, writes: "They were industrious peo-

---

11 Some children did not give their age, but all children were between 11 and 14 when writing the essays.
12 This interpretation was confirmed by several of the officials when I asked them about the intentions of the contest.

ple, bound to their traditions full of religious values [...] a mountain people that valued brotherhood and love. And the main thing that has prevented progress in the village is emigration!" (XII).

The children create paradise-like pasts in their stories. "In times long gone by one could meet people here with pure hearts free of the manifold problems that plague humanity today" (Matteo, 14, XII).

Considering this diction, it is unnecessary to even attempt to find any sense of historical reality. Instead I want to look at the ways in which the stories are told. Narrated past is – according to Stuart Hall (1994: 201ff.) – one element in the process by which communities, common culture and identity are conceptually connected. Transferred to "my field" a "narrated Tramonti" is laid down in the histories presented which ascribes meanings, symbols, events and myths to the town – points of reference for a common identity.[13]

The task of writing a narrative account of Tramonti, is – to use the notions of late-modern cultural theory – an appeal to construct local identity discursively. The historical models constructed by the children – the "historical Tramonti" – is as much a product of their experiences and imaginations as their image of "the north" of which we have already heard. Both are a product of experiencing and tackling migration.

Not only past prosperity but also its loss (through migration) is a central motif in these local historical discourses. Marianna writes that the old trades and agriculture have "disappeared more or less completely" and are "practically non-existent today" as a result of migration (XII).[14] But how do we interpret the following statement, made by 14-year-old Giuseppe? "Emigration is to blame for," he begins, and continues listing the common images of loss. He then concludes his statement with the words " the fact that I will buy myself a nice car!" (XII).

Binary discourses

The children clearly assess migration ambivalently and switch between condemnation and idealization. Two discourses and two different knowledge profiles exist side by side.

---

13 Hall describes the narration of nations in his essay. This narration creates a link between locales and landscapes and the events, symbols and myths, which represent shared worries and triumphs and provide specific locations with meanings, that become fixed in people's memories as the common points of reference for a common identity (Hall 1994: 202).

14 The children follow the arguments of the Tramontini Franciscan friar Salvatore Fierro. He is considered the official local historian and his numerous publications, titled, for example, "Tradizioni che scompaiono" (Dissappearing traditions, 1989) can be found in nearly every living room, church and store in Tramonti.

"Emigration is to blame for everything" (Tiziana, 11, XII).
"[It is] a difficult phenomenon that has struck our Tramonti!" (Jolanda, 13, XII).
"[...] the entire country must thus stand up to fight it, [...] this exasperating phenomenon!" (Bonaventura, XXI).

L'emigrazione is in their narratives a diffuse, threatening figment that has befallen the community like a natural catastrophe or – the narratives being produced in Italy after all – like a grand political conspiracy.

The "responsibility" of which everyone speaks, (responsibility for loss, poverty, over-ageing etc.) is not attributed to the migrating individuals, to the relatives whom the children feel attached to and from whose remittances their families profit, but to a catastrophic, yet abstract and unrelated process of *emigration*. Individual people rarely appear in the children's narratives. Instead, yet another motif is employed when dealing with the responsibility of migration as a condemnable process: "It is above all the young people that leave the village" writes Pascuale (XII). And Francesca, Fiorina, Gina, Maria and Sonia say that "to stop migration we need to make the youth understand that when they, who are the soul and future of the village, leave, when the youth of this village, which is ours, but also theirs, continue to leave, then it will never change" (XII).

The authors of this petition to the "youth" – between 11 and 14 years of age – seemingly do not consider themselves part of this group of young people. The village is "ours, but also theirs," they petition (a little moralizing, as if spoken by authoritative adults) the anonymous – the other – group of youth. They themselves ("we") are not part of those considered endangering Tramonti through migration.

Whenever migration is critically discussed in public it is related to an anonymous group of "migrants." When youth debate in abstract terms about youth's lack of responsibility, they reproduce the official lesson learned at school – and illustrate the results as a disaster with all their imaginative skill. But it is not the relatives in the north, of whom the children speak. They appear in the narratives only when dealing with positive aspects of migration – which is then no longer labelled as *emigrazione* either. After Giuseppe, 14, described the loss of the past glory of Tramonti (*tutto per la colpa de'll emigrazione* – "emigration as at fault for everything"), he concludes that he himself has planned his career as a pizza baker in the north, "[...] since I can earn a lot of money there and with this money I will buy myself a nice car!" (XII).

Children engage in two discourses simultaneously. The official discourse represents the institutionalized doctrine which was established by local authorities and which is taught at school. It emphasizes the negative results of migration and aims at strengthening the local economy and local identity. The informal – and less official – discourse deals with the subjects of migration, with relatives and friends, personal relationships, but also with dependencies, needs and desires.

These two discourses are each founded on different knowledge; and biography studies has argued[15] that knowledge of past events is in fact "changeable." In our example a "counter knowledge," which is closer to actual performance and more subject-centred can be found opposite official knowledge. Fragments of this "counter knowledge" can be detected even in *C'era una volta Tramonti* ("Once upon a time in Tramonti"), where joining the official discourse is called for. Marianna explains: "Life in Tramonti was in fact very difficult since one had to work all day to earn the minimum necessary to survive. This life of privation forced the population into emigration (XII)." And even today, life in Tramonti is not easy and offers little pleasure. "Many Tramontini who live in the north want to go back to Tramonti," says Filomena, "but what are they to do in a town with nothing?" (XII).

From the point of view of the children, emigration in the sense of "leaving/abandoning" is bad, but most children agree that the migrants returning for summer vacation bring – in addition to their financial resources – good things to Tramonti as well. "I live in Corsano, a small hamlet of Tramonti and I have many friends who return from the north in the summer; we have a lot of fun on the marketplace, we play and ride together on our bicycles and buy ice cream. In the evening I wash, eat and then I go to some party with my parents," reports 13-year-old Patrizia (XI). 11-year-old Benito writes: "Tramonti is really nice in the summer, the saint's days festivals take place then because the people who emigrated to the north organize them when returning for the summer" (XI), and Angelo, 11, writes: Then "the tourists come from the north and from foreign countries, Germany and Venezuela and populate *il Pendolo* [his hamlet] again. Usually we are only 50 people, but in the summer we are more than 100" (XI).

The otherwise deserted squares and bars swarm with people and often the *APE*, the three-wheeled carts of the grandparent generation, are parked beside the Ferraris of their children from the north. These weeks spent together are nonetheless not just intended to demonstrate the achieved wealth of the migrants. Gioacchino, 12, puts it this way: "In the summer, Tramonti is revolutionized" (XI).[16]

These stories are not about "migrants," even though it is them whom the children are talking about. For some, they are "tourists," for others "friends" from the north who "repopulate" the town and make it more pleasant, organizing parties and livening up Tramonti, as Stefani, 12, says. She then goes out with relatives from far away "almost every evening. Summer in Tramonti is very lively because the village is repopulated with relatives from far away. I

---

15 Cf. Alheit 1989: 139ff.
16 Gioacchino argues: "In the summer, Tramonti is revolutionized because the tourists and especially those from the north organize many parties and football tournaments for us children and for their parents. When my friend Anthonio comes, we horse around together in the village square; then we go to the sea and horse around even more."

have fun because my aunt and my cousins usually come to visit; we play together, go to the sea and go out almost every night" (XI).

Young women and girls in particular greet these effects of the migration process, which the official canon might tend to look down upon. While the latter tends to oppose the disappearance of traditions as a result of migration, the girls welcome the fact that some "traditional" norms are seen less rigidly by their relatives from the north. 14-year-old Paola explains: "The boys have many more opportunities to have fun than the girls. I have a friend, who, when she asks if she can come along for a walk, has to take her brother along because her parents have a completely antiquated mentality" (XI). Her friend Umberta, 14, writes:

There are still parents here with completely antiquated mentalities, who do not want to let you go out, out of fear that when a boy sees you on the street, he won't be able to go past without asking you to marry him. Then there are parents, who let you go out, but only to mass and you have to return directly after it has finished and in case you are five minutes late, you'll be in trouble. The people need to understand that the world has changed! (XI).

Many girls are very decisive in their demands for more personal liberties and changes in the infamous *mentalitá antica*.[17] Contacts with the "tourists" from the north offer many of them the opportunity to share the (female) migrants' more elaborate freedom of movement and action, however limited the time may be. 13-year-old Annunziata explains how daily life changes when relatives visit:

Normally I have to stay at home every day [...] do chores into the evening and not go out. It is not so bad in the summer. Then my brothers come from the north and I can stay with them. I have a lot of fun because they are so nice and so funny. In the evenings I stay with them until midnight and then I go home. The summer is a nice time of year because you meet many people and get to know them and I like it very much to be together with new people (XI).

These freedoms are all normally forbidden. Gioacchinos description of a "revolutionized" Tramonti is confirmed by Chiara, 14: "Every summer is a sweet memory for me because I enjoyed more freedom" (XI). These liberties are nevertheless only permitted in the company of people who live outside the town but are inside the family. The family is the most important social structure in Tramonti and also functions as a surveillance group; when Annunziata is out with her cousins, she remains within the sphere of family control. Perceptions of femininity as something that needs to be guarded, and of men

---

17 One of the boys of the same age also commented on traditional gender roles, although he himself, as a *ragazzo*, was little affected by their negative aspects. His comments are thus of a different nature: "Women, especially in the south are still tied to the household because of ancient traditions and are thus less free than elsewhere. Men, on the other hand, have firm control over women" (IX).

obliged to assume this responsibility also exist in the north, but they seem to be more open to change.

Young women, in any case, expect to gain more liberties with migration. In many cases they have completed school or professional training but are not able to find work in Tramonti. Patrizia, 23, studied law and would like to work in the north. However, she does not want to leave her parent's household unmarried and her decision to leave would only be accepted by her family, if it were organized within customary parameters. For women this means marriage with someone from the north, preferably a Tramontino.

She is ambivalent in her assumption of the situation. She disagrees with getting married only to meet the conditions for female migration, even more so as the role of wife and mother would leave her with just as little time to practice as a lawyer in the north as in Tramonti. Ideally, she would like to get married with a man from the north out of love, then emigrate to live with him and thus be able to work in her own profession as well.

The opportunities migration offers young men and women from Tramonti have already been heavily "traditionalized". Young men work as pizza bakers in the *ristoranti* of their relatives; young women largely remain in the sphere of reproduction. Thus, migration is not a decision for or against traditional gender roles. On the contrary, these roles determine the modalities of migration. Nevertheless, migration to the north allows young women in particular to challenge and modify traditional gender more so than in Tramonti. Reforming the "antiquated mentality" seems easier with relocation, which is, of course, only considered to be temporary.[18]

The claim that migration destroys tradition, as made in the official discourse in Tramonti, is thus not correct. Traditions are in fact reproduced in the process of migration which is largely controlled by traditionally powerful informal institutions, namely the families. These make use of traditional gender role patterns and rituals (such as marriage) in steering migratory processes. And to some extent thinking about one's own migration has become a local tradition in itself. To not want to migrate as a child (for the right reasons) could then at some stage be considered a violation of (family) tradition. And once the decision to migrate has been made, a traditional path is to be followed (migrating to the north, to an uncle, to work in a pizzeria, through marriage etc.).

---

18 Southern Italy is considered a classical Mediterranean region in social sciences, cultural – and children's studies. It's understood as a very "traditional" culture, social structures marked by clientelism and religiosity. Cf. the debate about Italian *familismo*, which, oscillating between disapproval (as in Banfield 1958, where it is labelled a "moral basis of a backward society") and idealization (cf. Schitteck 1979; Baake & Fracasso 1992) has dominated the academic discourse on Italy and childhood in Italy.

Migration as tradition

Migration has for a long time been the dominant tradition in Tramonti. The children know this as well, and they are involved intensively in its reproduction. Beside the "story of Tramonti," there's also a "story of migration," although this is not told under the topic *C'era una volta Tramonti*. It appears when they are asked to describe their town to a tourist. It also appears in the (other) essays since they knew, these were not going to be marked by their teachers or sent to the county administration. Here the central motif is not one of loss as in the story of Tramonti but one of the "*arte della pizza*" (the art of the pizza) (Margareta, 14, XI).

"So many have left," writes Massime, 11, "and today they all have a pizzeria" (VIII). Today the "pizza bakers of Tramonti are famous all around the world and have restaurants in all the big cities of the north" (Giosué, 11, VIII). In these stories specific names and individuals are mentioned around whom the children design the founding myth of "the tradition of important pizza bakers from Tramonti" (Maria Pia, 13, XII).

"In 1951 Giordano Luigi from [the hamlet of] Campinola founded the first pizzeria in Northern Italy which was also the first pizzeria owned by someone from Tramonti. By 1954 he had a whole chain of restaurants, which he entrusted to his poor relatives from Tramonti, who understood that this was an easy way to earn money!" (Filomena, XI). Others "say the first emigrant was Amatruda Aniello from Cesarano who was called Cinquanta because he left in 1950 [...] yet others claim, it was Fierro Giovanni from Pietre. So everyone from Tramonti worked in this new business, even if it required enormous sacrifice and a lot of responsibility" (Francesco, VIII).

Even if the emigration of these famous ancestors depopulated Tramonti, so the argument, they did manage to make the region world famous. Il Cinquanta and his contemporaries introduced the world to the symbol of local culture, the pizza.

The motif of the pizza has been institutionalized in the course of time in the Corporazione Pizzaioli di Tramonti, the union of pizza bakers from Tramonti with statutes, formal membership and, above all, pizza recipes policies. The emblem of the organization carries the motto "The Pizza in tradition – Tramonti all over the world." The local specialty has grown to become an icon of local tradition. The members of the union belong to a transnational community, which on the one hand draws on the common origin of its members from a single town but on the other hand only becomes a community as a result of its collective absence form the latter. Of the 271 founding members (who all have their own restaurant), only five live and work in Tramonti. The union is one of the social institutions that organizes and structures the transnational social space of migration.[19] Whether making pizza had always been a specific Tramonti tradition or only became one as a result of the emigration of

---

19 Cf. Pries 1997.

many Tramontini – whether it was actually migration which led to the invention of this local tradition that is[20] – remains open. No doubt, however, that establishing the *Corporazione Pizzaioli di Tramonti* made the profession of the pizza baker acquire local cultural contours and made it a point of reference for local tradition.

Illustration: Emblem of the "Corporazione Pizzaioli di Tramonti"

A whole series of further symbols, stories and institutions exist, which represent the positive aspects of Tramonti's history of migration and which the children of Tramonti relate to with pride. Walking through the hamlet of Cesarano in 1997, I met a group of primary school children in the street. With excited gestures they led me to the big attraction in the hamlet, the ruins of a house destroyed in the big earthquake in 1982, whose walls stood defiant of the traffic on the through road. I admired these, somewhat puzzled, until the children showed me a shining plaque fixed to the wall. It was, it seems, a symbolic site of the origins of migration. The plaque revealed that Mario Cuomo's mother was born in this house. Mario Cuomo, probably the most famous migrant from Tramonti, was once governor of New York State and is today an honorary citizen of Tramonti. His name is seldom left unmentioned in a conversation about *l'emigrazione*.

A magazine for the community of Tramontini around the world was founded in 1988, the TPE or *Tramonti per Emigrati, il magazine degli Italiani*

---

20 Hobsbawn & Ranger 1983.

nel mondo [tutte le regioni] (Tramonti for emigrants, the magazine of Italians around the world [all regions]).[21]

I will now return once more to the two unequal spheres of knowledge the children express in the two discourses I have designated official and informal. Does their parallelism involve an immanent potential for conflict?

Identities

"I would also like to go north and make pizza," wrote 12-year-old Umberto, "so that I learn something and, anyway, to do something. But I can't leave my home and I don't want to either, because I have gardens here, I am alone with my mother and I have to cultivate our gardens. I don't ever want to leave the Costiera Amalfitana" (X).

Are Umberto's conflicting emotions and considerations common among the children of Tramonti? Or, to use the dramatic terms of Italian rhetoric, does the experience of migration leave children with an *identitá strappata*, a disturbed identity?

Migration scholars have indeed debated vehemently about the negative effects of migration on the identity of children.[22] "Bicultural socialization" would run the risk of children being torn between two cultures (Schrader 1979), making the process of integration and assimilation into the host country more difficult, possibly leading them to develop "marginal personalities" and severe psychological illness as young adults (Branik 1982: 23). Such pessimistic assumptions have been challenged repeatedly.[23]

"Segmented" (Pries 1997) or "hybrid" identities (Bhabha 1990), which unify contrary segments have long since been understood as not being a priori conflictual. Stuart Hall (1994: 180ff.) understands the postmodern subject as a collection of "several, sometimes contradictory or unresolved" or "fragmented" identities. Tomaso Morone describes, for example, how Italian children in Germany develop their own differentiated status consciousness as migrant children, which helps them to position themselves socially and culturally.[24]

Despite Umberto's melancholy rhetoric, I share the opinion that the fractured knowledge the children have of Tramonti and their own history does not necessarily lead to problems. In over 200 essays, Umberto's was the only one which explicitly mentioned a conflict.

Identity, writes Iain Chambers (1996: 32) is a "fiction," a "particular story that makes sense." In Tramonti, identity is only in danger – to pick up one

---

21 Applying Pries' model of transnational social space (1997), the TPE could be classified a part of the material infrastructure of the Tramontini migrant network.
22 Cf. Schrader 1979; Branik 1982; Wilpert 1980; Morone 1996; Portera 1996.
23 I.e. Wilpert 1980; Morone 1996; Portera 1991, 1995, 1996.
24 Morone 1996: 53.

question asked initially – when it is allowed to follow a single model or a single narrative only. The stories told by the children of Tramonti grow out of an experience which encompasses more than one centre, and more than one system of knowledge. They develop in the process of encounter, in a space which despite being shared by closely interrelated family members reveals gaps and room for manoeuvre. In these gaps other stories, languages, and identities can be experienced.

The experience of this social space between Tramonti and the north enables the children to find their way and localize themselves in a heterogeneous world which comprises of both the local culture, i.e. the localized traditions of Tramonti *and* a delocalized environment which exists in the context of migration and its specific traditions, transregional migrant economics and which connects them to the ways of global culture. Or, as Christina, daughter of one of many Italian restaurant owners in Germany said to me: "Identity? Home? Well, I don't have either – no, wait, actually both, there the north, Germany and here Italy, that is my home!"

Conclusion

The children of Tramonti "write" migration. In their essays they create their own versions of local history, which clearly includes moments of ambivalence. However, in no way can these narratives be reduced to the conflict potential concealed in them. More than inner conflict these stories reveal how creatively the children of Tramonti deal with their heterogeneous environment.

They manage to weave together two apparently contrary discourses. On the one hand they energetically reproduce the official discourse depicting migration as a critical issue, as the cause of many misfortunes. With a great deal of imagination, mythical local histories and motifs of loss are created and solutions sought and suggested (e.g. the reproduction of tradition for the benefits of tourism). *L'emigrazione* is viewed as a threatening fiend raging in Tramonti like a natural catastrophe, independent of individual actors.

On the level of personal relations an informal discourse dominates. It is about subjects and their needs and desires, their successes, relationships, role models and friends. A lucrative life in the cosmopolitan north is confronted with a difficult life in the old and beautiful, but somewhat boring Tramonti.

But this does not remain a simple unanchored contrast. Emigration may have "severely damaged our old Tramonti" but now it is the migrants who "beautify" the town, "enliven" and even "revolutionize" it where it is dominated by antiquated rules. Migration connects the remote town in the mountains (*tra i monti*) with the wider world. The migrants, who come from every family in Tramonti and who have officially been given the role of having destroyed the town thus become as good and as important as those, who remain in the town and acquire, if not equal, at least close to equal status positions.

I consider this the specific contribution of the children to the development of a balanced system of social relationships within their personal environment.[25] The local ties of those who remain in the town and their knowledge and feelings about traditional cultural resources are seen as "cultural capital" equivalent to the "economic capital" of the migrants from the north.

The traditions of the *patrimonio culturale* (cultural heritage) and migration processes are not automatically mutually exclusive. Traditional gender roles for example, are both reproduced as well as transformed by migration. The issue is not one of two completely separate worlds – a traditional Tramonti on the one hand and a modern or global world of migration on the other. Both "worlds" are closely and inseparably intertwined in the subjects and their experiences. It is above all an issue of two economic strategies – migration, which has long become a tradition in Tramonti – versus the late-modern idea of making "tradition" itself an economic location factor by reviving or, if necessary, inventing traditions. This strategy followed by the county with the support of the schools, is closely related to the marketing tactics of the global tourism industry.[26]

Many children demonstrate in their essays that they see through the broader intentions of the project, i.e. the revival of traditions and their economic potentials. Several participants in the contest mention marketing strategies right away, their essays sounding like contributions to a publicity campaign. Federico, 14, articulately connects local identity and tourism. The "good-humoured" and "happy" mentality of the Tramontini – a result of the breathtaking natural environment – should be seen as a true incentive for tourism he claims.

> The air that one breathes here and the smell of the spring flowers flatters the spirit like good news. Everyone is happy and this happiness is passed on to the people who visit this picturesque town every year. Tramonti is blessed with so many beautiful things, the mountains, the agriculture, and the famous pizza bakers in the north and finally the hospitality, which reveals the pleasant nature and the charm of the Tramontini all over the world (XII).

Frederico demonstrates that the pizza, the symbol of the migrants bears a quality that makes it highly attractive in the context of tourist promotion. The

---

25 Pries (1997) describes the balanced "third system or social positioning" of transnational social spaces. However, literature on Southern Italy has to date often been surprisingly simplistic in its analysis. Speculations about the jealously and resentment felt by villagers who do not profit from the migration of their neighbours figure prominently. Behrmann & Abate (1984: 57) consider migration the most radical instrument of social differentiation. From time to time generally "internalised attitudes [...] of resentment and jealously," e.g. of Sicilian migrants are debated (cf. Zimmermann 1982: 129). Faith in the system of social security through migration and the example of migrating relatives seems to be more important in Tramonti, among children especially.

26 On late-modern tourism strategies see Cohen 1995; Errington & Gewertz 1989; Nash 1996.

migration of the *pizzaioli di Tramontini* simply needs to be added as an official narrative of success to the list of local traditions in Tramonti.

It has long been so for the children. Tramonti could market itself as a traditional mountain town and as a centre of a global migrant network, as the capital of pizza bakers from around the world, a stone's throw away from the breathtaking Amalfi coast. "If we try," says 12-year-old Simone, "Tramonti could soon become a little Switzerland" (XII).

Despite the danger of provoking a somewhat too enthusiastic conclusion, I close this essay with Simone's prediction. It demonstrates how in their narratives of their town and migrants the children of Tramonti prove to be highly creative, imaginative and critical (co)designers of their world.

This paper was translated from German to English by Andreas Hemming.

References

Ackermann, Andreas 1997: Ethnologische Migrationsforschung: Ein Überblick. *kea* 10, Ethnologie der Migration: 1–28.
Alheit, Peter 1989: Erzählform und 'soziales Gedächtnis.' In: Alheit, Peter & Erika M. Hoernig (eds.): *Biographisches Wissen. Beiträge zu einer Theorie lebensgeschichtlicher Erfahrung*. Frankfurt/Main: Campus: 123–147.
Baacke, Dieter & Ippazio Fracasso 1992: *Italienische Jugend. Einblicke in Lebenswelt, Lebensräume und Kultur*. Weinheim & München: Juventa.
Beguinot, Corrado 1994: *Comunità Monatan "Penisola Amalfitana." Piano Progetto Ambiente Recupero Riuso Territorio*. Napoli: Giannini.
Behrmann, Meike & Carmine Abate 1984: *Die Germanesi. Geschichte und Leben einer süditalienischen Dorfgemeinschaft und ihrer Emigranten*. Frankfurt/Main & New York: Campus.
Bhabha, Homi 1990: The third space. In: Rutherford, Jonathan (ed.): *Identity: Community, Culture, Difference*. New York: New York University Press: 207–221.
Branik, Emil 1982: *Psychische Störungen und soziale Probleme von Kindern und Jugendlichen aus Spätaussiedlerfamilien. Ein Beitrag zur Psychiatrie der Migration*. Weinheim & Basel: Beltz.
CDT (Comune di Tramonti/SA) 1991: 13. *Censimento Generale della Popolazione del 20 Ottobre 1991*. Tramonti (SA).
Chambers, Iain 1996: *Migration Kultur Identität*. Tübingen: Stauffenburg.
Cohen, Erik 1995: Contemporary tourism – trends and challenges. Sustainable authenticity or contrived post-modernity. In: Butler, Richard & Douglas Pearce (eds.): *Change in Tourism. People, Places, Processes*. London: Routledge: 12–29.
Dracklé, Dorle 1996: Kulturelle Repräsentationen von Jugend in der Ethnologie. In: Dracklé, Dorle (ed.): *Jung und wild. Zur kulturellen Konstruktion von Kindheit und Jugend*. Berlin & Hamburg: Reimer: 202–224.

Du Bois-Reymond, Manuela et al. 1994: *Kinderleben. Modernisierung von Kindheit im interkulturellen Vergleich*. Opladen: Leske & Budrich.

Errington, Frederick Karl & Deborah Gewertz 1989: Tourism and anthropology in a post-modern world. *Oceania* 20: 37–54.

Fierro, Salvatore 1989: *Tradizioni che Scompaiono*. Napoli e Tramonti: publisher unkown.

Glick Schiller, Nina et al. 1997: From immigrant to transmigrant: Theorizing transnational migration. In: Pries, Ludger (ed.): *Transnationale Migration*. (Soziale Welt, Sonderband 12) Baden-Baden: Nomos: 121–140.

Glogauer, Werner 1993: *Die neuen Medien verändern die Kindheit*. Weinheim: Deutscher Studien Verlag.

Hall, Stuart 1994: *Rassismus und kulturelle Identität*. Ausgewählte Schriften 2. Hamburg: Argument.

Hardman, Charlotte 1993: Auf dem Schulhof. Unterwegs zu einer Anthropologie der Kindheit. In: Loo, Marie-José van de & Margarete Reinhart (eds.): *Kinder. Ethnologische Forschungen in fünf Kontinenten*. München: Trickster: 7–17.

Hobsbawm, Eric & Terence Ranger (eds.) 1983: *The Invention of Tradition*. Cambridge: Cambridge University Press.

Kearney, Michael 1995: The local and the global: The anthropology of globalization and transnationalism. *Annual Review of Anthropology* 24: 547–65.

Kearney, Michael 1996: From the invisible hands to visible feet: Anthropological studies of migration and development. In: Cohen, Robin (ed.): *Theories of Migration*. Cheltenham/UK: Edward Elgar Publishing: 4–404.

Mead, Margaret 1970: *Jugend und Sexualität in primitiven Gesellschaften*. München: dtv.

Morokvasic, Mirjana & Hedwig Rudolph (eds.) 1994: *Wanderungsraum Europa. Menschen und Grenzen in Bewegung*. Berlin: Edition sigma.

Morone, Tommaso 1996: Italienische Migrantenfamilien in Deutschland. Die Bewältigung des Kulturwandels. *Migration und Soziale Arbeit* 2: 48–53.

Nash, Dennison 1996: *Anthropology of Tourism*. University of Connecticut: Pergamon.

Portera, Agostino 1991: *Europei senza Europa. Storia e Storie di Vita di Giovani Italiani in Germania*. Catania: Coesse.

Portera, Agostino 1996: Identitätsbildung im multikulturellen Raum. Empirische Untersuchung über Risiko- und Schutzfaktoren der Identitätsbildung Jugendlicher italienischer Herkunft in Südbaden und in Süditalien. *Migration und Soziale Arbeit* 2: 54–57.

Portera, Agostino 1995: *Interkulturelle Identitäten. Faktoren der Identitätsbildung Jugendlicher italienischer Herkunft in Südbaden und Südtalien*. Köln, Weimar & Wien: Böhlau.

Postman, Neil 1982: *Das Verschwinden der Kindheit*. Frankfurt/Main: Suhrkamp.

Pries, Ludger 1996: Internationale Arbeitsmigration und das Entstehen Transnationaler Sozialer Räume: Konzeptionelle Überlegungen für ein empirisches Forschungsprojekt. In: Faist, Thomas, Felicitas Hillmann & Klaus Robinet-Zühlke (eds.): *Neue Migrationsprozesse: Politisch-institutionelle Regulierung und Wechselbeziehungen zum Arbeitsmarkt*. Zentrum für Sozialpolitik Bremen: Arbeitspapier Nr. 6/1996: 20–29.

Pries, Ludger 1997: Neue Migration im transnationalen Raum. In: Pries, Ludger (ed.): *Transnationale Migration* (Soziale Welt, Sonderband 12). Baden-Baden: Nomos: 15–44.

Richter, Dieter (ed.) 1998: *Fremdenverkehr und lokale Kultur. Kulturanthropologische Untersuchungen an der Küste von Amalfi*. Bremen: Kea-Edition.

Salt, John 1987: Contemporary trends in international migration study. *International Migration* XXV (3): 241–252.

Schitteck, Claudia 1979: Vom Kinderalltag in der Toscana. *Ästhetik und Kommunikation* 38 (Dezember): Kinderalltag: 31–46.

Schrader, Achim 1979: *Die zweite Generation. Sozialisation und Akkulturation ausländischer Kinder in der Bundesrepublik*. Königstein: Athenäum-Verlag.

van de Loo, Marie-José & Margarete Reinhart 1993: Wir alle kommen aus der Kindheit. In: Loo, Marie-José van de & Margarete Reinhart (eds.): *Kinder. Ethnologische Forschungen in fünf Kontinenten*. München: Trickster: 7–17.

Weiss, Florence 1995: Kinder erhalten das Wort. Aussagen von Kindern in der Ethnologie. In: Renner, Erich (ed.): *Kinderwelten. Pädagogische, ethnologische und literaturwissenschaftliche Annäherungen*. Weinheim: Deutscher Studienverlag: 133–147.

Wilpert, Czarina 1980: *Die Zukunft der zweiten Generation. Erwartungen und Verhaltensmöglichkeiten ausländischer Kinder*. Königstein: Hain.

Zeiher, Hartmut J. & Helga Zeiher 1994: *Orte und Zeiten der Kinder. Soziales Leben im Alltag von Großstadtkindern*. Weinheim & München: Juventa.

Zimmermann, Emil 1982: *Emigrationsland Süditalien. Eine kulturanthropologische und sozialpsychologische Studie*. Tübingen: Mohr.

Zinnecker, Jürgen 1990: Vom Straßenkind zum verhäuslichten Kind. Kindheitsgeschichte im Prozeß der Zivilisation. In: Behnken, Imke (ed.): *Stadtgesellschaft und Kindheit im Prozeß der Zivilisation*. Opladen: Leske & Budrich: 142–200.

Small Heroes. Rap Music and Selective Belongings of Young Haitian Immigrants in Montreal

Heike Drotbohm

Introduction

While the role fulfilled by music in the construction of personal and ethnic identities has received significant attention in recent anthropological literature, the perspective of children and young people has been widely neglected. The culture of hip-hop[1] in particular, with its group dynamics, competitive elements as well as its spirit of resistance against the world of adults constitutes a reflective tool for children and young people. The identification with this youth culture serves as a significant means for the (re-)creation of "black" tradition and ethnicity. From the moment it became understood as a vehicle for the "voices from the margins" (Rose 1994) just over 10 years ago, the interest in hip-hop within academia has become more established, mainly in the United States and in Canada,[2] but also in Europe[3] and other parts of the world.[4]

My fieldwork focused on the Haitian community in Montreal, Canada, and how it recreated "Haiti." I was particularly interested in the reconstruction of Haitian history and gender ideologies within the migrant community and in discovering how it relates to both home and host society.[5] From the beginning of the 1990s, much research has been carried out on the first generation of Haitian immigrants, mainly to the United States, and they provided one of the most significant case studies in the development of the concept of "transnationalism" (Glick Schiller et al. 1992, Basch et al. 1994). By means of physi-

---

1 While the culture of hip-hop consists of rap music, breakdance, graffiti and dj-ing, rap music has shaped urban black youth cultures most significantly all over the globe. This article will concentrate on the analysis of rap songs.
2 Kage 2002; Lipsitz 1999; Ross & Rose 1994.
3 Klein & Friedrich 2003; Menrath 2001.
4 Auzanneau 2001; Kimminich 2004; Weller 2003. These authors have been working on rap music in Gabon, Senegal, and Brazil, respectively.
5 Data was collected during my Ph.D. fieldwork in Montreal (2002, 2003). I thank the University of Marburg, Germany for supplying me with a doctoral grant and the Centre d'Etudes Ethniques, CEETUM, at the University of Montreal, for their support during my stay in Montreal.

cal movement, personal networks and political ideologies, Haitians in Montreal live their lives as transmigrants, commuting between "home" and host society. In doing so, they forge and sustain multiple social relations that link Haiti with Haitian settlements – within Canada and in other parts of the world, i.e. Paris, Miami, New York City or Boston.

The city of Montreal has attracted 80 per cent of all new immigrants in the Province of Quebec in recent decades and immigrants make up between 20 to 25 per cent of the metropolitan area population today (Meintel 2000: 15). An estimated 50,000 to 70,000 Haitians have come to Montreal since the mid 1950s. They were fleeing political persecution, structural violence and *la mizè* – the increasing poverty in one of the poorest countries in the western hemisphere (Dejean 1990).

I was interested in the differing and sometimes conflicting perspectives within Haitian families in Montreal, i.e. in the differences in attitudes, interests and needs with regard to gender and generation. The following article aims at exploring how children in particular perceive and define their position between Haiti as their parents' reference culture, and Canada as their host society, a society within which they are labelled as immigrants, in spite of having been born there. Writing about "Haitian children" in Montreal, I mainly refer to children belonging to the second, in some cases third generation of Haitian immigrants – that is the children and, in some cases the grandchildren of former immigrants.[6]

I will focus on the following questions: How do children perceive their position betwixt and between? How do they construct an ethnic identity? Is ethnic identity important to their concept of self? Which roles do home and host society play in the process of shaping children's identities? Finally: what role does rap music play in the construction of self among young Haitian immigrants?

Haitian families and identities in Montreal

The Haitian Community in Montreal falls into two broad categories, which run parallel to class and race differentiations rather typical for post-slavery-societies.[7] There are working class and "undocumented labourers" on the one hand, and skilled middle-class professionals working as teachers, doctors or nurses, on the other. Generally speaking, the former group tends to live on the margins of society, with little opportunity for upward social mobility while the latter is better off financially and also tends to be more comfortable with its

---

6   Most of them are officially Canadian citizens; few have not been "naturalized" and remain Haitian citizens. Cf. Mannitz in this volume, who is pinpointing the problem of labelling children and grandchildren of former immigrants as "second and third generations of immigrants."
7   See also Basch et al 1994: 183–198; Waters 2001.

Haitian heritage.[8] Many Haitians refer to their children as "wealth,"[9] since children – particularly among Haitian immigrants – are supposed to fulfill the expectations and desires of their parents.[10] Family life tends to engender strong challenges for all, more so in families with poor working class background, where both parents are forced to work fulltime. On the whole, parents' perception of life in Canada differs from children's perception. Flore Zéphir describes the trauma, frustrations and disappointments many Haitians face upon arrival in Canada. For months and often years, most first-generation immigrants have to come to terms with low-paid jobs, prejudice and little opportunity for upward social mobility, as well as with linguistic and cultural barriers. On top of that they often fear to lose their children to what they consider to be a foreign cultural world – Canada that is. At the same time, their children, by means of rapid acculturation and acquisition of language skills acquire the role of "experts" whom they depend upon. This paradoxical inequality often produces frustration on the parents' part, frustration that sometimes results in child abuse.[11]

Haitian children in Montreal are highly diversified as a group and include those born and raised in Canada as well those who were born in Haiti but came to Canada at an early age. Like the first generation of Haitian immigrants, they are stratified in terms of social class, which in turn affects their ethnic identifications. By and large, children from a middle-class background tend to claim a certain degree of Haitianness, which is expressed by declaring pride in one's Haitian roots. Those children show a preference for a Haitian lifestyle and participate in Haitian social activities at home or within their ethnic community. Be it their culinary preferences, their choice of music or their religious affiliations – Haiti serves as a source of ethnic identification.[12]

There are also weaker forms of Haitianness, which Zéphir (2001: 99) calls the "undercover phenomenon." It means hiding one's Haitian roots by passing as an African Canadian. These children speak inner-city Black English, many of the girls wear short skirts, the boys wear baggy pants and gold chains. Alex Stepick (1998: 60) calls this response "cultural suicide", which he claims to be the result of the continuous confrontation of Haitian children and youth with negative stereotypes about their own group. They are accused of being prone to gang violence and drug abuse, of being dirty and smelly, and, most severely, HIV positive.[13]

---

8   Zéphir 2001: 146.
9   "Timoun yo ce canet banc malere," translated as "the child is the bank account of the poor," is a common Haitian proverb.
10 Stepick 1998: 22; Zéphir 2001: 50.
11 Stepick 1998: 23; Zéphir 2001: 125–145.
12 Potvin 1999.
13 In the 1980s and 1990s the North American media spread the message that the HIV/Aids-transmitting risk groups consisted of the "Four Hs" – Heroin addicts, Haemophiliacs, Homosexuals, and Haitians (Richman 1992: 192; Stepick 1998: 35).

These two different strategies of identification serve as my frame of analysis. While the rap songs I am dealing with have been produced by Haitian university students with middle-class backgrounds, the children I worked with in order to understand the perception of these songs live in a poor working class area of Montreal. I will try to show how through hip-hop, group solidarity and community consciousness is (re-)produced and differences between these two groups of young Haitian immigrants are levelled out.

Moune morne: The people from the mountains

In the following case study I will present one of the most popular hip-hop groups in Quebec, called "Muzion – moune morne." Their first album, "mentalité moune morne – ils n'ont pas compris," appeared in 1999, the second, "J'Rêvolutionne," in 2003. The group is composed of four rappers of Haitian descent – two female and two male. Since the mid 1990s, Muzion, who rap in French, English and Haitian Créole, have gained a lot of respect and "street cred"[14] among children and youth of Haitian origin in Montreal. All members of the group have a middle-class background. J Kyl, for instance, one of the female members, was studying law at one of Montreal's universities and interrupted her studies in order to concentrate on her musical career. She and the three other members view hip-hop as an educative tool. They work in close contact with their local community, St. Michel, and invite children and youth to participate in their projects. Thus, through their music, they get in touch with the local population.

The following excerpt from the song "rien à perdre" demonstrates some of their ideas.

> **Rien à perdre – Nothing to lose**[15]
> Not one day without a song
> How many tell me: 'you would have made a good lawyer, what went wrong?'
> But I have an artistic soul, a spirit too mystic, nearly autistic for the lyrics
> unconstrained, I chose rap to live my rebellion
> Displaying my poems, making them run under an amazing beat
> Hip-Hop does for me everything that the rest won't do
> Gives me 3 times 16 bars of noise, which beats at the head of those,
> who otherwise wouldn't listen to me
> I keep the kids off of the street, they're running to my music
> I make them hear my voice so loud, in public
> Represent the oppressed, you say that's bullshit?
> But how many raise their arms when I take the mic' for rhyming.

---

14 "Street cred" (abrev.) = "street credibility," one of the main concepts of Hip-Hop-Culture.
15 Excerpt from "rien à perdre," from the album "mentalité moune morne," 1999 (my translation). See appendix for all original song versions.

During the two summers of my fieldwork in Montreal, Muzion's songs were played all day long on the local ethnic music stations. Children and young people also sang their songs at festivals, parties and other private events. Nearly every Haitian child I talked to knew Muzion – their story, their music and their messages. In using the three languages of their environment, Muzion's songs describe life under Montreal's plurilingual urban conditions. They constantly employ code-switching and language borrowing and maintain symbolic references of identification.

In order to understand the relevance of hip-hop for children, one needs to consider its function in group dynamics and communication. Alison James hints to the importance of group dynamics for children, who learn to negotiate the conflicting cultural demands between individuality and conformity within their peer-groups. She furthermore declares "talk" to be the primary medium of social exchange among children. Children's habits of talking and playing with words describe the inherent codes, which relate to specific categories of thoughts (James 1995: 59–60). Thus, it is not surprising that rap music in particular can serve as a source of empowerment and inspiration, given that it works with specific codes, linguistic varieties, mixings and neologisms.[16]

Both aspects, peer-group dimensions and their communicative skills, help children to advance from childhood to adolescence, from a more private way of life within the family to a more social way of life in the wider community. In many societies institutions such as the family, school, churches or youth associations help children through this phase of transition. However, as a result of the specific conditions mentioned above, in many Haitian families these institutions hardly exist, much less function. Instead, it is hip-hop's group dimensions that provide spaces for ritualizing the transition from childhood to adolescence. In all my interviews with children in Montreal, specific hip-hop-groups, i.e. their "crews" and "posses" served as a local source of identity and group affiliation within the "hoods."[17] As such they also function as a substitute for the missing or inadequate family support system. Hip-hop also serves children's competitive needs. They can compare their agility and skill, their strength and endurance.[18] In rap-music, breakdance and graffiti "battles," they aim at judging each other's creativity, originality and innovative potentials.[19]

As mentioned, the four members of Muzion have a strong attachment to their community and feel responsible for Haitian children in the streets. In one of my interviews with J Kyl, she explained to me that the term "moune morne" or "mornier" referred to the maroons, the slaves who had fled the sugar plantations two centuries ago and continued their lives as rebels in the mountains of Haiti. While in Haiti the term is employed to describe poor peasants

---

16 On the use of local vernaculars within rap music, see also Auzanneau 2001.
17 From "neighbourhood," also used in French and Haitian Créole.
18 Regarding children's desire for competitive occasions, see also Hardmann 1993: 73–76.
19 Rose 1994: 41–61.

living in the rural areas, in Montreal, many Haitian parents use it to let their children know that they consider their manners uncivilized and wild. Muzion, however, use the term in a positive way, J Kyl explained and confessed proudly: "Yes, I am mornier, yes, I will fight for my freedom, yes, I live like a peasant, because I am not materialistic."[20]

In this statement, two main aspects of children's and young people's identity constructions are pin-pointed: they define themselves as opposed to their parent's world, which they experience as intimidating and hostile, and they refer to Haitian history and to heroes of the Haitian revolution – the latter serving as role models.

Thus, "family conflicts" on the one hand and "black power" on the other are experienced as major issues in the social lives of Haitian children and serve as focal points of reference with regard to identity construction. In the following I will analyze some of Muzion's songs, focusing on these two major themes. During my interviews with the children, the lyrics of Muzion's songs served as a point of entry to discuss their perspectives and attitudes concerning these issues.

The seven children I mainly talked to were between 10 and 14 years of age and lived in St. Michel, a multi-ethnic working-class quarter of Montreal.[21] The following descriptions and citations result from two meetings organized by Muzion, who knew the children through their own project activities.[22] We met in a public park, where we sat on the ground, listening to Muzion's songs on a small CD-player. We listened to a couple of songs, the children singing the lyrics or humming the melodies. Then I interrupted the music and we discussed the songs' messages.[23]

---

20 This and all following children's statements have been translated from French/Haitian Créole into English.
21 Except from the members of Muzion, all names mentioned in the text are pseudonyms.
22 The members of Muzion were interviewed separately and did not take part in the meetings with the children.
23 While all the following songs have been translated from a mix of French/Haitian Créole/English into English, I would like to point out that translations of rap-songs tend to remain partly inadequate. Rappers often produce abstract stories with catchy phrases, storing fragments of associative allusions. Rap language contains images, ideas and icons, which encompass re-contextualizations that emerge from dialogues between rap musicians and those who listen to their music.

Family conflicts

L'éducation – Education[24]
An alcoholic father, a choleric son with a devil's look
All alone, without accomplices, getting furious, hitting too easily.
A mother, selling her body, a girl, stretching her body easily
In the bed of a pig, the first night, he takes her out
An abusive father disrespecting his wife, his son disrespecting his mother
Ephemeral authority and his mates applauding.
The family, first source of all our actions,
The most beautiful thing or the most ugly,
depending on whether or not there's love involved in our education.

Tel père, tel vice – Such father, such shame[25]
A naïve life of 10 years
Depressive mother, absent father, dictator style, cutting looks
What's wrong, son? Say you're afraid! He's bringing fear to the whole house
He's getting even more brutal by the time he has to pay the rent, the bills
What a mess, nobody is laughing anymore, when the door-bell rings.
The mother sets up the table, the child running to bed
Lying under the covers, cramping, this jerk of a father
Might come to play with him, his hands in his pants...
Refrain: After all you've done wrong, you want me to forgive you?
You say you love me? How dare you forget the past!
I don't believe you when you say you're sorry.

Muzion touch upon the issue of family and intergenerational conflicts in many of their songs. "L'éducation," among other songs, accuse parents of inadequate communication vis-à-vis their children. Muzion develop an image of autistic, violent and isolated fathers, who long for other worlds and other women, and an image of mothers, who lose their identity in their day-to-day worries about their jobs and their children's lives. Lack of respect and self-control on both sides, the songs tell us, teaches children violent worldviews and sexualized modes of behaviour.

In my discussions with the children they confirmed this general picture and described severe conflicts within their families, between their parents as well as between parents and children. The children claimed most of the tension and quarrels in Montreal's Haitian families resulted from their parent's frustration on the one hand and their own desire for more freedom and less control on the other. Particularly their fathers suffered from the unexpected changes that result out of unemployment, low social and economic status and the loss of authority. Tom, a boy of thirteen years said: "It's true what they say. Normally it's important, the respect; sure one has to respect the other. But

---

24 Excerpt from "l'Education," from the Album "mentalité moune morne," 1999 (my translation).
25 Excerpt from "Tel père, tel vice," from the Album "mentalité moune morne," 1999 (my translation).

at the same time it's not only me, who is obliged, it's also my parents, they also have to have respect. And that's what they say, Muzion."

In his explanation Tom refers to the fact that Haitian children in Montreal profit from a more permissive educational system in Canada but at the same time suffer because their parents nevertheless try to raise their children according to Haitian traditions of strict generational hierarchies.

The issue of sexual abuse was another difficult topic which came up. Again, Muzion's lyrics helped me to imagine the violent conditions many Haitian children face and my young interviewees to discuss their fears and suspicions. When I read the lyrics of "Tel père, tel vice" to them, Emile, a 10-year-old boy, started talking about his elder brother. He left his family a couple of years ago to join one of the local street gangs that roam the streets of Montreal-Nord and St. Michel making a living from drug dealing and carjacking. Sometimes when they meet, Emile and his brother talk about the situation at home and about the brother's desire to re-start an ordinary life and continue school. Emile said the situation at home got even worse after his brother had left, because his father felt ashamed of his son's gang activities and, according to Emile, at times even hid or denied his elder son's existence: "It's the severest punishment for my father, that my brother went away and lives his life. But it's true: sometimes my father is like a dictator; that scares me. I understand my brother, but I miss him a lot."

Emile uses the song to talk about his feelings, such as his fear of violence and his solitude. When discussing the lyrics, most of the children agreed with Emile's negative perception about their everyday lives at home and started talking about their experiences. They all longed for a less conflict laden "home," i.e. a place of security and refuge. Most of them, girls as well as boys, felt closer to their mothers than to their fathers, since the former showed a lot more interested in their children's lives. Vanessa, aged 12, complained that the only issue her father would talk about was Haiti. Even though her father has lived in Canada for more than 20 years, she said, he was obsessed by the idea of eventually returning there. And she added: "Sometimes that scares me, because I do not know anything about Haiti and I know that there's much criminality over there." Vanessa felt threatened by the idea of having to "return" to a country she does not know. A couple of other children also mentioned their parents had never started a real life in Canada, but remained fully attached to their homeland instead. These different ties – the parents being attached to their home country, their children feeling more at home in their host society – are a common phenomenon within immigrant families in general.[26] The children's narrations made this gap running through Haitian immigrant families very apparent.

Both songs discussed here carry different images and judgements concerning mothers and fathers. When I touched this issue, it quickly became clear that gender plays an important role in the perception of family conflicts. Myr-

---

26 Rumbaut & Portes 2001: 6.

lène, aged 14, explained, that only Haitian fathers acted in such a violent manner, while Haitian mothers generally felt much more attached to their children. She told us that she was happy to know that her mum would never take her to Haiti, but would always stay in Canada with her children. Vanessa agreed, saying her mother would never leave Canada either because she wanted her children to get a good education. She witnessed many violent conflicts in her family as well, but knew her mother would either try to calm down her father or would leave him one day to live on her own with her children, as many Haitian women in Montreal have already done.

Other girls mentioned that since their parents lived according to Haitian traditions and values, they treated girls and boys differently. While their brothers were allowed to stay out even at night, girls would be much more controlled. Eve, aged 13, mentioned that she felt her mother did not trust her and had started to observe her even on her way to school to find out whether she had a boyfriend. Referring to the songs, one of the girls said: "For me, with Muzion, I know that they're Haitians, like me, they are blacks, and they live through the same things as we do. Sometimes, in their songs, things become clearer. Sometimes, it's strange to see that it's just around the corner. And I talk about it with my friends; it's great to see a Haitian girl talking like that, which is not our parents' ideal!"

Muzion serve as a representation of young and modern Haitians, who do not – and do not want to – live up to their parent's expectations. The two female members of Muzion in particular present an image of Haitian girls inconsistent with Haitian traditions and ideals. Their habit of wearing baggy pants and dreadlocks like their male peers as well as their unbridled performances on stage cause huge concerns among Haitian parents in Montreal. For Haitian children, however, they serve as role models and their attitudes and behaviour are perceived as integral parts of the lives and identities of young Haitians in Montreal.

In summary, by means of discussing two of Muzion's songs dealing with family conflicts, four major issues were elucidated as being central to the social lives and identities of Haitian children in Montreal. First, the lack of respect both between parents and between parents and children. Second, the issue of sexual abuse and violence in general. Third, marked differences in attitudes and perspectives between different generations, effecting different ties with regard to home and host society, parents and particularly fathers feeling attached to their home country, children feeling more at home in Canada. Fourth, the parent's reproduction of Haitian gender ideologies and hence, the different treatment of girls and boys.

Black power

J'Rêvolutionne[27]
You see one million rowing slaves. That's us!
One million children, men and women. Us!
Without chains, without the lash of the whip. That's what makes us move:
the fury in our souls, that's us!
Humanity which crosses ebony and ivory, that's us!
A whole army of oppressed, who yell 'war'
Who are tired of being the ridiculous mass! White or black
We take back our power
But who zombified me, confiscated my spirit... Tame?
Only when this written dream can live, I will stay here without hope...
I don't have any tears left when I cry
We don't mind the scandal
I dream the revolution Boukman[28] style
Wherever I go, I will settle down among ourselves
Hit the volume, beat the tam-tams in the mountains.
We're running applauding these guys
Dead! (For to serve us as cover)
Free! (all saints like Louverture)[29]
We will die this time all the same
Between ghettos and aristocracy
As long as there's no flag. And too many fatherlands!
We will be nothing but Negroes against Nazis oppressors
As long as we're condemned for our sex, our race, our class,
For the god, to whom we pray and whom we worship
As long as my texts harass and annoy the coward
Who doesn't understand what we say and the brothers say
Everywhere, in all the countries, decay,
They die under the betrayal, the beatings
Where're you from? I am there! We want war – And that's all!!!

Black pride, rebellion and violent images about the legacy of slavery are common tropes in hip-hop culture in general and constitute the most important topic in Muzion's songs. Like many other hip-hop groups, they embrace the idea of blackness in ways that parallel the rise of black consciousness in the 1970s in the United States. They popularize an afrocentric movement through lyrics that link the daily problems of racism, economic oppression and black marginality in contemporary American society.[30] Furthermore, they connect

---

27 Excerpt from the song "J'rêvolutionne," from the Album "J'rêvolutionne," 2003 (my translation). J'rêvolutionne, a neologism, could be translated with: I dream the revolution.
28 Boukman was a vodou priest, who inspired the Haitian slaves to rebel against their white masters during the Haitian revolution, a rebellion, which resulted in the declaration of the state of Haiti in 1804, the first independent black nation in the world.
29 Toussaint Louverture was a soldier during the Haitian revolution, who managed to unite the black masses and to mobilize them against their white enemies.
30 Rose 1994: 21–34.

contemporary racial discrimination with the historical experience of slavery, drawing upon both as a source for black rebellion and resistance. Muzion work with explicitly aggressive contents, a common phenomenon in hip-hop-culture.[31] In the song discussed here, they do not just mix French, English and Haitian Créole, but also interweave cultural elements originating in the African American movement in the Americas, from Haiti, and from their distinct youth culture.

As for the reconstruction of a particularly Haitian identity in the diaspora, specifically Haitian symbols are drawn upon – e.g. "Boukman" and "Louverture," two Haitian heroes from the Haitian revolution. Their fury and rage are not being addressed primarily to evoke worldwide solidarity among coloured people, but to bring to light historically rooted issues of a particular Haitian relevance and, thus to evoke Haitian ethnicity on a transnational level.

I started my discussion with the children by questioning the relevance of the "old" Haitian heroes for the life of a Haitian girl or boy in Montreal today. I asked them whether they knew about these Haitian heroes and whether they had talked about them at home. Tom, aged 13, explained that his parents had told him some things about Haitian history and the slave rebellion, but that he particularly liked the sound and the general atmosphere of the songs: "When I listen to Muzion, I am glad to be Haitian. Their pride and all that, that's good. Haiti, this is not the same thing for my parents, for Muzion, it's much cooler." He laughed, then raised his arms and shouted "Men Moun Yo!" ["I am here!"].

I also raised the issue of the aggressive tone of the song, asking "What kind of war are they talking about?" Altogether they started giggling and Sammy, a boy of 14, got up, raised his arms and started performing the last part of the song with lucid hip-hop-style movements. Then he sat down again and the children started discussing the importance of those famous rebels and their use of violence for their everyday life. After several minutes of chaotic shouting about, some order returned and Sammy started talking about his experiences at school: "We, at school, the blacks, we are rebels too, you see? Sometimes it's like this, we get together, but we're not a street-gang. Anyhow, we're against the others, we have to fight all the time!"

Sammy relates to one of the common tropes of Caribbean culture, the rebellious maroon. Referring to "maroon resistance" is calling for class-based solidarity as well as for enduring resistance against the dominating American way of life. Sammy continues explaining that at school he would always be Haitian, although he's proud to be a Canadian citizen: "Haiti, it is like your mother. You might have your problems with her, you might even fight with

---

31 For instance, Rose (1994) analyses the way rap and rap-related violence are discussed in popular media, showing how this specific discourse is part of a more general discourse on black people. See also Gilroy (1991: 110), where he deconstructs the media's ideological perspective on black crime.

her, but you will never leave her, you will be with her all your life, it's biology, you can't escape it."

Sammy's equation between one's Haitian descent and the relationship to one's mother shows that despite ambivalent feelings, ethnic ties are perceived to be like maternal ties, biological and inescapable and thus need to be accepted as such. Moreover, he explained that the main reason why the children at school constantly reminded him of his Haitian descent was the negative image Haitians have in Montreal.

The music and lyrics produced by Muzion help him to view Haiti as well as his family in a more positive light. Sammy assumed that many black people would be better off today if they were as courageous as the Haitian slaves during the revolution. Indeed, most of the other children I talked to where impressed by the radical stance the slaves took and shared a vision of a better life achieved through united resistance and black power.

Particularly the three girls complained that their Quebecois identity was not accepted among many of their white friends. Myrlène explained that she had never really felt Haitian because she grew up mainly with white friends and hardly knew other Haitians. But the day other children made fun of her on account of her skin-colour, she started reflecting upon her Haitian roots. The music, she told me, helped her to find something "Haitian" which was different from her parents' Haiti, something more positive and meaningful. Again, this statement implies ambivalence between a negative "Haiti" associated with one's parents and a more positive "Haiti" associated with connotations and meanings, that may serve as a source of identification for oneself. The latter need to be discovered and music is an important means of such discovery.

In order to deepen the analysis of these ambivalent attitudes and feelings, I would like to introduce one more Muzion song – "La Vi Ti Nèg" – meaning: "the life of a small nigger." It depicts miserable living conditions, violence and broken families as part of Haitians' life in the diaspora, but it also pleads for a positive memory of and solidarity with the homeland. Since its release in 1999 this song has become Muzion's most popular hit, which may be the result of both its captivating rhythm and its simple message:

La Vi Ti Nèg – Life of a small nigger[32]

It's one love / like the pearl of the Antilles my clan is shining
As did the folks / who destroyed power in 1804[33]
Black & proud to be I see those people capable
To realize that everything is only camouflage
but you don't have to worry because we're united
You can lean on me even when the load is heavy
A handshake for me before the countdown starts
Where are we from?
1 Recognize your power. Black, your fury,
think well about where you are and where you want to start from
2 Never lower your head. It's your planet. Do what you have to do from A to Z.
3 Recognize where you're coming from and give a lot of support
To the crews who for you don't fear the dead.
At the end of your power, you need your allies
To eradicate the bad and go before the wind. That's what you have to do!

Cry, cry, I've already cried
Now, nobody will make fun of me
You pretend not to know me
But I recognized you from Delmas[34]
Where we drank coconut milk
Where you ate a mango
Now you don't know where you are
I saw you crying. What has happened to you?
I don't recognize your accent
Everywhere you go you do crazy stuff / You have made yourself enemies
Now you speak French / You studied good, forgot your créole
You want to make your family believe that everything is fine
And that you're able to make lots of money
Your mouth lies / You're a liar
In Haiti, you ate well
Now you live in a room with cockroaches
Jescome[35] who just arrived / You don't have money to go to the market
Every day you eat flour with milk

Move on, move on / Do you think I'm just kidding?
Move on, move on / Get up and come to see what's happening
Move on, move on / Do you think I'm just kidding? Haitian!

I look for a job, / The white guy says I stole his money
I look for a house, You say I'm dirty / That's why I go home
At school, the teacher said I am stupid / My whole family is broken

Refrain: Life's not easy / That's why we unite

---

32 Excerpt from "La Vi Ti Nèg" (French and Haitian Créole), from the Album "mentalité moune morne", 1999 (my translation).
33 The year 1804 is the year of Haitian independence.
34 A rich residential area of Port-au-Prince, Haiti.
35 Haitian expression for someone, who only recently arrived in Canada.

Like "J'rêvolutionne," this song addresses the issues of family life and black pride, pinpointing the transnational dimension of Haitian ethnicity in Montreal. But in contrast to many other of Muzion's songs, "La Vi Ti Nèg" raises the issue of ethnic consciousness and pride specifically with respect to Haitian community life in Montreal. In bringing up class-related issues, i.e. language, food, and lifestyle, Muzion call for the recognition of Haitian origins and for class-transcending solidarity within the Haitian community. The common attitude among many migrants, that they should fulfill the ideal of the successful immigrant and thus deny migration-related losses and failures in order to meet the expectations of others, is rejected. Instead, Muzion depict the typical immigrant who struggles to make ends meet while being torn between the immigrant community in Canada, Haiti and the family-members left behind there and the host society as such. In this song, they deal especially with the ambivalent feelings towards Haiti, which most Haitians are forced to leave for economic and political reasons, but which still plays an important part in many of their lives.

Most of the seven interviewed children shared this ambivalent feeling towards their parent's home country. This is also due to the fact that their parents themselves (re-)produce contradictory and inconsistent images of Haiti. On the one hand, Haiti is depicted as a dramatically poor and violent country where people are regularly massacred and tortured. On the other hand, Haiti is depicted as the first black independent nation in the Western Hemisphere that has the potential to serve as a model for all black nations in the world. It seems the first generation of Haitian immigrants has passed this somewhat paradoxical depiction of Haiti on to their children. Among the latter an even greater variety of depictions and meanings of Blackness and Haitianness exists since they feel more attached to their host country than their parents and are thus more influenced by ideas developed within the black Canadian community than they are. In the discussion about the meaning of the song "La Vi Ti Nèg" Vanessa explained:

For me, with Haiti, it gets on my nerves too what they say all the time about criminality and all that. But in the songs, what is important is that we are here today, we have to learn that Haiti worked in the past. And today, we can also work, we have to unite, that's what will give us power. Our parents, they are always stressed, they always work and all that. But we, young people, we can do things in a different way. They, Muzion, they do it. Everybody knows them, they are proud to be Haitians and they make a lot of money.

Conclusion

By means of the songs – using them as a primary source of information and as a means for discussing their messages with children – I could identify the major issues that affect immigrant Haitian children in Montreal in their endeavour to localize themselves socially and culturally in an environment characterized by ambivalent ties and demands. The songs and the children's reflections upon them give insight into their perceptions of their own social reality between home and host society.

Through listening to music and experiencing music as a way of life, immigrant children are better able to find their own social selves in the world they live in. They may construct selective belongings in order to position themselves socially vis-à-vis their host society, their immigrant community and their parent's country of origin. They use hip-hop as a reflective tool for dealing with the relevant issues affecting their lives, such as family life or black power.

With regard to their family lives the image of Haiti that children develop is a rather stereotypical and negative one. It serves as a symbolic icon encompassing the parents' generation's conflicts in establishing themselves in Canada, conflicts also effected by their desire to maintain Haitian traditions and values and to return to Haiti one day. Children consider their parents' ideologies and traditions as out-dated and as incompatible with life in Montreal. Their parents' desire to return to Haiti evokes fears in them of being deported one day to a "home" country they have never been to.

We also learn about divisions along gender lines when focusing on problems within the family. The images of mothers and fathers depicted in the songs differed considerably and highlighted major conflicts. In the discussions girls and boys related differences of attitudes and behaviour in terms of gender – i.e. different relationships to their mothers and fathers – thus portraying social and cultural diversity as linked to gender as well.

With regard to "black power" Haiti serves as an imaginary homeland. Contrary to its depiction when related to family issues, it appears as an image one can draw upon for the production of black pride. By means of the songs, Haitian children are encouraged to learn about the Haitian revolution and the heroic deeds of their ancestors, who fought for Haiti's independence and made it the first black nation in the world. The conflicts they experience within their families as well as vis-à-vis the Canadian host society trigger the "invention" of Haiti as an imaginary land characterized by black unity and black power.

By relating to Haitian history through music, children may develop a feeling of belonging to the Haitian community. At the same time they remain part of their Canadian environment. The accounts of the children revealed that a transnational Haitian identity exists side-by-side with a genuine feeling of belonging to the Canadian society. These attachments do not go without conflict but nevertheless bear positive connotations in their inter-relatedness.

Haitian children are aware that their lives are shaped by "culture," "culture" being in their view something that needs to be situated somewhere between their parents' "heritage" and their own cultural creations, ascriptions and belongings.

The class-transcending qualities of hip-hop may serve as a social link between youth from a well-to-do middle-class and children from a poor working class background. Particularly for children, who spend a lot of their time on the streets, hip-hop can serve to reconstruct black history and culture, and to fulfill to some degree their desire to belong somewhere. Sometimes it is only through hip-hop that Haitian children and youth get to know about the history of slavery and about Haitian history in general. Especially the heroic aspects of the Haitian revolution can help to create a positive identification as blacks and as descendants of rebels and revolutionaries.[36] Through the ideals and ideologies attached to hip-hop, social values such as respect, trust, and credibility may be conveyed to children – values many children do not acquire through their parents.

The analysis of children's perception and interpretation of their music helps to elucidate the social dynamics within their peer-groups as well as between themselves and their parents and the larger society. I agree with those who claim that societies need to be understood from different angles and that the insights children can provide make our understanding of the social dynamics within societies more complete.[37] Like "gender," "generation" can serve as an analytical tool that opens up new perspectives on social phenomena and can therefore contribute to the development of new theories in the social sciences and anthropology in particular.

Appendix

Rien à perdre
Pas un jour sans ligne
Combien m'disent: 'T'aurais fait une bonne avocate yo qu'est-ce t'as bloqué?'
Mais j'ai l'âme artistique, un esprit trop mystique presque autistique aux lyriques désinvoltes et j'ai choisi le rap pour vivre de ma rivolte
Apposer ma poésie, la faire couler sur un beat frappa
Le hip hop fait pour moi c'que tout le reste ne fera pas
Me laisse 3 fois 16 bars de fracas qui frappe à la tête de celui qui autrement ne m'écouteras pas
Garder les jeunes hors de la rue stocké sur ma musique
Faire entendre ma voix très haute là, sur la place publique
Représenter la masse opprimée, tu dis qu'ce bullshit ?
Mais combien lèvent leurs bras quand j'prends le micro pour rimer?

L'éducation
Un père alcoolique, un fils colérique au regard diabolique
Solo pas d'acolyte s'énerve et frappe trop vite
Une mère qui vend son corps, une fille qui étend son corps facilemen
Dans l'lit d'un porc la première nuit qu'il la sort dehors

---

36 On hip-hop's relevance in creating ethnic consciousness and historical reflection, see also Weller 2003. In German cities, a growing number of youth projects use hip-hop as an educative tool in order to attract young people from the streets and use the language and style of hip-hop to gain the youth's attention.
37 Caputo 1995; Hardmann 1973: 76; Haudrup Christensen 1994.

Un père abusif qui dérespecte sa femme, le fils dérespecte sa mère
Autorité éphémère et ses potes l'acclament
Une famille, la première source de toutes nos actions
La plus belle chose ou la plus l'aide dépendant d'l'amour dans l'éducation.

Tel père, tel vice
Une vie naïve de 10 ans
Mère dépressive, un père absent style dictateur au regard tranchant:
'Qu'est ce que t'as fils? Dis que t'as peur!' Il dicte la peur dans tout le foyer
Et devient d'autant plus bestial quand vient le temps de payer les bills, le loyer
Quelles conneries! Dès qu'on entend la sonnerie, plus personne ne rit.
La mère place le couvert et l'enfant court dans son lit.
Couché sous ses draps, il constipe à l'idée que ce con de type
Viendra jouer avec lui, la main dans son slip...
Refrain: After all you've done wrong, you want me to forgive you ?
You say you love me? How dare you forget the past!
I don't believe you when you say you're sorry.

J'Rêvolutionne
Tu verras un million d'esclaves qui rament C'est nous!
Un million d'enfants, d'hommes et de femmes: Nous!
Sans chaîne, sans coup de fouet. C'qui nous fait bouger:
la rage dans nos âmes c'est nous!
L'humanité croise l'ébène et l'ivoire c'est nous!
Une seule armée d'oppressés qui crient «War!»
Y'en a marre d'être la masse dérisoire! Blancs ou noirs,
On reprend le pouvoir sur nous!
Mais qui m'a zombifiée, confisquée, mon esprit... Docile?
Sauf si ce rêve écrit vit, J'reste prise sans espoir ici...
Je n'ai plus de larme du tout quand j'braille.
On fout le scandale.
J'rêvolutionne, Boukman style
Où que je m'en aille, Chez nous je m'installe.
Mets le volume, cogne le chant des tam-tams dans les mornes.
On courre en acclamant ces hommes
Morts! (pour nous servir de couverture)
Libres! (tous saints comme Louverture)
Nous mourrons tous égaux c'fois-ci
Entre les ghettos et l'aristocratie.
Tant qu'il n'y aura d'un drapeau et trop de patries,
Nous ne serons que des négros contre des bourreaux nazis.
Tant qu'on sera jugé pour notre sexe, notre race, notre classe,
Pour le dieu qu'on prie et vénère
Tant que mes textes vexent et fâchent le lâche
Qui n'a pas compris ce qu'on dit et que des frères
Partout, de tous les pays, s'écroulent
Meurent sous le mépris, les coups.
Kote Moun Yo? Men Moun Yo! On veut la guerre – Et puis c'est tout!!!

La Vi Ti Nèg – Life of a small nigger

C'est one love / comme la perle des Antilles mon clan brille
En tant que les gens qui ont anéanti / le pouvoir d'autruit en 1804
Black & proud to be, j'vise les gens aptes
À reconnaître qu'aujourd'hui c'est camouflé
mais faut pas s'soucier car nous sommes associés
yo tu peux t'accoter sur moi si la charge est lourde
Un coup de main aux miens avant le compte à rebours
On part de où?
1 reconnaît ta force. Black, ta rage,
pense bien à où est-ce que tu l'amorces
2 baisse jamais la tête. C'est ta planète. Fais ce que t'as à faire avec de A à Z
3 reconnaît d'où tu sors, donne beaucoup d'support
aux crews qui pour toi s'en foutent de la mort.
À bout de tes forces, t'as besoin de tes alliés
Effacer le mal et aller devant l'vent. Cé sa li yé!

Kriye kriye ou, mwen kriye deja
Kounye-a pa gen moun kap manke mwen d'éga
Pran poz ou pa konnen'm
Mwen té konn wè ou bo zon Delma
Koté ou té ap bwè bon dlo kokoyé
Ou te ap manjé mango
Kounye-en ou pa konn koté ou yé
Mwen wè je ou nen dlo / Sa ki pran ou?
Mwen pa sa rekonèt aksen ou
Wap mache di bétiz, / ap fè lenmi ak prop san ou
Tonbe pale franse / gro klas lekol bliye kreyol
Montre fanmi lakay wap bien Mennen / se kob la kap monte
Bouch ou senti / Ou ap bay manti
Ayiti, ou te konn manje
Kounye-en ou rete nen yon ti piès kay plen ravèt
Jescome ki fèk parèt / Pa gen kob fè makèt
Chak jou manje farin ak lèt

Avanse, avanse! Ou konprann m'ap ranse?
Avanse, avanse! Kanpe vini wè sa kap pase
Avanse, avanse! Nou konprann m'ap ranse?
Aiysyen! M'al chèche travay, / blan en di se kob li m'ap volè
M'al chèche kay, yo di mwen malprop
Se pou mwen touen lakay
Lekol, mèt la di mwen se kretin / Tout fanmi'm gaye

Refrain: Lavi na pa fasil / Sé pou sa nou rasanble.

References

Amit-Talai, Vered & Helena Wulff (eds.) 1995: *Youth Cultures: A Cross-Cultural Perspective.* London & New York: Routledge.

Auzanneau, Michelle 2001: Identités africaines: le rap comme lieu d'expression. *Cahiers d'Études africaines*, Vol. XLI, No. 3: 711–734.

Basch, Linda, Nina Glick Schiller & Cristina Szanton Blanc 1994: *Nations Unbound. Transnational Projects, Postcolonial Predicaments and Deterritorialized Nation-States.* Amsterdam: OPA (Overseas Publishers Association).

Caputo, Virginia 1995: Anthropology's silent 'others:' A consideration of some conceptual and methodological issues for the study of youth and children's cultures. In: Amit-Talai, Vered & Helena Wulff (eds.): *Youth Cultures: A Cross-cultural Perspective.* London & New York: Routledge: 19–42.

Dejean, Paul 1990: *D'Haiti au Québec.* Montréal: Cidihca.

Drotbohm, Heike 2000: *Timoun-yo ce canet banc malere. Die Situation, Probleme und Potenziale von Jugendlichen im ländlichen Haiti, dargestellt an zwei Gemeinden des Départements du Nord.* Unpublished study, carried out for the German Society of Technical Cooperation, GTZ. Eschborn 2000.

Drotbohm, Heike 2005: *Geister in der Diaspora. Haitianische Diskurse über Geschlechter, Jugend und Macht in Montreal, Kanada.* Marburg: Curupira.

Foner, Nancy (ed.) 2001: *Islands in the City. West Indian Migration to New York.* Berkeley & Los Angeles: University of California Press.

Gilroy, Paul 1991: *'There Ain't No Black in the Union Jack.' The Cultural Politics of Race and Nation.* Chicago: University of Chicago Press.

Glick Schiller, Nina, Linda Basch & Cristina Szanton Blanc (eds.) 1992: *Towards a Transnational Perspective on Migration. Race, Class, Ethnicity, and Nationalism Reconsidered.* Annals of the new york academy of sciences, Vol. 645. New York: The New York Academy of Sciences.

Hardman, Charlotte 1993: Auf dem Schulhof. Unterwegs zu einer Anthropologie der Kindheit. In: Loo, Marie-José van de & Margarete Reinhart (eds.): *Kinder. Ethnologische Forschungen in fünf Kontinenten.* München: Trickster: 60–77.

Haudrup Christensen, Pia 1994: Children as the cultural other: the discovery of children in the social cultural sciences. *Kea, Zeitschrift für Kulturwissenschaften*, Bd. 6, Kinderwelten: 1–16.

James, Allison 1995: Talking of children and youth: language, socialization and culture. In: Amit-Talai, Vered & Helena Wulff (eds.): *Youth Cultures: A Cross-cultural Perspective.* London & New York: Routledge: 43–62.

Kage, Jan 2002: *American Rap. Explicit Lyrics – US-HipHop und Identität.* Mainz: Ventil.

Kimminich, Eva (ed.) 2004: *Rap: More Than Words.* Frankfurt a.M.: Lang.

Klein, Gabriele & Malte Friedrich 2003: *Is This Real? Die Kultur des HipHop.* Frankfurt/Main: Suhrkamp.

Liell, Christoph 2003: Jugend, Gewalt und Musik. Praktiken der Efferveszenz in der HipHop-Szene. In: Luig, Ute & Jochen Seebode (eds.): *Ethnologie der Jugend.*

Soziale Praxis, moralische Diskurse und inszenierte Körperlichkeit. Münster, Hamburg & London: Lit-Verlag: 123–153.

Lipsitz, George 1999: *Dangerous Crossroads. Popmusik, Postmoderne und die Poesie des Lokalen.* St. Andrä-Wördern: Haniball.

Loo, Marie-José van de & Margarete Reinhart (eds.) 1993: *Kinder. Ethnologische Forschungen in fünf Kontinenten.* München: Trickster.

Luig, Ute & Jochen Seebode (eds.) 2003: *Ethnologie der Jugend. Soziale Praxis, moralische Diskurse und inszenierte Körperlichkeit.* Münster, Hamburg & London: Lit-Verlag.

Meintel, Deirdre 2000: Plural identities among youth of immigrant background in Montreal. *Horizontes Antropológicos*, Porto Alegre, ano 6, n. 14: 13–37.

Menrath, Stefanie 2001: *Represent What... Performativität von Identitäten im Hip-Hop.* Hamburg: Argument.

Muzion (songs and lyrics) 1999: *Mentalité moune morne.* BMG Canada, Québec and ViK Recordings.

Muzion (songs and lyrics) 2003: *J'rêvolutionne.* BMG Canada, Québec and ViK Recordings.

Potvin, Maryse 1999: Second generation Haitian youth in Quebec: Between the 'real' community and the 'represented' community. *Études Ethniques au Canada*, Vol xxxi, No. 1: 43–72.

Richman, Karen 1992: "A *Lavalas* at home/A *Lavalas* for home": Inflections of transnationalism in the discourse of Haitian President Aristide. In: Glick Schiller, Nina, Linda Basch & Cristina Szanton Blanc (eds.): *Towards a Transnational Perspective on Migration. Race, Class, Ethnicity, and Nationalism Reconsidered.* Annals of the New York Academy of Sciences, vol. 645. New York: The New York Academy of Sciences: 189–200.

Rose, Tricia 1994: *Black Noise. Rap Music and Black Culture in Contemporary America.* Middletown: Wesleyan University Press.

Ross, Andrew & Tricia Rose (eds.) 1994: *Microphone Friends. Youth Music, Youth Culture.* New York, London: Routledge.

Rumbaut, Rubén & Alejandro Portes (eds.) 2001: *Ethnicities. Children of Immigrants in America.* Berkeley, Los Angeles: University of California Press.

Stepick, Alex 1998: *Pride against Prejudice. Haitians in the United States.* Boston, London: Allyn & Bacon.

Waters, Mary C. 2001: Growing up West Indian and African American: Gender and class differences in the second generation. In: Foner, Nancy (ed.): *Islands in the City. West Indian Migration to New York.* Berkeley & Los Angeles: University of California Press: 193–215.

Weller, Wivian 2003: *HipHop und ethnisches Bewusstsein in den Peripherien Sao Paulos – Brasilien.* In: Luig, Ute & Jochen Seebode (eds.): *Ethnologie der Jugend. Soziale Praxis, moralische Diskurse und inszenierte Körperlichkeit.* Münster, Hamburg & London: Lit-Verlag: 155–176.

Zéphir, Flore 2001: *Trends in Ethnic Identification among Second-Generation Haitian Immigrants in New York City.* Westport, Connecticut & London: Bergin & Garbey.

LIMINALITY AS LINGUISTIC PROCESS.
IMMIGRANT YOUTH AND EXPERIENCES OF LANGUAGE
IN GERMANY AND THE UNITED STATES

H. Julia Eksner and Marjorie Faulstich Orellana

Introduction

If it is an adult they think that younger people don't really know how to translate. They just look down on them and by showing them that a kid translates it kind of raises up my spirits a bit. It kind of gets back at them. [...] He will look down on him and he will be like, ha, ha, ha, and he will start laughing at the little kid. And if the little kid does show him he can translate it kind of raises up the kid's spirits. It gives [him] more encouragement for the next time (Sammy).

12-year old Sammy, the son of immigrants from Mexico to Chicago, is one of millions of children of immigrants in the United States and Europe who, in the process of growing up, use language to negotiate multiple relations and forge new identities. These youths sometimes utilize their knowledge of two languages to mediate between their parents and speakers of the "majority" language. At the same time, like all people, they deploy language to negotiate their *own* identities with these adults, and with each other, as well as to *contest* identities that are wrested upon them. Each of these linguistic processes – mediation and contestation – is shaped by the youths' positions of liminality along the lines of immigration status, language, and age.

In this paper[1] we will build from anthropological theories of liminality, providing a critical evaluation of this concept as a useful heuristic for understanding the linguistic practices of immigrant children. Entailed in this is a brief discussion of how the concept of liminality has hitherto been used to explain the experiences of immigrants, particularly immigrant youth, in anthropological and socio-linguistic research. Centrally, this paper will explore the power-laden ways in which the limen becomes situated linguistically, and how new identities are constructed from this locus, by looking at the language practices of Turkish adolescents in Berlin (Germany) and Mexican-origin children in Chicago (United States).

---

1 Acknowledgements: Thanks to Nina Glick-Schiller, Daniel Monterescu, and Jennifer Reynolds for thoughtful feedback, to Remzye Uykun for her translations from Turkish into German, and to Olivia Pils for the photograph of the Turkish youths' graffiti art in the Berlin field site.

Using these two cases as points of leverage, we develop a comparative analysis of immigrant youths' experiences in two different national and cultural contexts, focusing on linguistic processes of mediation and contestation. We center our analysis of mediation in the study of Mexican-origin children who serve as language and culture brokers for their families in the Midwestern United States. Our analysis of contestation is based on the ways in which the Turkish youths clustered in a Berlin youth gang use language to contest and recode stereotypes put on them by dominant society. We draw from multiple, mutually illuminating sources of data, including field notes based on participant observation, open and semi-structured interviews, inferred personality characteristics tests, survey data, transcripts of focus groups, children's journal entries and transcripts of youth engaged in a range of talk.

We begin our discussion with a brief elaboration of the construct of liminality, from its inception to its portrayal in current anthropological, sociological and sociolinguistic inquiry. We then go on to identify three key theoretical concerns about the construct of liminality: first, issues of power; second, the conceptualization of change; and third, the multiplicity of identity processes. We consider how these three issues play out in the experiences of immigrant youths and their language practices, and through grounded theorizing aim to contribute to an elaboration of theories of liminality, partly by joining Turner's concept of liminality with more recently-forged hybridity theories.

The concept of liminality

The concept of liminality was originally formulated by Turner (1969), who took up van Gennep's (1960 [1909]) model of "rites of passage." Elaborating on Durkheim's (1912), and later Eliade's (1959) dichotomization of human experience in sacred and profane, Turner used this concept to describe a phase through which an individual passes during processes of social transition. Liminality is a condition in which individuals are stripped off their ordinary identities, roles, and positions. During a liminal period the characteristics of the "ritual subject," as Turner calls it, are "ambiguous;" he or she is "betwixt and between" (Turner 1969: 94).

Rites of passage are periods of ambiguity that accompany every change of place, state, social position and age of an individual. A rite of passage is a three-part process that includes first the separation of the individual from one of his previous social statuses, second, the *limen* (lat.) or threshold phase, and third, the aggregation of the individual into a new status. During the first phase, the individual symbolically detaches from an earlier status in the social structure and/or a set of cultural conditions. "Liminality," the second stage, is a state experienced by the individual during a rite of passage. It is a condition of not having full membership in a status.[2] In the third phase the ritual cycle is completed and the ritual subject is again a member of a "relatively" stable state, with the binding norms and values connected to it.

Turner had a closely defined understanding of liminality. In his conceptualization "liminal personae" do not fit the categories that are available for societal classification. It is exactly for their "betwixt and between"-ness (Turner 1969: 94), their lack of membership in established categories, that liminal persons are assigned and represented by numerous symbols in societies that ritualize these transitions. On the symbolic plane liminal transitions are often represented as death, darkness, invisibility, and being in the womb (95). The behavior expected of liminal persons is passivity, humility and obedience. Classic examples are initiates in traditional societies and soldiers in modern day armies. They are in a state of absence of personal rights, and they cannot challenge unjust treatment. Their former self is ritually deconstructed and a new self that will lead them through the new life stage is constructed from its ruins. During the transition stage, liminal personae develop "an intense comradeship and egalitarianism" (95) and rank and status distinctions disappear. For Turner the experience of liminality is part of the normal developmental process of every individual: "social life is a type of dialectical process that involves successive experience of high and low, communitas and structure, homogeneity and differentiation, equality and inequality" (97). Importantly, each society is made up of "multiple personae, groups, and categories," each of these with a separate developmental cycle, so that at any given moment an individual might be both in liminal and structured states.

When a group of people goes through a liminal phase together, *communitas* is created. A brief elaboration of the notion of communitas is of interest here, because in this article we are specifically addressing social processes and practices. Communitas is not "community" in its prevalent connotation, but essentially the complementary opposite of societal norms and classifications: "[C]ommunitas emerges where social structure is not" (126). The opposition between structure and communitas hence does not describe the difference between the inner sphere of family or neighborhood life ("community") and the outer sphere of official institutions and the public sphere. Communitas means that there are no institutionalized rules or norms. Communitas is outside of the defined statuses of "structure," it is "spontaneous, immediate, concrete" as opposed to "norm-governed, institutionalized, abstract" (127). Crucially, as we can see, communitas can only become evident "through its juxtaposition to, or hybridization with, aspects of social structure" (127).

Turner is then situated in a structuralist functionalist approach in which the liminal phase culminates in the reestablishment of structure and social order. However, this process is dialectic, and for Turner the notion of hybridity is entailed in this dialectic. The opposite is part of that which it opposes. Commu-

---

2 Turner defines a state as "any type of stable or recurrent condition that is culturally recognized." It opposes the "transitions" between these states.

nitas (and hybridity) for Turner are not simply resistant forces, but communitas is what makes structure possible.

Theoretical work related to the notion of liminality includes Mary Douglas' (1966) work on purity and dirt and the danger inherent in their conflation and Max Gluckman's (1997)work on rituals of rebellion and the inversion of power structures during seasonal rituals. These early anthropological writings, according to Werbner (1997), showed how hybrid symbolic acts challenge cultural orders from a position within society. Other work in this line include Barth's (1969) analysis of the creation of identity via processes of opposition and boundary construction; Bakhtin's (1968 [1940]) analysis of popular mass culture and carnival as subversive and challenging inversions of popular discourse; and Park's (1950) concept of the marginal man. Each of these theories can provide insights into the experiences of people who do not experience themselves as full members of particular social groups, even as each differs in their central focus in the way they address the experiences of individuals versus social groups; the movement of people between spheres versus their experiences on the margins, and power and change.

In the context of immigrant and minority cultural and language practices, the notion of liminality was first framed in essentialist models of identity that were instrumental in creating discourses about the "deficiency" of immigrant children. The notion of cultural and cognitive deficiency proposed that minority and immigrant children come into mainstream society with a lack of skills in one or more domains (linguistic, cognitive, developmental, social).[3] This deficit model, which previously dominated work across disciplines on the linguistic and cultural practices of minority and immigrant children, has since met a devastating critique from the fields of education, psychology and cultural studies. In a postmodernist reaction to the dominating Eurocentric view on minority children's cultural and linguistic practices (and in its implications of their cognitive potential), the notion of *new ethnicities* and with it the concept of *hybridity* was introduced.[4] The term hybridity describes the idea that immigrants and ethnic minorities are not merely caught in a deadlock between cultures; rather this state of "in-betweenness" is a positive, socially productive historical process in which new cultural practices are forged in their own right. Werbner (1997) stresses the unbounded, impure characteristics of hybridity as opposed to essentializing notions of monolithic identities implied in normative theories surrounding immigration and immigrant identities. Hybridity theory emphasizes the creativity of the cultural practices of the "new ethnicities." The central idea involves looking at what these formerly stigmatized social groups have to offer in and of themselves, and not at how they compare to the dominant group.

In post-colonial theory it is Bhabha (1994) who has reconceptualized the notion of cultural hybridity. Bhabha introduces the concept of mimicry to

---

3 For a critique see Cazden 1970, 2001.
4 Hall 1996 [1989], 1994; Hall & du Gay 1996.

conceptualize the subjectivity of the liminal experience, the "social articulation of difference, from the minority perspective" (2). He argues that cultural identities are not pre-formulated, a-historical cultural traits that are mapped onto conceptions of distinct ethnicities. Rather, for Bhabha cultural identities are continually negotiated through the interface and exchange of cultural performances that produce recognizable representations of cultural difference. For Bhabha a third space is created at the heart of first world cultures and Third World postcolonial states. This is a liminal, hybrid space for the production of cultural meaning. The concept of mimicry subverts Fanon's (1952) dichotomic theory of oppressor and oppressed, while still speaking to a hegemonic context that demands assimilation, in which there is no room for difference. Liminality – as subversion – here takes the form of (subtle) mimicry, *"as a subject of a difference that is almost the same, but not quite.* This is to say that the discourse of mimicry is constructed around an *ambivalence*; in order to be effective, mimicry must continually produce its slippage, its excess, its difference" (Bhabha 1994: 85).

Mimicry is neither unidirectional, nor static. Rather, it presents a practice of political agency appropriating forms of cultural representation. In sociolinguistic theory, Rampton (1999) shares this focus on slippage and describes social and linguistic interactions as constant flows of structured practices that can be breached and interrupted, and because of this, day to day life presents dozens and dozens "of small-scale opportunities for minor adventures into liminality – opportunities, indeed, for the reworking of oppressive relations which liminality is seen to permit" (Rampton 1997: 6). In his study on the use of Stylized Asian English among multiethnic urban youth in Great Britain, Rampton (1995: 158f.), draws on theories of liminality to interpret the use of stylized language as a form of ritual interaction. According to Rampton, stylized talk as a youth cultural language practice centers on issues of social order. He introduces three different kinds of interaction rituals that use stylized language – rituals of disorder, differentiation and consensus. These three functions – the anti-structural, the differentiating and the consensual – are taken from a number of discussions of ritual.[5] Rampton (1995) points out that collective ritual, here in the form of language practices, function as attempts to resolve deep social anomalies and contradictions. These processes surrounding structure and anti-structure – as theorized by Turner – become meaningful in the context of youths' use of formalized speech as well.

Recent work employing the concept of liminality then uses Turner's concept as well as hybridity theory to theoretically grasp processes of adolescence, ethnicity and identity. This work includes considerations of adolescence as "liminal,"[6] "liminal ethnicities,"[7] and studies on liminal cultural,[8] and

---

5 See Goffman 1967.
6 Amit-Talai & Wulff 1995; Bucholtz 2002; Skelton 1998.
7 Back 1996; Hewitt 1992.
8 Gilroy 1987; Puzar & Markovic 2001.

multilingual language practices[9] These recent conceptualizations are important developments in our understanding of immigrant positionalities, because they address the tensions of immigrant subjectivities and practices without reifying and fixating immigrants in stable identity categories, or normative host-newcomer dualisms. However, both the original and these recent conceptualizations fail to consider how, at the local level, liminal practices may play out in very different, possibly contradictory ways, and how they might include practices of both accommodation and defiance at the same time. Liminal practices may then be both hybrid practices that merge different cultural forms into a "bricolage" (Hebdige 1979: 102ff.), and practices of contestation that newly forge apparently "authentic" ethnic traditions (Williams 1990). In this paper we will look at language practices that appear to be dichotomous in this way; we, however, consider both to be linguistic practices that arise from being "betwixt and between."

Practices of mediation and contestation

Examining liminality as linguistic practices means looking at how liminal positionings in society are responded to culturally. We have described prior sociolinguistic research on positionalities of in-betweenness and marginality. As we turn to our cases, we want briefly to introduce the social and historical contexts in which these particular youths grow up, and note some similarities and differences. Similarities in the social and historical contexts of Berlin and Chicago include challenges for immigrant communities to establish access to institutional networks and resources of the dominant society, and ethnicization and racialization of both immigrant populations in the dominant discourse.[10] In the United States and Germany immigrants can be found at all levels of society; nevertheless the Latino and Turkish immigrant families in our case studies are positioned in the lower socioeconomic levels in society, as indeed are the majority of their counterparts. Resulting from this is low symbolic, cultural and educational capital of immigrants, and low linguistic prestige accorded to their language.[11]

Important differences between these immigration contexts include the fact that the sites vary in the relative progression of historical stages of immigration in that the Turkish youths generally were second and third generation immigrants, while the Latino children were the 1.5 generation,[12] i.e. some of them had been born in the United States, while some of them had only recently arrived with their parents. The complexities of the local sites also include the fact that the Chicago data is drawn from ethnographic fieldwork conducted in two different communities in the Chicago area.

---

9   Androutsopoulos 2002; Eksner, to appear; Rampton 1995, 1999.
10 Çağlar 1995; Urciuoli 1998.
11 Bourdieu 1977.
12 Portes & Rumbaut 2001.

Differences in the research foci in each site also have importance for the kinds of phenomena we observed: the Mexican children were observed mainly at home and in school, while the Turkish youths were observed in a youth centre and on the neighborhood streets. Accordingly, the youth were involved in different kinds of activity settings, where different language practices would flourish: in activities with families or in classrooms (in the case of the Mexican youth) versus hanging out in the street (in the case of the Turkish immigrant study). This has implications for the presence or absence of adults in the activity settings described as well as for other differences in practice. For example, while hanging out in the street different participants are involved in the activity, different situational identities are constructed, and different actions are pursued than when translating back and forth for a mentor while negotiating over a public aid form with a government agent.

Lastly, in addition to differences in social and historical contexts, it is important to consider differences between the groups that we studied. The Turkish youth were somewhat older (ages 16–18) and in mid to late adolescence, while the Mexican youths were 10- to 12-years old, just entering the liminal phase of adolescence. Further, the Turkish youths in Berlin were self-proscribed members of a local youth gang (the "36"). In contrast, the Mexican youths were identified on the basis of a school survey in which they self-identified as translators for their families.

It is this range of activities and variations in immigration histories and contexts that gives empirical power to our grounded discussion of the concept of liminality. By comparing two immigration contexts, and contemplating the liminal experiences and practices connected to them, we are able to illuminate the dimensions of liminality in ways that would be impossible with a single case. All of these remarks also add up to explain why we use the Berlin case to describe processes of contestation, because on an overall continuum these adolescent Turkish youths' practices are situated more at the end of contesting practices. In contrast, the practices we observed with the Latino children are overall more closely linked to mediating activities. This does not mean that each group does not engage in the other activity, or that each practice cannot be used in the service of the other (as indeed the opening quote by Sammy suggests; Sammy uses his skills as a mediator to *contest* his positioning by others*)*. Further, we do not mean to imply that these differences in the expressions of liminality are culturally pre-determined or that they map deterministically or easily onto either cultural group or context (Germany or USA; Mexican or Turkish). Rather, it is the unique combination of developmental stage (which includes identity formation and autonomy from the family) as well as socio-cultural and class context that shapes the forms of cultural practices around language that are produced.

Research sites

Our first research site is located in a Turkish ethnic enclave in Berlin, Germany, a neighborhood also known as "Little Istanbul." During the late 1990s, socio-linguists, politicians, and the media in Germany have busily discussed a new language code as being the second and third generation immigrant youths' Creole variety of German. Discourse depicted and continues to depict the majority of the speakers to be of Turkish origin and the new code is characterized by the "toughness" and "aggressiveness" of the streets. Some writers declared this apparent new code to be a phenomenon related to pidginization; some labeled it mere semi-lingualism. Both the media and official institutions described the speech of German Turks as bad, uneducated and unintelligible. At the same time pop-cultural discourse celebrated a new stereotype of a tough, empowered, yet semi-literate, inarticulate jargon – "'lan-talk"[13] or "Kanak Sprak"[14] (Zaimoglu 1995, 1997, 1999) – supposedly spoken by immigrant Turks of the second and third generation. The data presented here is pulled from a larger body of research on how German Turkish youths' linguistic and social practices are related to their notions of collective identity that are created in engagement with and contestation of discourses about their liminal positioning in German society (Eksner, to appear).

The youths in the study were predominantly male teenagers aged 14–18 years and involved in a neighborhood youth gang. In contrast to other neighborhoods in Berlin, where Turkish youths grow up with closer contact to peers of other nationalities, and often are completely bilingual, most of the youths in the Berlin-Kreuzberg field site were dominant in the language used at home, Turkish, and usually also interacted in Turkish among themselves (Eksner, to appear). Most of the children are successive bilingual speakers, with Turkish learned first and German acquired later. However, the youths have several codes and registers at their availability, and the "new pidgin" is only one situational code reserved mainly for conflict interactions with members of the out-group, particularly German and Arab youths. As in other cultural settings, the youths' code and register use is connected to specific linguistic realms: they used several linguistic strategies, i.e. different registers and codes, according to the demands of the respective situation. There were three different spheres of relations that demanded different linguistic strategies: First, the inner sphere of class-equal familiar and familial relations, secondly, the outer sphere of authority and class/race imbalance, and thirdly an outer sphere of reversed authority and dominance by the Turkish youth. We will discuss in more detail how the code used in this outer sphere of reversed authority has

---

13 "'Lan" from "oglan" means "boy" in formal Turkish, it is often being used to mean "gay" in slang language. Both "'lan" and "oglan" (my son) are slang terms that Turkish male youth in Berlin frequently use to address each other. "To speak 'lan" is how this code is frequently called among German youth.

14 A derogative term used for immigrants, from the Melanesian ethnonym "Kanak."

performative power attached to it that transforms language into a tool of contestation.

In the second case study we are building on a line of research carried out by sociolinguistic, psychological and educational researchers interested in the experiences of immigrant children in the United States who translate for their families. Since the 1990s there has been an increased interest in what researchers have called "family interpreters,"[15] language and culture "brokers"[16] or "para-phrasers."[17] Researchers have considered the social and linguistic processes involved as well as the psychological and educational consequences of this practice.

Illustration 1: Claiming territory and power, wall with graffiti by the "36 Juniors"

Para-phrasing, like other forms of social interaction, takes many different shapes as it occurs in different contexts, relationships, and activity settings. Most often, youth translate for their parents (usually their mothers) or other close family relations; but they may negotiate for that parent in interactions with a wide range of others, including teachers, social workers, lawyers, government officials, store personnel, doctors, dentists, and strangers on the street. The texts children translate include official letters, medical and insur-

---

15 Valdés 2002; Valdés, Chávez & Angelilli 1999.
16 Buriel, Perez, DeMent, Chavez & Moran 1998; Cooper, Denner & López 1999; Tse 1995; 1996; Weisskirch & Alva 2002.
17 Orellana 2001; Orellana, Dorner & Pulido 2003; Orellana, Reynolds, Dorner & Meza 2003.

ance documents, letters from school, application forms for store credit and legal materials. These exchanges may take place in public spaces, before audiences, or in the privacy of families' homes. Children may deploy mostly English as a mediational tool (e.g. when translating written or oral texts, or when going out in the world to do things for their parents simply because they can speak English), or both English and their home language (e.g. when they negotiate conversation), in different configurations. Power relations in these situations are differently configured, which shapes the nature of the mediational demands on youth, as they must negotiate their own relationship with each speaker as well as the communication between different adults. There are different kinds of mediational demands on children when they translate, for example, between a parent and a lawyer, a teacher and a student, or an aunt and a neighbor. But in all cases children have to listen as well as speak in order to represent each perspective and accomplish the task at hand.

As this initial introduction of our two research sites demonstrates, structurally comparable experiences of immigrant childhoods in the US and Germany can lead to different practices situated in subjective feelings of marginality.

Theoretical concerns

While the concept of liminality seems immediately heuristically useful in characterizing these experiences, as we detail our cases we will use grounded theorizing to further elaborate the topic. With this discussion we want to indicate ways to conceptualize liminality in a more differentiated way than has hitherto been the case, and better unite it with other theories of hybridity. We will consider three major theoretical concerns, which fall into the following broadened categories: (1) issues of power, (2) the conceptualization of change, and (3) the multiplicity of identity processes.

Power

While for Turner the liminal phase is a phase of loss of status, powerlessness, and obedience, "new" liminality theories, speaking to hybridity and defiance, operate with complementary categories: appropriation, power (of the streets), and disobedience. There is a mismatch then between these two conceptual frames. As our, and other, case studies reveal, adolescent social practices clearly show the impact of power relations, or structure and in-betweenness often comes hand in hand with powerlessness. Immigrant child translators in Chicago are mediators between their parents and English speakers because of socioeconomic and structural conditions that have kept their parents largely monolingual. Turkish teenagers in Berlin are stereotyped and experience prejudice that is similarly connected to their socioeconomic standing and segregated lives in Germany. They create a situational code that appropriates and at the same time defies these stereotypes. This, however, neither implies that they are unconscious of power relations (or that they don't adhere to the demands of power inequality), nor that their cultural responses are truly agentic political responses to these relations.

Stylized Turkish German as contestation

We introduced three different spheres that demanded different linguistic strategies of Turkish youths in an ethnic enclave in Berlin: the inner sphere of class-equal familiar and familial relations, the outer sphere of authority and class/race imbalance, and lastly an outer sphere of reversed authority and dominance by the Turkish youth. Particularly during situations of conflict with members of the out-group, the boys would intentionally use a third register, apart from Turkish and German, which I have called Stylized Turkish German[18] (STG) and which is the object of ongoing debate about "pidginization" in Germany. STG, which is used in the outer sphere of reversed authority and dominance by the Turkish youth (outer sphere 2), will be the focus of the following discussion.

The language ideologies of the youths reflect the dominant discourse that strongly prefers standard German pronunciation and describes (ethnic) accents as negative. Accents are complex signs of difference in which several semiotic principles converge: they are perceived as outlining contrasting cultural positions and create a frame of reference and interpretation in which a person's looks, language and actions are judged.[19] To say that a person sounds typically Turkish means the person is likely to mean or do just what one would expect from a Turk. In contemporary Germany a Turkish accent is strongly associated with exclusion. People who speak with such an accent can be ridiculed, treated as if they are stupid, and put down by standard speakers. Accent as a marker of ethnic identity also indexes social capital. The youths showed keen awareness of these different ways that accents crucially influence their social positioning.[20] While accounts of accommodation to standard, or as they called it, "good" German were frequent among the youths, in the sphere of reversed power relations, accent was redefined as a sign of power and strength in the face of the interlocutor.

It is the peculiarity of outer sphere 2 interactions that the rules and power inequalities of outer-sphere 1 are suspended or superseded by reversed norms.[21] Here the Turkish youth feel themselves to be in a (real or imagined) position of dominance. The relations in outer sphere 2 are not connected to institutions or authorities as those of outer-sphere 1 are. Instead they take place in uncontrolled territory that cannot be claimed by German mainstream society, as for instance the territory of the neighborhood Kreuzberg 36 or the youth center. Typical interactions take place on the street, in parks, in public

---

18 This term is modeled after Rampton's (1995) "Stylized Asian English."
19 Urciouli 1998.
20 Eksner, to appear.
21 Bakhtin 1968 [1940].

places, with people who have no institutional or network control over them. These interactions include other youths, especially youths that are not part of the same networks, thus Germans and other foreign youth.

There are two main characteristics of conflict situations with non-peers. First, conflict situations are carried out in ritualized speech that reflects exactly their notions about others as they are mirrored and indexed in language. Second, they employ linguistic strategies of insult and counter-insult to compete over masculinity.[22] Not only could code switching be observed, in their interviews most boys also stated that they spoke "hard" or "tough" in situations of conflict. The following is an excerpt from an interview with 18-year old Murat (M).[23]

JE:[24] Are there any situations, in which you talk harder than you talk now with me?

M: Naturally there are, yes. For example, if I see a guy here, who, let's say, is getting on my nerves or something, or who wants to confront me, or something like that, then I'll talk a little bit harder... While now... now I'm giving an interview, let's say, I'm still talking more friendly. Now I'm still talking friendly, you know... Then, let's say, another one comes, like this:
[Murat's voice rises to higher pitch, and gets louder. Facial expression and body language more tense] Hey! ... What's up! Whyya staring at me ...
[lowered voice and pitch again] naturally I'll talk hard with him, that's automatic. Not... yes... uh... uh... *[and back to original pattern]* I won't talk like that, because then he thinks softballs. ... What's up.

STG then is a code created to represent "toughness" in language; a "foreignized" German with Turkish paralinguistic features. Its properties are closely modeled on the discourses surrounding indexes of Turkishness and the Turkish language. The interpretation of STG as a situational register is supported by the fact that the youths have achieved different levels of linguistic competence in German, while they all "hypocorrect" their linguistic production in the performance of STG. The concept of hypocorrection, as introduced by Baugh (1999), originally referred to African American Standard English speakers who, in an attempt to perform an inner-city African American identity, will shift style towards African American Vernacular English, resulting in the creation of hypocorrect – as opposed to *hyper*correct – utterances and linguistic overcompensation beyond the target linguistic form. In a similar way, STG is used to mark a certain, "non-German" identity in the face of speakers who are not Turkish. The situational identity that is created through this register use is a form of meta-identity.

STG closely resembles ethnolectic varieties, where basic structures are acquired, while phonetic features ("accent") and lexical items alone provide the "ethnic overlay" (Fennell 1997; Labov 1972). However, STG stands inde-

---

22 Dundes 1972; Tertilt 1997.
23 Interview in Standard German.
24 JE = Julia Eksner.

pendently from the parents' immigrant language, and it is therefore not a Creole that developed of their parents' speech. It can also not be seen as a kind of substratum effect. The function of language has shifted from a learner or interlanguage to its function as an identity marker via the emergence of a situational "xenolect." A xenolect, which Holm (1988) defines as "slightly foreignized varieties spoken natively." It does not rely on radical restructuring of language, but on a small – "but symbolically significant" (Fennel 1997) – amount of influence from immigrant languages to render it different from the standard.

STG is employed in interactions of situational dichotomization as a register that carries xenolectic characteristics. With this it primarily serves as a social semiotic.[25] Several short examples of naturally occurring conflict situations will serve to illustrate ritualized speech as social semiotic. The first situation, which we will discuss, takes place with members of the out-group.

One evening, five of the older boys were standing in the entrance of the neighborhood center. They were talking to each other in Turkish, while code switching to and borrowing from German all along. Because they knew each other, they presupposed each other's accents and code switching, which are both indexes of their shared location and background. For the boys the neighborhood center is "theirs;" it is the former "headquarters" of the local gang, the "36" and the boys know all the regulars, have keys to some of the rooms, and regard the Germans, mainly adults, who use some of the space for their dance or music practice, as outsiders. While the youths were standing in front of the building, a German man and a German woman, in their mid-thirties, appeared in the window above them. To the Turkish boys they were presumably identifiable as typically "German" because of their light skin and hair, their choice of clothes, the way they moved, and the simple fact that they were not known to them as regulars. The man in the window waved to the boys, which was probably prompted by the boys holding and filming with a video camera. The boys acted on the looks of the German man as a creative index, thereby establishing an inside-outside line across the following interaction (Standard German/Berlin dialect: normal letters, STG: bold, Turkish: small caps):

C: [sweet, tempting voice] Fall... fall...
[German man is waving from a window in the building to the camera.]
T: [performative, Berlin dialect, loud for the camera] What kind of asparagus[26] is this, I'm fucking your mother. Fuck, fuck...
[The man can't hear what the boys are saying. He closes the window. One of the boys whistles to get his attention. The man opens the window again.]
I'm fucking your mother, yes, I'm fucking your mother. I'm fucking your mother. OK, HONEY, BYE BYE).
[The man is waving again. The boys laugh.]
Some people like it when you fuck their mothers.

---

25 Fennel 1997.
26 Derogative for skinny, "weak," German.

> *[The German woman appears in the same window and waves like crazy. We can only guess her motives for this action...]*
> Haha... THEY ARE GIVING IT TO YOUR FATHER A LOT[27].
> Somebody's touching you down there, right... ha. *[laughs]*

While this example might seem crude, it is both exemplary of the youths' language practices, and, if looked at in more detail, shows linguistic richness. The boys started out their comments with a rhetorical question in the local Berlin dialect, thereby both demonstrating proficiency this register, and sharing their assumption that the two adults in the window are Germans from Berlin. They then addressed the Germans in a deliberately aggressive way, shouting to them in a very curt and offensive form of German that appears simplified. The Germans could probably overhear some of the louder comments. In two instances, when they used particularly crude insults, which they may not have felt appropriate to say to the face of their interlocutors (or to the camera), they switched back to Turkish (see underlined). When the Germans left the window, the boys continued their usual pattern of interaction. While the German adults might have interpreted the whole situation in terms of code (i.e. "deficient language skills"), the underlying dynamics were generation, ethnicity and class. The boys here employed strategic or "metaphorical" switching (Blom 1972) between different codes.

In the following interactions, conflict interaction took place in a less mediated way, here however among youths in the in-group themselves. Because STG is not the code used for in-group conflict, we catch only short glimpses before the boys switch back to Turkish to continue the conflict or before they resolve it. In the first example, Çem (Ç) and several of his friends are playing computer games at the neighborhood center. A register switch from jokingly commenting on his friends to a half-serious conflict occurs. Çem is teasing Halil as "gay," because he does not act up for the camera. Halil gets up and without much ado, and no words, boxes Çem in the stomach. Çem's register switch ensues during this action (Standard German/Berlin dialect in normal letters, STG in bold, Turkish small caps):

> Ç: Yo, we're inside, man, what's up? Everybody's shooting already, yeah, come on... yeah. You're all lazy, man...
> *[Çem zooms in on Halil]*
> *[voice starts to get into higher pitch]* What's up with you, hey you faggot. *[laughs]* Hey, it's you I'm talking to. Yeah. Exactly you. GET LOST, I SAID. *[Halil gets up]*.
> **'Lan!!** *[suddenly very high pitch, loud]* **Fuck off, I said, 'Lan!!**
> *[voice suddenly drops, calmer]*...STOP.

This interaction points into the direction of how "tough talk" is used among the boys. The performance of STG can be glimpsed in the first phrase uttered by Çem, immediately after Halil attacks him. He however immediately switches into Turkish (italics), since STG is not the conflict code used with in-

---

27 Allusion to anal penetration.

group members. It might also have been perceived as too aggressive for the context of originally playful in-group-conflict.

In a last example, we find STG to be used as a ritual of consensus, which again points to its role as social semiotic. In the interaction below we find a formulaic – ritualistic – exchange of phrases. STG is used in joking provocation between two friends and acquaintances of the same social status. While the youths were all participating in a representation of them to the outside world (by making a video), one of the boys, Tarkan, was holding back and not really playing along. In this interaction Rahman (R) challenges Tarkan (T) in a friendly and consensual manner, thus inviting him to properly participate in the ongoing activity. STG was used as a regulative and consensual register, reminding Tarkan of where he was, with whom he was hanging out and simultaneously symbolically referring to and enacting the emblems of being "ghetto."

In this excerpt the older boys are spending their Friday night by roaming through the streets of the neighborhood, documenting their paths with a video camera. Rahman (R) is filming the others and then focuses in on Tarkan (T). Tarkan makes a sign of refusal with his hands, but Rahman continues to film Tarkan. He then initiates interaction by teasingly addressing Tarkan in STG (while before they had been speaking Turkish). Tarkan picks up the genre and responds with a strong accent himself (and exactly despite the fact that he is one of the youths who is almost completely bilingual):

R: *[loud]* "What's going ooonn [= stretched sound] here, what's going ooonn, heey...
[higher pitch] heey... what's goin ooonn here, what's going ooonn... You a
[higher pitch] victim or were you victimized?"
T: *[loud]* 'Maaan! You a victim you.'
R: *[loud, high pitch]* "Or did you, or did you victimize?"[28]

Rahman makes these switching practices explicit and points to the performative efficacy of using stylized speech. We want to cite this excerpt in length, because several of the social relations and issues addressed in this paper are also addressed in his statement:

JE: Be tough? Yes, I become angry too, but I don't know if I do the same things as you do, or you. How do you do it? Show me. What would you say then?
R: *[dismissive]* I don't know what I'd say.
JE: Well I would talk like this: Hey, are you stupid or what? Don't mess with me! That's what I would say.
R: Nuuh, I would say: HASIKTIR 'LAN!
JE: What?
R: HASIKTIR 'LAN!
JE: What does that mean?

---

28 The trope of "victim" is a very strong one in this ingroup. Rahman tries a wordplay by turning the passive "victim" into an active verb "victimize," which in German obtains the meaning of "sacrifice." The intended meaning is "Did you victimize somebody?"

R:	Fuck off.
JE:	But would you say that to a German?
R:	To a German I would do, yes, I wouldn't say anything, I would just hit him in his face, that's it. Immediately.
JE:	If you wouldn't hit him, though, but you would talk.
R:	I would then use such... such a strange accent and say: 'LAN SIKTIR...
JE:	What strange accent?
R:	Like Turkish-German, somehow. All different. How should I... how should I explain this. I don't know how I can explain this, but I would say, 'LAN SIK-TIR *[high pitch, curt]* GIT...
JE:	And why would you stress it that way?
R:	Because he's supposed to take me serious.
JE:	And he will take you serious, if you stress it that way?
R:	Yes, yes. Exactly.
JE:	Why is that?
R:	Because he's afraid then. [...]
JE:	And then I also wanted to know why you think this is this way. Why is it especially intimidating?
R:	Because you come across hard somehow. With that I want to show, that I'm serious, and then it happens, d'you understand?

In this interview excerpt we can observe how Rahman, just as Murat earlier, stresses the efficacy of language as performative/performance. Speech acts in STG can thus be understood as performative in the sense described by Austin (Austin 1975). The youths understand utterances in STG as acts in an interactive continuum. To sum up, discourse about liminality, in conjunction with everyday life and labor experience, is self-reflexively appropriated and mapped onto language to index collective group identity and express (linguistic) difference from Germans and what they represent. In using different speech styles in different contexts, "we" and "they"-codes are enacted; they reflect culturally constructed oppositions between categories of speakers. Different codes are employed to index situational shifting identities: in using standard German, migrant children stress their equality and rights to occupation or political rights. In using their non-native languages, the familial background, or the cultural heritage and connection to it, is stressed. In using stylized German, the authority of all images and discourses connected to it, is invoked and a youth identity of deviance and "otherness" is presented. At the same time, this novel form of speech is not only symbolic of a newly forming social entity, but also instrumental in creating it,[29] i.e. while STG arises from a position of liminality in German society, it is also instrumental in symbolically and materially reproducing this liminality.

Mediational processes in para-phrasing

Where the Turkish youth described above self- stereotyped as talking "hard," in acts of contestation, the mediational work of the Mexican immigrant youth with whom we worked might be characterized metaphorically as ways of talking "soft." On the surface, these practices may appear diametri-

---

29 Gal 1987.

cally opposed. But we want to argue that these divergent practices arise from similar relationships between participants and structures of power; they only represent different ways of engaging with those structurations of power.

In some (though by no means all) mediational encounters children are expected to speak on behalf of their families to people who have the power to offer or withhold a range of resources, goods, information, or other services. The children that we worked with had translated for their parents in schools, government and public aid agencies, doctor's offices, as well as stores and restaurants. (They also engaged in many private translation acts at home with their family; these were different kinds of mediational events that we have analyzed elsewhere; they do not involve the same kind of "soft talk" that we see in public encounters.) In their efforts to secure resources for their families, children in these encounters sometimes exaggerate politeness norms and soften their parents' words. As Luz, a 19-year-old who had translated for her family for many years put it in an interview: "I became a huge 'May I help you' kind of person." Luz talked of softening her father's "vulgar" language when she translated for him:

Once we got into the office an English speaking person would ask my dad questions and even though he understands lots of English he made me answer the questions. And that wasn't too easy because I had to interpret what my dad wanted me to say without sounding rude or ignorant. My dad doesn't speak proper Spanish either so I had to watch what I was going to say to this person carefully. I couldn't use the derogatory comments my dad had so I had to sort of fix what he wanted me to say to the person. So I just had to be like, 'Oh my father is very upset because he paid this much and bla, bla, bla.

This "soft talk" involves a careful balancing of seemingly contradictory goals. Luz is attempting to protect the image of her father, express her own viewpoint, advocate for her father's rights, but avoid the kind of confrontation that could keep the family from securing the resources they need. She describes another time when she filed a complaint on behalf of her mother when applying for social service benefits:

And it's like what do you say? I can't say the lady was a meany you know. I can't say things like that. I have to like, watch what I say and things like that. So then I put that my mother was feeling uncomfortable with the lady there. I remember that day and I remember the tension I felt as I listened to my mom angrily complain about the lady, and the pressure I felt to translate properly. I didn't know what to say. I wanted the complaint to sound like it came from a grown-up, my mother, but I also wanted to stress how rude she was. But then again, I didn't want to be rude myself. I ended up writing that she was very impatient with our situation and that my mom felt very uncomfortable with her and that it was hard for her to express herself and to understand the lady. I made it sound grown-up-like, but I stressed the main point.

While this mitigated language may be most commonly applied when soliciting aid from government agencies, the youth we observed also softened and edited their parents' words when they translated for them in seemingly more benign public encounters, such as in stores.³⁰ Beatríz described going with her mother to shop for gloves:

And my mother would say, you know, ask the lady for the certain type of gloves, and I would say, 'It doesn't exist.' You know, making it up. Because my mother ... would ask somebody to assist her, but she'd know exactly what was the material that she wanted, and I of course had no idea, no clue, so I would tell the lady, 'My mother is looking for these type of gloves,' and she would look at me like I was nuts. And of course I was saying it the way my mom was saying it, and it wasn't correct. It wasn't being pronounced correctly. So then, I would look her straight at my mom, and the lady, everybody was frustrated. And my mother would just point, having the lady take out all these different gloves, and my mother would say tell her that these are a bit too small and I need them a size bigger.

Beatríz told of changing her mother's words in order to minimize the annoyance that she saw her mother causing for the store clerk. Her modifications also seem designed to improve her mother's image vis-à-vis the clerk: "I thought she was being a nuisance and I thought, 'I don't want this lady to think that way about my mom. I saw it as protecting her image." She gave an example of how she would modify her mother's words: "I mean she would say, 'Oh, this leather feels too rough.' And I would have to tell the lady that, and I would, I would change it a little bit and I would say that, 'Oh, she says these don't fit.'"

*Illustration 2: Journal entry by a 10-year-old "para-phraser"*³¹

---

30 The 10- to 12-year-old children that we worked with seemed less able to engage in such metalinguistic and metacultural reflections.

We see this kind of mediation in interaction in an audio-taped situation recorded by 11-year-old Estela. In this encounter Estela is in a music store with her father, who wants to rent a musical instrument to play in a band with other men from his hometown. Estela translates while the store clerk points to a number of instruments, indicating their prices, but providing little other information. An analysis of the first part of this encounter is developed in Reynolds and Orellana (under review); we argue there that the clerk's emphasis on the cost of the instrument seems shaped by his assumptions about this family's ability to pay. In another segment of the transcript, we see a further emphasis on the cost of the instruments, even as the salesperson picks up on what he assumes the father "owes" to others:

Dad: I know! But I owe, I...
Salesperson: You owe Victor?
Dad: Yeah, I (have) money in the bank but I wanted credit.

This emphasis on the family's ability to pay frames the initial encounter and continues to mark the entire event. Following the description of instruments, Estela helps her father to fill out a lengthy application for store credit. This involves deciphering the meanings of things like "monthly and gross earnings;" "source of income;" "applicant's employer; if military show branch and pay grade." During the long process of filling out the form, Estela turns the tape recorder off and on several times. Later she explained to the research team that this was because her father was getting upset and saying bad words. She wanted to edit the bad words from the tape. This suggests that Estela was aware of her power to mediate her father's image vis-à-vis the research team as well as vis-à-vis the store personnel.

The store clerk, who provides no assistance with the application, takes the completed form and shortly returns to announce that credit has been denied. We take up at this point in the transcript to show how Estela – who may well be exhausted from the translation and emotion work (Hochschild 1983) that she has done – continues to serve as mediator between her father and the clerk. In this next section of the transcript, Estela and her father try to negotiate another form of payment. Here Estela seems not only to mediating her father's words *to* the salesperson, she seems to work as well to soften the salesperson's words to her father.

---

31 Text in the picture: April 30, 2001 – Today I translated to my mom about a letter that they send her in my brothers school. The letter said that my brother should bring gym shoes with rubber buttons, only. It said that we cannot send with sandals, flip flops, jelly shoes, or open toe shoes. How I tell about translating is because every time I translate I feel like I am talking to somebody. Text in the bubbles (left to right): 1. I wonder why they can't bring sandals, flip flops, jelly shoes, or open toe shoes? 2. You shouldn't let Chavito bring sandals, flip flops, jelly shoes, or pen toe shoes. 3. Ok.

Salesperson:	This is a thousand.
Estela:	*Dice que eso es, es mil.* [He says that this is, this is a thousand.]
Salesperson:	With tax.
Estela:	*Con las taxas.*
Salesperson:	You got enough on there?
Estela:	*Dice que si tienes um, um, dinero que puedas.* [He says that if you have, um, um, money that you can.]
Dad:	Yeah! I, I...

The salesperson has asked a challenging question: "You got enough money on there (a credit card)?" Estela frames the question more optimistically to her father, by saying: "If you have money *you can*." She is cut off by her father, however, who has tracked the English conversation, and who seems to react indignantly to the salesperson's implied suggestion that he might be buying something he cannot afford.

Estela goes on to negotiate for her father about how he might pay for this instrument. The salesperson suggests putting it on a store credit card, but Estela's father sees this as essentially the same as paying cash, and says so: "*Entonces es como, es como pargarlo en cash*" ("Then it's like, it's like paying in cash."). Estela softens the potentially challenging nature of this statement when she renders it in English to the sales clerk by converting it to an ambiguous statement that could be read as something her father intends to or wants to do: "He's like, he's paying in cash."

But Estela's father speaks in English to clarify that he wanted *credit*; Estela, still taking up the role of mediator, repeats his statement in English to the clerk. The clerk merely says he is sorry. Estela's father does not press the point further, and both Estela and her dad thank the man as they leave the store without credit and without the instrument that they came to rent. Estela ends this stretch of soft talk on a cheery note as she renders an upwardly inflected "Bye!"

Dad:	I, I wanted credit.
Estela:	He wants credit.
Salesperson:	Yeah, I'm sorry.
Dad:	OK! That's okay.
Salesperson:	But, uh, well, you know where we're at. So...
Dad:	Yeah, ok, thank you.
Salesperson:	Thank you.
Estela:	Uhuh, bye!
Salesperson:	Bye.

The two cases we have presented reveal that even though youth counter and redefine hegemonic interpellations, they are not empowered to change the present structure. Nor for the most part do they seem aware of its existence or of the processes that they are involved in. The effects of structuration are strongly discernable in the use and pragmatics of STG. Similarly, they are evident in the ways that child translators sometimes take up voices of authority and represent those to their parents. We may therefore see the youths as (more or less) unconscious *historical actors* that are responding to and influential of their historical context without being aware of the implications of their actions. However, as our discussion of the youths' recoding of dominant discourse and their social practices has shown, in trying to understand the creation of new vernaculars, and specifically STG, we cannot completely stress the impact of structure either. Rather, we would agree with Woolard, who states that "linguistic practices stem from someplace in between both these poles" (Woolard 1985: 745f.).

Building on this, we understand immigrant youths' cultural practices to be *both* powerless and empowered, i.e. youths are constrained by structure while they may create spaces in which to defy it as well. Neither force is absolute, nor totally absent. For example, when children translate for their parents, a practice that is shaped by structural conditions of inequality, they at the same time may experience power over language and over participants in the translating event. In contrast, readings that understand liminality in terms of "defiance" and oppositional youth cultures only, particularly in the U.S. tradition (Bucholtz 2002), tend to not consider the constrained nature, i.e. the at least partial powerlessness, of these practices.[32]

Further, such readings play down the fact that these practices are a reaction to structures created by dominant adult practices in their lives, in our cases stereotypes about Turks in Germany or global immigration flows that propel Latino laborers and their families in the United States. In these readings the role of agency is over-emphasized at the expense of real-life power relations and constraints posed by these. For example, current thinking about youth practices carefully avoids a developmental teleology and asserts that these adolescent practices are focused on themselves and are not simply a developmental stage on the way to adulthood.[33] These current understandings of adolescent liminality emphasize the "here-and-now of young people's experience, the social and cultural practices through which they shape their world" (Bucholtz 2002: 532), and the research attention is shifted to "inside the borderlands, inside liminality" (Rampton 1999: 8). However, such theoretical approaches tend to neglect the fact that to be liminal is always to be liminal *to something*; liminality is inherently a position of relatedness. In other words, to see youth practices as self-contained disregards what makes the practice happen: the power of adults over those acting on the "inside" (i.e. the juxtaposition of communitas to structure). Individuals are part of the societal "marketplace" in which power and status is accorded according to possession of various forms of capital (Bourdieu 1977). The power that comes with ownership of different forms of "dominant capital," here adult group membership that is linked to certain practices, cannot simply be ignored or seen as disconnected from the practices on the "inside" of youth culture/communitas.

---

32 Defiant hybrid practices as described earlier by Hall and more recently by Rampton and others (such as immigrant youths' language practices) are not liminal practices, they are rather liminoid (Rampton 1999; Turner 1974).
33 Haavind 2001; Rogoff 2003.

Further, to play down the idea that adolescent practices are in some ways directed towards adult practices (under the impact of transformation and change), and even defined by their exclusion from the adult sphere, is to equally deny the power relations inherent in adult-adolescent relations. Youth practices are often not aimed to be the adult "real thing," but they are still created within and parallel to a hegemonic social sphere that is perceived as "adult" and that serves as reference point. They are exactly characterized by their difference in ideology and practice to the "official" adult world (in both minority and dominant culture). Similarly, studies of youth cultures in different contexts have found that divisions between youth and elder and "conflictual and consensual" are often not clearly differentiated, but permeable and flexible.[34]

Theories that reduce adolescent practices to distinctive practices and identities which are not oriented to adults at all, assume adolescents to exist in an enclave, influenced and unconcerned with their membership in larger society, and neglect to see that identities are crucially made in opposition.[35] This does not necessarily imply that youth cultures and practices should be reduced to the notion of "oppositional youth cultures" or on the other hand to mere imitations of adult culture. Rather the point here is that there is mutual influence of both, adult and adolescent practices, on each other. Adolescent culture is created in reaction to adults' norms and behaviors, and adult culture is a result of adolescent practices. But it is power that defines the structure within which youths create these practices.

Change and multiplicity

Turner's theory of liminality is fundamentally about processes surrounding the change of status of individuals in society; hence it is a theory about change. While Turner discussed the structural conditions that make possible individual change, via the creation of communitas and anti-structure, he was primarily concerned with the individual's trajectory in this process. However, as discussed above, the concept of liminality has been considered particularly with attention to socio-historical processes of change, as for example connected to global immigration flows.

In its application to immigrant experiences and conditions of culture contact, there therefore has been a change in unit of analysis: while for Turner each *individual* experiences structure and communitas, the concept is now applied not only to the individual developmental cycle, but to *groups* of individuals and their access to group membership. The effect of this is that, because the phenomena described are different in kind, the temporal aspect ("phase") – which is a crucial aspect of Turner's concept of liminal phase and its cyclic character, is pushed to the background or lost.

---

34 Bucholtz 2002.
35 Barth 1969; Elwert 1989, 1995; Irvine & Gal 1999.

We therefore face another paradox: the concept of liminality was originally conceived as a way to describe one phase in a teleological and unidirectional process, yet now it is being applied to situations that are neither teleological nor unidirectional. The liminal cycle in its developmental usage is usually completed and does not stop in the liminal phase, i.e. adolescents who are members of the group biologically and socially mature at a certain point in time. On the level of collective membership this teleology cannot hold true. Many authors legitimately claim that there are cases in which collective membership is not established and groups of people permanently remain marginal to dominant society. In fact, this is exactly the case to which the concept of liminality is most often applied. The question is then if this marginality can be conceptualized as (permanent) liminality, as it so often is, or if this might make it in some ways the wrong concept for the analyses for which it is used.

One problem with this conceptualization is that this analytical lens takes entities such as cultural groups, and cultural group memberships in these entities, as a given, *and* ignores that "group" is basically a term for people engaged in a shared set of cultural practices (with diffuse and changing boundaries). Another concern we have is that the idea of a permanent liminality implies the notion of permanently *non-liminal entities or states*, a notion that contradicts history and historical change. It fundamentally neglects the fact that cultures are not historically stable units and that in fact all new cultural groups of practice have been produced by deviance from established, official, or institutionalized forms of practice.

Further, the cyclic notion of change inherent in Turner's conceptualization is lost when the notion of (implicitly) permanent liminality is used to describe the "failed" integration of immigrant and minority individuals and groups. When immigrants try to gain access to group membership claimed by dominant society, society often excludes them. We do not find a cyclic integration into and release from structure as described in Turner's model. What this fissure shows is that an individual can become part of structure, *if, and only if* s/he has been part of this structure before. This is implicitly assumed in Turner, but it is not made explicit.

The negotiation of power and access to resources in immigrant communities may hence lead to a superficially permanent liminal state. However, this analysis is stopped in its tracks because it does not consider larger historical changes that are the result of these liminal practices. Practices, which are not part of the categories and classifications available within structure, are initially labeled as liminal. However, with time and historical change, new categories are created. Permanently liminal practices become categorized, and to some extent legitimate, non-liminal states. This is exactly what happens with many of the "hybrid" practices that are described as liminal.

Liminality refers to temporary exclusion, but these are permanent, new social practices. They are new cultural forms. It is exactly in this way that culture is created and change has happened throughout history. The underlying semiotic process in this has been called fractal recursion (Irvine & Gal 1999).

There is a fissure – either forced or voluntary – from the structure. The liminal person will be part of an alternative, new structure; a new locus for identity is created. It is because of this that immigrant youths with newly consolidated identities are not truly liminal – i.e. homogeneous, powerless, obedient, and without social status. The youth find a voice and construct new identities, i.e. they have defined and created new *structures* from which to speak and act.

Although the application of the concept of liminality to phenomena on a social level seems intuitively clear, we still regard it to be conceptually difficult and possibly misleading. But also on the individual level, Turner's conceptualization might structure ways of thinking about individual change that lead to the erasure of the important processes surrounding development across the life span. Turner, in his original conception of liminality, focused on the transitions between stages and the movement of individuals from one societal stage to another, such as from childhood to adolescence. This is in accordance with (cognitive) developmental stage theories such as Piaget's (1975). Turner suggests a relatively unproblematic progression across stages, with the first step involving a separation from the starting identity (e.g. "child") and placement into the limen. From there, cultural rituals assist the movement through the "flat" or "ambiguous" stage before official recognition in the new category (e.g. "adult"). Similarly, for Piaget it is a "crisis," a kind of liminal phase, through which the child has to pass in order to arrive at the next stage. However, developmental stage theories have been exposed to substantive critique on the basis of assumptions of teleology and the normative structure proposed by the chronological order of these stages.

As with the "kanak sprak" of Turkish youth in Germany, the phenomenon of child language brokering has not only garnered the attention of sociolinguists; it has also been a topic of discussion in the U.S. media, and has received some consideration in political debates as well. In popular discussions (and as well in much research), the focus has been on the burdens that this mediational work imposes on youth, insofar as it takes children into the realm of adult responsibilities, knowledge and information. In popular and academic work alike, there is discussion of the "adultification" of children and of "role reversals" between parent and child. The perspective is premised on particular Western, middle-class cultural notions of adult-child relations, in which children are viewed as relatively helpless objects requiring adults' protection and socialization (Zelizer 1985). From a "mainstream" cultural perspective, children speaking for adults in "adult" domains of knowledge can present itself as a violation of established orders. Efforts to regulate against such disorder include recent legislation that has been proposed in the state of California denying state funding to any medical clinic that allows children of clients to act as translators. Our point here is not to judge such legislation or the cultural viewpoints that frame it; rather it is to point out the anxiety that may be provoked for some people when immigrant youths speak from the positions that they have found themselves placed in.

Turner's model further invites closer consideration of the ways in which liminal persons are considered to pass in and out pre-defined stages. While Turner's model may appropriately characterize the transition to adulthood in cultures that have preserved relative homogeneity or cultural "consensus," it is less useful for understanding the liminal experiences of youth in places where there is a juxtaposition of different beliefs about the nature of particular stages, and of divergent practices to identify or transform them, such as is often the case in immigrant communities. In immigrant communities, individuals' and families' beliefs and practices about childhood, adolescence and adulthood, and the transitions between them, may diverge from each other as well as from those of the dominant culture, and rites of passage that ensure smooth transitions across stages may be absent or contradictory.

We have discussed earlier how Bucholtz (2002) identifies a shift in anthropological theory away from transitory processes and toward an interest in adolescent youth culture in its own regard. Increasingly, researchers attend to age-based cultural practices. However, this conceptualization does not eliminate the inherent problem of "stage theories;" it only fixes attention on the practices that take place within a given stage, however defined.

Research on hybridity, as detailed above, represents a similar critique within cultural studies. Here, the focus is on the nature of hybrid practices, on the ways in which new cultural forms are produced, and on the mixing of cultures; gone are the assumptions of smooth progression from one cultural orientation to another, of neat processes of assimilation or acculturation. But even here, there remains some tendency in the field to consider hybridity as a resolution of stages in itself. For example immigrant youth may pass through a stage of "bicultural ambivalence" before resolving their cultural identities. The ambivalence stage would constitute the limen, biculturalism the resolution.

Despite the shifts toward an interest in practices and recognition of ambiguities, complexities, and hybridities, we would argue that stage-based models of development, such as Turner's model, still permeate research on adolescence across the disciplines. The very concept of adolescence is based on a stage theory of human development, and it provides inadequate recognition of variance across cultures, contexts, time, and situations in the marking of this category, or its meaning.

The youth we studied – ranging in age from 10 to18 – are in a contested zone between childhood and adulthood. How they are seen – as children, adolescents, youth, or young adults – is shaped by context and setting (the larger context of racialized immigration in each country as well as more specific settings such as those of home, school, street, or language brokering encounters). It is shaped as well by the linguistic and social practices these youth engage in, even as these in turn are influenced by the youth's readings of their social contexts. For example, the Turkish youth's "hard" talk can be seen as both a response to and a reinforcement of a particular view of these youth as "over-mature" or "street-wise" – as not children but not young adults either. The youth's words and actions are not oriented toward assimilating unproblematically into the (mainstream) adult world, and they are not read as such by outsiders.

The work that immigrant youth do as language brokers, on the other hand, represents a different kind of threat to the established order; these youth are readily positioned as "children" who have been thrust prematurely into adult worlds. Their innocence is highlighted, and they may be seen as immature instead of over-mature. (Note: neither conception of their maturity may match how the youth view themselves, nor how their families view them.) Part of what these children must negotiate in their mediational work is how to speak appropriately *as children* to adults, even as they speak *for those adults* to each other.

Whether openly contesting, or attempting to mediate, it is the voices of liminal subjects, arising from their betwixt- and betweenness, that is disquieting to the public.

But in neither case do we see clean separations from the stage of "childhood" into the limen, or neat transitions into adulthood. And yet diverse contemporary literatures – in anthropology, sociology, psychology, and education, as well as Turner's conceptualization via the concept of liminality as under discussion here – still treat adolescence as a stage, and assimilation as a process, that is teleological in nature and that presumes the resolution of liminal tensions.

Lastly, we would like to address the issue of multiplicity. For Turner individuals are simultaneously members of many different groups, while *each* individual experiences structure and communitas at multiple times in his/her life. Turner therefore recognizes that liminal positionalities do not include all aspects of a person's identity and that they hence do not translate into liminality in all spheres of the individual's life. Nevertheless, Turner's work does not pursue this multiplicity and there is a lack of descriptive and theoretical attention to how each individual, and each social group, experiences liminality to different extents, in different combinations, and at different points in time.

Possibly as a result of this original conceptualization, the way in which the concept of liminality is often mapped onto immigrant youths' experiences does little to help us understand how these liminal positionalities differ. As our case studies show, multiple liminalities as adolescent, gendered, bilingual, ethnicized immigrants are based on a complex system of memberships, exclusions and transitional phases. It is a qualitatively different experience to be a fluently bilingual male Latino adolescent in the U.S. or a Turkish dominant girl in Berlin-Kreuzberg. Similarly, there is a qualitative difference between being a monolingual German speaking Turkish boy living in an ethnic enclave in Berlin (a rare case, but existent) and a bilingual Latino boy forced to interact in a predominantly English-speaking environment on his families' behalf.

The environments and contexts in which children and adolescents live give meaning to the practices that they are involved in and this makes for the subjective experience of liminality. These qualitative differences of power and powerlessness are conflated in the concept of liminality as it is commonly used.

To sum up, we want to alert the reader to the pitfalls, which are inherent in the use of the concept of liminality, both in regard to the implicit conceptualization of change and multiplicity. In applying the concept and its assumptions to our case studies, we show that it is not able to account for the experiences of these youths and that it simultaneously continues to structure our thinking about them. Even more than in our consideration of issues of power in the conceptualization of liminality, it is in the domains of change and multiplicity that this concept seems to side-track current conceptualizations.

Conclusion

The analysis of linguistic practices is ultimately the study of how cultural groups are positioned in society and how they respond to this positioning. While the practices described in this chapter emerge from different contexts and are created by different participating groups, they both speak strongly to the impact of power relations on immigrant youths' everyday lives. The effects of power inequality, in the form of low socio-economic standing, and lack of symbolic, social and educational capital, have emerged at multiple points in our discussion of these youths' practices. We have shown how Turner's concept of liminality is in many ways on target when applied to immigration contexts, particularly because it considers the lack of status of the liminal personae. Nevertheless, the difficulty with resting the analysis of contemporary immigrant experiences on this concept is that it inadequately addresses other aspects of those experiences, such as change and multiplicity. On the other hand, contemporary research in the fields of sociolinguistics and anthropology that further develops Turner's concept by considering these dimensions, has often under-theorized the central aspect of power inequality in the everyday experiences of immigrant youths.

What the field should be working towards then, we propose, is a theory that addresses immigrant youths' experiences particularly as they relate to power. Such a theory is well-advised to consider and make use of both Turner's theory and contemporary deconstructivist theories, but it needs to push further in the conceptualization of these experiences. As we have shown, the concept of liminality is in many ways not the right one for the phenomena we are trying to understand. We discussed some of the elements that such a theory *would* need to address, including the role of change, and the multiplicity of liminal experiences. Further, this theory needs to conceptualize power inequality as non-transitory experience (even as it is continually contested). Turner's concept of liminality has a temporally bound character and does not get at this permanence. The strong importance we accord to considering power inequality lies in the fact that almost all cultural and linguistic practices that research in immigration contexts tries to understand, are fundamentally influenced by this experience of power inequality. Some practices, such as the ones discussed in this chapter, are even centrally shaped by such experiences.

We therefore believe that in order to understand immigrant youths' language practices, it is not enough to understand adolescence, cultural practices and the construction of ethnic identities as separate constructs. Rather, because immigration contexts are (post)-colonial spaces, in which different groups mutually engage in contestations over the status quo of power distribution, it is important to understand how power weaves through the different aspects of immigrant youths' lives and personaes and how it shapes their ultimate structuring.

A theory of immigrant youths' experiences should consider multiple intersecting historical trajectories of subjects who are differently positioned in relation to structures of power, and their dimensions in everyday interactions[36]. It should enable us to understand both power contestation in immigration contexts, and its relational aspects, while avoiding the conceptual traps we have outlined above. With this we would be then analyzing activity settings, in which actors in particular contexts engage in shared practices, or activities, that are subject to continuous change on the social and individual level.[37] An analysis of the activity settings in which immigrant youths engage in a range of linguistic and cultural practices would then allow us to avoid being sidetrapped by essentializing ideas about identity or development, or blindness towards the shaping effects of power on these practices.

References

Amit-Talai, Vered & Helena Wulff 1995: *Youth cultures: a cross-cultural perspective*. London & New York: Routledge.
Androutsopoulos, Jannis 2002: jetzt speak something about italiano. Sprachliche Kreuzungen im Alltagsleben. *Osnabrücker Beiträge zur Sprachtheorie* (65).
Austin, John L. 1975: *How to do Things with Words*. Oxford: Claredon Press.
Back, Les 1996: *New Ethnicities and Urban Culture*. London: UCL Press.
Bakhtin, Mikhail M. 1968[1] [1940]: *Rabelais and His World*. Cambridge, MA: MIT Press.
Barth, Frederic (ed.) 1969: *Ethnic Groups and Boundaries: The Social Organization of Cultural Difference*. London: Allen & Unwin.
Baugh, John 1999: Hypocorrection. Mistakes in the Production of African American Vernacular English as a Second Dialect. In: Baugh, John: *Out of the Mouths of Slaves. African American Language and Educational Malpractice*. Austin: University of Texas Press.
Bhabha, Homi K. 1994: *The Location of Culture*. London & New York: Routledge.

---

36 Pratt 1991.
37 Cole 1996; Engestroem 1999; Wertsch 1991.

Blom, Jan-Petter & John Josef Gumperz 1972: Social meaning in linguistic structures. In: Hymes, Dell & John Josef Gumperz (eds.): *Directions in Sociolinguistics*. New York: Holt, Rinehart and Winston: 407–434.

Bourdieu, Pierre 1977: *Language and Symbolic Power*. Translated by Gino Raymond & Matthew Adamson. Cambridge, MA: Harvard University Press.

Bucholtz, Mary 2002: Youth and Cultural Practice. *Annual Review of Anthropology* 31: 525–552.

Buriel, Raymond W., William Perez, Terry L. DeMent, David V. Chavez & Virginia R. Moran 1998: The relationship of language brokering to academic performance, biculturalism, and self-efficacy among Latino adolescents. *Hispanic Journal of Behavioral Sciences* 20(3): 283–297.

Çağlar, Ayşe S. 1995: German Turks in Berlin: social exclusion and strategies for social mobility. *New Community* 21(3): 309–323.

Cazden, Courtney B. 1970: The Neglected Situation in Child Language Research and Education. In: Williams, Frederick (ed.): *Language and Poverty. Perspectives on a Theme*. Chicago: Markham Publishing Company: 81–101.

Cazden, Courtney B. 2001: *Classroom Discourse. The Language of Teaching and Learning* (4 ed.). Portsmouth, NH: Heinemann.

Cole, Michael 1996: *Cultural Psychology. A Once and Future Discipline*. Cambridge: Belknap Harvard.

Cooper, Catherine R., Jill Denner & Edward M. López 1999: Cultural brokers: Helping Latino children on pathways to success. *The Future of Children* 9: 51–57.

Douglas, Mary 1966: *Purity and Danger*. London: Routledge.

Dundes, Alan, Jerry W. Leach & Bora Özkök 1972: The Strategy of Turkish Boys' Verbal Dueling Rhymes. In: Gumperz, John J. & Dell Hymes (eds.): *Directions in Sociolinguistics. The Ethnography of Communication*. New York: Holt, Rinehart and Winston: 130–160.

Durkheim, Emile 1912: *The Elementary Forms of the Religious Life*. London: George Allen & Unwin.

Eksner, Helene Julia (in print): *Ghetto Ideologies, Youth Identity and Stylized Turkish German. German Turks in Berlin-Kreuzberg*. Hamburg: Lit-Verlag.

Eliade, Mircea 1959: *The Sacred and the Profane: The Nature of Religion*. London: Harcourt Brace Jovanovich.

Elwert, Georg 1989: Nationalismus, Ethnizität und Nativismus – über die Bildung von Wir-Gruppen. In: Waldmann, Peter & Georg Elwert (eds.): *Ethnizität im Wandel*. Saarbrücken: Breitenbach: 21–60.

Elwert, Georg 1995: Boundaries, Cohesion and Switching. On We-Groups in Ethnic, National and Religious Form. In: Brumen, Borut (ed.): *Mediterranean Ethnological Summer School (MESS)*. Ljublajana: 150–121.

Engestroem, Yrjv, Reijo Miettinen & Raija-Leena Punamaeki (eds.) 1999: *Perspectives on activity theory*. Cambridge, MA: Cambridge University Press.

Fanon, Frantz 1967 [1952[1]]: *Black Skin, White Masks*. New York: Grove Press.

Fennell, Barbara A. 1997: *Language, Literature, and the Negotiation of Identity: Foreign Worker German in the Federal Republic of Germany.* Chapel Hill & London: The University of North Carolina Press.

Gal, Susan 1987: Codeswitching and Consciousness in the European Periphery. *American Ethnologist* 14: 637–653.

Gennep, Arnold van 1960 [1909[1]]: *The Rites of Passage.* London: Routledge and Kegan Paul.

Gilroy, Paul 1987: *There Ain't No Black in the Union Jack': The Cultural Politics of Race and Nation.* London: Hutchinson.

Gluckman, Max 1971: *Order and rebellion in tribal Africa; collected essays with an autobiographical introduction.* London: Cohen & West.

Goffman, Erving 1967: *Interaction Ritual.* Harmondsworth: Penguin.

Haavind, Hanne 2001: *Contesting and recognizing historical changes and selves in development.* Los Angeles (unpubl.).

Hall, Stuart 1994: Cultural Identity and Diaspora. In: Williams, Patrick & Laura Chrisman (eds.): *Colonial Discourse and Postcolonial Theory.* New York: Columbia University Press: 392–403.

Hall, Stuart 1996 [1989[1]]: New Ethnicities. In: Morley, David & Kuan-Hsing Chen (eds.): *Stuart Hall: Critical Dialogues in Cultural Studies.* London: Routledge: 441–449.

Hall, Stuart, & Paul du Gay (eds.) 1996: *Questions of Cultural Identity.* London: Sage Publ.

Hebdige, Dick 1979: *Subculture. The Meaning of Style.* London & New York: Routledge.

Hewitt, Roger 1992: Language, Youth and the destabilisation of ethnicity. In: Palmgren, Cecilia, Karin Loevgren & Goeran Bolin (eds.): *Ethnicity in Youth Culture. Report from a symposium in Stockholm, Sweden June 3–6, 1991.* Stockholm: Youth Culture at Stockholm University: 27–41.

Hochschild, Arlie Russel 1983: *The Managed Heart. The Commercialization of Human Feeling.* Berkeley and Los Angeles: University of California Press.

Holm, John 1988: *Pidgins and Creoles.* Cambridge: Cambridge University Press.

Irvine, Judith T. & Susan Gal 1999. Language Ideology and Linguistic Differentiation. In: Kroskrity, Paul V. (ed.): *Regimes of Language. Ideologies, Politics, and Identities.* Santa Fe, New Mexico: School of American Research Press: 35–84.

Labov, William 1972: *Sociolinguistic Patterns.* Philadelphia: University of Pennsylvania Press.

Orellana, Marjorie Faulstich 2001: The Work Kids Do: Mexican and Central American Immigrant Children's Contributions to Households and Schools in California. *Harvard Educational Review* 71 (3): 366–389.

Orellana, Marjorie Faulstich, Lisa Dorner & Lucila Pulido 2003: Accessing Assets: Immigrant Youth's Work as Family Translators or "Para-Phrasers." *Social Problems* 50 (4): 505–524.

Orellana, Marjorie Faulstich, Jennifer Reynolds, Lisa Dorner & Maria Meza 2003: In other words: Translating or "para-phrasing" as a family literacy practice in immigrant households. *Reading research quarterly* 38 (1): 12–34.

Park, Robert E. 1950: *Race and Culture*. Glencoe, IL: Free Publisher.
Piaget, Jean 1975: *The Development of Thought: Equilibration of Cognitive Structures*. New York: Viking Press.
Portes, Alejandro & Rubén G. Rumbaut 2001: *Legacies: the story of the immigrant second generation*. Berkeley, New York: University of California Press.
Pratt, Mary Louise 1991: Arts of the Contact Zone. *Profession* 91: 33–40.
Puzar, Aljosa, & Igor Markovic (eds.) 2001: *Limen. Journal for theory and practice of liminal phenomena*. On-Line Journal. http://limen.mi2.hr.
Rampton, Ben 1995: *Crossing. Language and Ethnicity Among Adolescents*. London and New York: Longman.
Rampton, Ben 1997: *Sociolinguistics and Cultural Studies: New Ethnicities, Liminality and Interaction, Vol. 4*. London: King's College London.
Rogoff, Barbara 2003: *The Cultural Nature of Human Development*. Oxford: Oxford University Press.
Skelton, Tracey & Gill Valentine (eds.) 1998: *Cool Places. Geographies of Youth Cultures*. London: Routledge.
Tertilt, Hermann 1997: Rauhe Rituale. Die Beleidigungsduelle der Turkish Power Boys. In: SPoKK (ed.): *Kursbuch Jugendkultur. Stile, Szenen und Identitäten vor der Jahrtausendwende*. Mannheim: Bollmann Verlag: 157–167.
Tse, Lucy 1995: Language borkering among Latino adolescents: Prevalence, attitudes, and school performance. *Hispanic Journal of Behavioral Sciences* 17: 180–193.
Tse, Lucy 1996: Who decides?: The effect of language brokering on home-school communication. *The Journal of Eduational Issues of Language Minority Students* 16: 225–233.
Turner, Victor 1969: *The Ritual Process. Structure and Anti-Structure*. Chicago: Aldine Publishing Company.
Turner, Victor 1974: Liminal to liminoid in play, flow and ritual. In: Turner, Victor: *From Ritual to Theatre: The Human Seriousness of Play*. New York: PAJ: 20–60.
Urciuoli, Bonnie 1998: *Exposing Prejudice. Puerto Rican Experiences of Language, Race, and Class*. Boulder: Westview Press.
Valdés, Guadalupe 2002: *Expanding Definitions of Giftedness: The Case of Young Interpreters from Immigrant Countries*. Mahwah, NJ: Lawrence Erlbaum Associates.
Valdés, Guadalupe, Christina Chávez & Claudia Angelilli 1999: *Receptive and productive competence: The Spanish and English proficiencies of young interpreters*.
Weisskirch, Rob S. & Sylvia Alatorre Alva 2002: Language brokering and the acculturation of Latino children. *Hispanic Journal of Behavioral Sciences* 24 (3): 369–378.
Werbner, Pnina 1997. Introduction: The Dialectics of Cultural Hybridity. In: Werbner, Pnina & Tariq Modood (eds.): *Debating Cultural Hybridity*. London: Zed Books: 1–27.

Wertsch, James V. 1991: *Voices of the Mind: A Sociocultural Approach to Mediated Action*. Cambridge, MA: Harvard University Press.

Williams, Brackette F. 1990: Nationalism, Traditionalism, and the Problem of Cultural Inauthenticity. In: Fox, Richard G. (ed.): *Nationalist Ideologies and the Production of National Cultures. American Ethnological Society Monograph Series, 2*. Washington, D.C.: American Anthropological Association: 112–129.

Woolard, Kahtryn 1985: Language variation and cultural hegemony: toward an integration of sociolinguistics and social theory. *American Ethnologist* 12 (4): 738–748.

Zaimoglu, Feridun 1995: *Kanak Sprak. 24 Mißtöne vom Rande der Gesellschaft*. Hamburg: Rotbuch Verlag.

Zaimoglu, Feridun 1997: *Abschaum. Die wahre Geschichte von Ertan Ongun*. Hamburg: Rotbuch Verlag.

Zaimoglu, Feridun 1999: *Koppstoff. Kanaka Sprak vom Rande der Gesellschaft*. Hamburg: Rotbuch Verlag.

CHILDHOOD DYNAMICS IN A CHANGING CULTURE. EXAMPLES FROM THE XAVANTE PEOPLE OF CENTRAL BRAZIL

Angela Nunes

The ethnographic data and reflections presented in this paper[1] are not about a people living through a migration process, but about a group of people in Central Brazil who were prevented from continuing their migrant way of life and had to settle down. They still suffer from the consequences of the sudden and violent change in all aspects of their social lives caused by having to give up a semi-nomadic existence that had determined their way of life for centuries. With a great deal of effort, however, they are finding ways to mend what was almost destroyed. Their hopes lie in the children. They say children can better bridge the past with the future. They say children have a wisdom that adults do not know much about.

Indigenous children and the Anthropology of Childhood

Despite efforts during the last 15 years to acknowledge the child as a social agent and childhood as a social phenomenon in the social and educational sciences, there is still a need to intensify and diversify the research that reveals the participation of children in the (re-)construction of social life, in any society. Expanded ethnographic research on childhood as such may not be the solution in and of itself, but theoretical and methodological consolidation of this new field of study will not be possible without it. Within this new theoretical framework, childhood is not considered a unique and closed concept but varied dependent on the social particularities of a given group. Thus, it must be understood from an intercultural perspective.[2] Findings resulting from research pursued within the framework of this approach are aimed to go beyond

---

1 I am grateful to Lynda Seeley and Helena Briosa e Mota for reviewing this paper, and to Rosário Carvalho for the discussions on the intercultural education programme for indigenous peoples in Brazil.
2 See, i.e., Caputo 1995; Hardman 1973; Hirschfeld 2002; James, Jenks & Prout 1997; James & Prout 1990, 1995; Jenks 1996; Mead 1975; Qvortrup 1994; Toren 1993.

theoretical contributions; they also aim at shaping the direction of childhood policies world wide.³

Indigenous children, however, have received less attention than any other group of children both by scientists and by the different organizations engaged in improving children's living conditions and ensuring their rights. The last UNICEF report specially dedicated to indigenous children, published in October 2003, states that:

> Around the world in rural and urban areas alike, indigenous children frequently constitute one of the most disadvantaged groups, and their rights – including those to survival and development to the highest standard of health, to education that respects their cultural identity, and to protection from abuse, violence and exploitation – are often compromised. At the same time, however, indigenous children possess very special resources: they are the custodians of a multitude of cultures, languages, beliefs and heritage. As this Digest discusses, the most effective initiatives to promote the rights of indigenous children build upon these very elements. Such initiatives recognize the inherent strength of indigenous communities, families and children, respect their dignity and give them full voice in all matters that affect them.⁴

This paper is based on long-term anthropological field research on indigenous childhood I conducted in Brazil. It tries to shed some light on a subject that is still struggling to find its place in the field of recent international childhood studies, but also in the field of more general ethnological studies of indigenous societies in Brazil.⁵

Institutional support of childhood issues in Brazil has mostly concentrated on poor children who abound in the streets of big cities and who have been considered a serious social problem for decades.⁶ As a consequence, these "problematic children" increasingly became the focus of attention among Brazilian educators, psychologists, jurists, and social workers. Sociologists did

---

3   Stephens 1995.
4   Innocenti Digest/Unicef 2003: 34.
5   Presently there are 216 different indigenous peoples living in Brazil in varied contact situations with the non-Indian Brazilian population, also termed the national society. Brazilian indigenous people speak around 180 different languages and the last census estimated a population of 350,000 persons (Ricardo 2000). According to Law 6.001 from December 19th 1973, "Indian [...] is defined as any individual with pre-Colombian descent or origin, who identifies him/herself, or is identified as belonging to an ethnic group, whose cultural characteristics are different from the ones of the national society," and an "indigenous community or tribal group is the set of families or Indian communities, either living in total isolation from other national community sectors or maintaining permanent or intermittent contact with the national society without being integrated into it." This Law is currently under revision. In the meantime, the statements above are considered to be valid. Anthropological literature uses "indigenous" and "Indians" as equivalent terms. The same designations are used by indigenous people/Indians in reference to themselves.
6   Alvim & Valadares 1988; Del Priore 1991, 2000; Martins 1993; Rizzini 1997a, 1997b, 2002; Rizinni 2000.

not get involved in the debate until the 1970s[7] and anthropologists have become engaged in the field only recently.

Dealing with so-called "street-children" or "street-kids" is certainly indispensable as long as there are children living on the streets. Nevertheless, considering that to date only "problematic children" have been at the centre of social science concerns, and in view of the lack of studies dealing with indigenous children, one may get the impression that the latter might not have received attention because they simply have no problems – at least not the type of problems that disturb the public order like those of "street-kids." Taking into consideration how distant Indian children are from the non-Indian society in ethnic, geographic, and social terms, the question arises of what we really know about them. Do they have problems or not? Do they give rise to problems or not? And as we do not have any answers so far that could appease our minds, we may ask whether – besides the potential "problems" that might be prevalent among indigenous children – there is anything else worthy of anthropological interest concerning childhood in indigenous societies.

An evaluation of Brazilian anthropological literature since the beginning of the 20th century reveals that its contribution to the knowledge about indigenous childhood are isolated and discontinuous. The information given is only of peripheral importance in the framework of the respective general research area.[8] Identification, systematization, and evaluation of this disperse data, which was largely obtained in the context of ascertaining data on the social organization of the different indigenous peoples, has shown how valuable it in fact is. It opens up research questions that have not been considered in Brazilian anthropology so far, research questions, from which one can proceed to study indigenous childhood.[9]

Recent ethnological research on indigenous childhood in Brazil is situated in the theoretical framework of the emerging anthropology of childhood, which points out that childhood studies also serve as instruments of reflection upon present social – particularly educational, economic, juridical, health, and gender – questions that affect not just children but all others with whom they share their social world.[10]

These studies have, indeed, revealed that indigenous childhood – like childhood in any society – must be studied as a topic in its own right, and that childhood in Brazilian indigenous societies is profoundly embedded in the

---

7 The first systematic and continuous studies by Brazilian sociologists about childhood took place at the beginning of the 1970s. One such study was ordered by the Court of São Paulo/Juvenile Court; the objective was to collect information about the juveniles who were provoking so many social problems (CEBRAP 1972). The other was carried out in Rio de Janeiro and had the same aims (Misse et al. 1973).
8 Nunes 1999, 2002.
9 Nunes 2004.
10 This means the child is considered a social agent. See details concerning the theory of an anthropology of childhood in the introduction to this book.

other aspects of social life.[11] To a great extent, these studies strengthen the paradigm of an anthropology of childhood as proposed by James and Prout[12] that childhood should be considered an important variable in social analysis, like any other variable. They also support a child-focused anthropology as proposed by Toren,[13] who argues that studies on childhood should not simply be multiplied but should rather be an integral part of social studies about any given society so as to be able to understand it as completely as possible.

The studies of indigenous childhood in Brazil mentioned above aim to apply these theoretical considerations. They desire to shed light on the specificity of Brazilian ethnological research and on the specificity of its empirical object – the more than 200 indigenous groups living in Brazil.[14]

Almost a decade after the beginning of the European research project *Childhood as a Social Phenomenon* (Qvortrup 1994), which led to sea change in social science studies of childhood, James, Jenks & Prout (1997: 26–33) identified four main approaches in contemporary childhood studies: (1) childhood as a social construction, (2) childhood as a world aside (3) children as a minority group, (4) childhood as a component of (all) social structures.[15] Studies about indigenous childhood can make use of all of these approaches and can contribute to their further development.

Firstly, in reference to the study of childhood as a social construction, the cultural variety and particularity of Brazilian indigenous societies constitute very diverse contexts that allow for comparative ethnographic research dealing with the question how childhood is socially constructed in different settings.

Secondly, as a world aside, what kind of "worlds aside" children construct under different social and cultural conditions and how these differences in the

---

11 Cohn 2000; Lopes da Silva, Macedo & Nunes 2002; Nunes 1999, 2004.
12 James & Prout 1990: 1–34.
13 Toren 1993: 462.
14 Cardoso de Oliveira (1986, 1998) describes Brazilian anthropology as a field of research that grew out of its particular empirical object: Indians, Africans, and Europeans. Knowledge was historically subordinated to the nature of these real objects, rather than to the nature of theory. Two traditions emerged from this specific situation: the ethnology of indigenous societies and the anthropology of the national society. Brazilian ethnology dedicated to indigenous societies started to define its particularity as scholars became aware of the fact that the classical analytical models constructed during the first half of the 20th century in Europe and based on African ethnographic data could not explain the social organisation and structure of South American indigenous societies, thus demanding the need for other explicatory models. Important contributions to this debate are the discussion on dualism in the South American lowlands, carried out between Lévi-Strauss (1960) and Maybury-Lewis (1960), and the analysis about the notion of Person undertaken by Kaplan (1977) at the XLII International Congress of Americanists, followed by Seeger et al. (1979), Lopes da Silva (1986), Carneiro da Cunha (1986), and Peirano (1991).
15 See details in the Introduction.

"worlds aside" relate to the larger social and cultural context can be investigated.

Thirdly, on the topic of childhood as a minority group, as a socially disadvantaged group, discriminated against and in need of political empowerment, indigenous children can serve as an excellent object of study – in fact they suffer from a double minority position: as children and as members of a minority group.

Fourthly, concerning the study of childhood as a socio-structural category present in all societies, studies dealing with specific societies in a local context can pick up the "universalist-versus-particularist-debate" and obtain new insights on the different forms and meanings social phenomena take on in relationship to the social and cultural context of the society they are part of. With regard to the latter, studies about indigenous childhood also offer an excellent framework to observe the interrelation between biological development and social conditions and structures.

Beyond the theoretical interests mentioned above, I would like to refer to the more pragmatic aspect present in my work about indigenous childhood and Brazilian anthropology in general. Scientific aims are interrelated with the social, juridical, and political issues that affect the individuals under study; research also aims at improving the latter's living conditions. Brazilian anthropologists are not merely passive observers. Instead, they have become indigenous societies' crucial allies and interlocutors. This approach keeps the needs of the people studied in mind and aims at giving them a voice in academic writing as well. Research about indigenous children could not be otherwise. Childhood topics in need of attention are many; most of them have not been addressed yet. I will concentrate on questions related to the introduction of formal school education in indigenous areas in Brazil, and – more specifically – in a village, where people with a semi-nomadic background, namely the Xavante, have settled down permanently.

Differentiated school education for Indian children

School education for indigenous people began in colonial times. According to Ferreira,[16] its first period lasted until the beginning of the 20th century. Its main objective was to deny existing indigenous diversity, to extinguish cultures and to train the indigenous population as a working force. The Church had an important role during this phase, and forcing the Indians to learn Portuguese was just one of the many practices for assimilating them into Christian civilization. The second period started in 1910, when the government created the SPI, the *Serviço de Protecção ao Índio* (Indian Protection Service), in an attempt to stop four centuries of extermination. Its objective was to integrate the remaining indigenous population into the national society. Several

---

16 Ferreira 2001: 71–111.

agendas aimed at development and at agricultural production were imposed on the indigenous population. Indians themselves had no say in any of the decisions made. However, most of these plans failed, including the plan to implement an educational programme aimed at adjusting the schools in indigenous areas to the needs of the respective people and community. Indian schools remained to be the same as the schools of the more established Brasilian society, but had to function under worse conditions and with less supplies.[17] Thus, school education alienated Indians from their cultural and social values by completely ignoring long established indigenous educational practices.

During the 1960s and 1970s, when Brazilian anthropology focused on indigenous societies acquired a certain standing, Indian leaders and anthropologists became aware of the fact that school education was a double-edged sword. It helped the Indians interact with the non-Indian Brazilian society by teaching them to read and write; however, it also provoked cleavages within the indigenous populations and had a negative impact on their social equilibrium. In establishing a solid partnership between Indians, anthropologists, and non-government organizations, Indian political resistance against social discrimination was strengthened considerably and provided a foundation for their struggle for a more appropriate school education system. As a result, Indians were to receive school education, which ensured respect for their cultural and linguistic particularities. Indian teachers were to receive special training and be in charge of directing their schools, teaching the Indian school children, and producing their own teaching aids and methods. Under the designation "differentiated school education for indigenous peoples," these rights were laid down in the new Constitution of the Republic proclaimed in 1988. These steps were followed by a period of active co-operation among anthropologists, linguists, historians, and NGOs, who – together with indigenous leaders and government representatives – further developed desirable educational practices and policies.[18]

Many significant institutional initiatives followed. Indigenous communities are now involved in developing projects and producing educational materials to be used for teaching purposes. The number of anthropological studies dedicated to education matters has increased as well, focusing especially on linguistic and cognitive aspects, as well as on ethno-science and ethno-knowledge.[19]

However – and paradoxically – this academic engagement did not significantly increase our knowledge about the children in the indigenous societies under study. The latter still do not have a voice or a say when it comes to de-

---

17 On the history of Indians in Brazil, including the period of SPI administration, see Carneiro da Cunha 1992.
18 The different contributions to indigenous education are dealt with in: Capacla 1995; Lopes da Silva 1981, 1987; Lopes da Silva & Ferreira 2001a, 2001b; Lopes da Silva & Grupioni 1995.
19 I.e. Carrara 1997; Emiri & Monserrat 1989; Ferreira 1992, 2002; Giannini 1991, 1994; Monte 1996; Tassinari 2001.

veloping educational methods and programmes. Indigenous children, understood as an ontological category in their own right,[20] and as social agents having a mind to develop and express thoughts and a voice to speak,[21] are just now beginning to become involved in Brazilian anthropological research.[22] Some old concepts of childhood socialization are seemingly difficult to overcome. One example is the International Labour Convention[23] concerning "Indigenous and Tribal Peoples in Independent Countries," which was ratified by the President of Brazil in April 2004. Children are mentioned only twice and only when education issues are concerned.

Art. 28.1: Children belonging to the peoples concerned shall, wherever practicable, be taught to read and write in their own indigenous language or in the language most commonly used by the group to which they belong. When this is not practicable, the competent authorities shall undertake consultations with these peoples with a view to the adoption of measures to achieve this objective.

Art. 29: The imparting of general knowledge and skills that will help children belonging to the peoples concerned to participate fully and on an equal footing in their own community and in the national community shall be an aim of education for these peoples.

Respect for indigenous languages is an official policy aim, as are consultations with the indigenous peoples when difficulties arise – however, it remains unsaid, whether the latter are meant to include consulting the children. Equal social participation in both the local and the national community is aimed at as well, and this is to be supported by adequate teaching. However, what children for their part can give to their communities and how they influence social life, is not mentioned. The rights of children to be heard, the comprehension and consideration of their understandings of their environment are matters, which are to date largely ignored. The International Labour Convention has considerable political importance world wide; it is regrettable that it does not consider social science findings about childhood in its statutes. One could argue that the latter were formulated in 1991, at a time when research only started to bring about major changes in the approach and understanding of childhood and childhood policies. But one could also argue, on the other hand, that in the meantime the new findings could have been included gradually, adjusting them to new and current demands. Thus, despite all positive achievements, to date, scientific as well as children's knowledge about the societies concerned are not included in the design and implementation of educational policies.

---

20 Jenks 1996: 10.
21 James & Prout 1990: 8–9.
22 Nunes 1999, 2004; Cohn 2000; Lopes da Silva, Macedo & Nunes 2002.
23 International Labour Convention No. 169, dated 1991.

The school as an ideal locus for the meeting of cultures

In order to convey a more vivid impression of the issues at stake and in an attempt to bridge theory and practice, I invite the reader to enter the daily life of a small Xavante village called Idzö'uhu, located in the Indigenous Area Sangradouro, Mato Grosso, in Central Brazil. Here people are involved in the challenging endeavour of planning an educational project.

The Xavante are identified in ethnological literature as one of the indigenous or Indian peoples of the South American lowlands.[24] First written sources about the Xavante – a semi-nomadic people of hunters and gatherers – date from the 18th century. According to these documents,[25] they were constantly moving from one area to another. As they lived in temporary settlements for only three to four years, surviving by undertaking seasonal excursions in search of resources, the Xavante could not inscribe their domination upon a certain territory. There is evidence, however, that since the beginning of the 19th century they were forced to migrate westward as a result of the occupation of their territory by the state and due to agricultural expansion. Options for gathering and hunting were reduced dramatically, and survival became difficult. Several documents testify that the Xavante did not want to make contact with non-Indians.[26] At the end of the 1950s, after centuries of fighting, the Xavante were tired of fleeing, suffering from hunger and of not being able to cure the many diseases that had befallen them. They took refuge in the missions that had been established nearby and the missionaries provided them with food and medical care. The Xavante built settlements in their neighbourhood, but did not have in mind to settle there permanently at first. However, due to the new territorial order that had been established in the meantime, it was not possible to return to the semi-nomadic lifestyle they were used to. Thus, the Xavante ended up being dependent on the missions for quite some time with no other chance than to accept whatever was imposed upon them by the outside world.

Only during the 1970s, when Indian political awareness rose and political action set in on a wider scale did things started changing. The Xavante today live in permanent settlements in seven protected areas in the State of Mato

---

24 The Xavante identify themselves as A'uwẽ, which is also their linguistic identification. It means "people" or "us." The designation Xavante is of Portuguese origin, the meaning of which is not known (Nimuendaju 1942). Although they are sometimes referred to as A'uwẽ-Xavante in the ethnological literature, the latter term is the one used more often, and is assumed to be their correct identification. The American anthropologist Maybury-Lewis was the first to pursue research among the Xavante people at the end of the 1960s (1967, 1979). Other important studies were undertaken by Graham (1990, 1995), and Lopes da Silva (1982, 1986, 1992).
25 See Lopes da Silva 1992.
26 On Xavante resistance to contact see Lopes 1988; Lopes da Silva 1992; Menezes 1982.

Grosso, Central Brazil. Almost 10,000 Xavante live in more than fifty villages of 100 to 1,000 inhabitants each.[27]

Things have changed since the times of the first closer contacts between the Indians and the non-Indian missionaries. This becomes apparent in the words of the education project's leader in Idzö'uhu when reflecting upon 19 years of experience in the mission school – the experience of studying to become a primary school teacher, of working as a teacher under the guidance of the missionaries and of now being engaged in the educational programme for the indigenous population:

> I thought that what I learned at the occidental school was something that would work out, would help us to see and solve our political problems, among ourselves and also with the non-Indian society. But this was an illusion. I say this because we, ourselves, we have a different view. For us, learning how to read and write means that we are prepared to defend ourselves. Not individually, but together. Learning how to read and write means having a minimum knowledge about life in the cities and [...] about relating socially with the surrounding societies, and vice-versa. However, from what I can see, this occidental school, instead of helping us, is confounding us more. I am sure it is. The school took a big space away from the children. Before, children were free to play, to learn about our culture, how to do things with their parents, to listen to the older ones. But school took this part [of education] away from us. Children do not have any time for that because they are always busy with school tasks and activities.[28]

Despite all the institutional and scientific support with regard to indigenous education, there is obviously a high degree of disappointment – the major reason being that it has been very difficult to put into practice what papers and documents state, or to see actual improvement. At the time we came to an agreement about my stay in the Xavante village concerned, the teacher leading the project said that until then, nobody – Indians, pedagogues, anthropologists or technicians from the Ministry of Education – knew exactly what the so-called "differentiated school education for indigenous peoples" actually was all about, nor did anyone know how to develop or apply appropriate new educational programmes. One of the obstacles was that the Indian teachers had not been asked to contribute their experience and knowledge in the process, another that suggestions coming from the villages were rarely accepted or even considered at the institutional level. The teacher I talked to was well aware that local projects needed professional support as well and, knowing I was an anthropologist with an interest in education issues, he invited me to observe the establishment of the differentiated school project in progress in his village. Of all the challenges that ethnographic field work in indigenous areas poses, what made this invitation particularly challenging was that he was

---

27 Ricardo 2000.
28 Testimony from Lucas Ruri'õ. Quoted with permission. Note his usage of the term "occidental school;" he is clearly familiar with social science terminology, which implicitly opposes western and non-western societies.

looking for support to objectify what he called "giving value to children's participation." He considered this aspect to be absent in the government's educational programmes. Both of us were in agreement: children's thoughts about the world around them, their ways of acting within and of changing it need to be known to design and implement any educational programme that would serve children's interests. If ethnology does not provide adequate information about Indian childhood, how could the education experts, sitting in their offices in Brasília, consider its particularities?

The Xavante village where this project took place had around 100 inhabitants, living in 12 houses made of wood and palm leaves. Each was occupied by an extended nuclear family.[29] There was no electricity supply and no running water. The village was founded by an old Xavante man, together with his sons and daughters and some other families, who had decided to separate from the main Xavante village located near the mission area. This main village was established at the end of the 1950s, when the first contact between Xavante people and missionaries took place. At the time the new settlement was founded, the main village had more than 1,000 inhabitants. The teacher I was working with told me that initiating an Indian education project would not have been possible in the main village because of the dominance of the mission school that was attended by all children, and because of internal disagreements among some of the Xavante political factions. It is common practice among the Xavante for a group to split for demographic or political reasons – a practice that has become more frequent since the semi-nomadic existence came to an end. In the village where I collected my data, the separation from the old village was a decisive step towards autonomy, and it was started by developing an educational project. The main objectives of this project were to:

- rescue the traditional Xavante knowledge developed as semi-nomads and to re-activate social and cultural practices already in a process of erosion – partly by adjusting them to the changes caused by ending their semi-nomadic lifestyle and becoming permanently settled.
- reflect upon the new knowledge gathered in the years of contact with non-Indian people – like the Portuguese language, school education, access to media, new technologies and different behaviours.

---

29 Xavante social organisation is based on two exogamous moieties that correspond to two clans. They follow a patrilineal rule of descent and an uxorilocal rule of residence. This dual social organisation is crossed by a complex system of age- and class-sets that, according to Maybury-Lewis (1967), are crucial for the understanding of the social structure of the Xavante. Cf. Graham 1990, 1995; Lopes da Silva 1983, 1986 and Maybury-Lewis 1979.

- combine both forms of knowledge in a way that takes into account whatever is advantageous in order to be prepared for dealing with the outside world while at the same time not losing one's own cultural heritage. The school as an open place for the whole community was meant to serve as an ideal locus for this meeting and mixing of cultures.
- create one's own didactic materials and to serve as an example for other Xavante communities in order to contribute to the development of differentiated school education for indigenous peoples in general, and to communicate Xavante culture and knowledge to wider Brazilian society.

The project was to be carried out by its leader, acting as mentor and co-ordinator, and by two other Xavante teachers: a woman working with children aged four to ten and a man working with children aged eleven to fourteen. They told me that their hope to keep Xavante culture alive depended on what the old men and women could pass on to the children. The teachers, as the intermediate generation that grew up under the influence of the missionaries and the missionary school, would merely be the ones preparing the ground for this endeavour.[30] They hoped that the children would stimulate their families to recall Xavante values and practices already abandoned or forgotten and – at the same time – to become aware of and prepare to deal with the changes and demands that had occurred with time. They believed that children were more open-minded and adjustable to what was new or unknown in general – whether it derive from without or from within their own culture and society. Thus, children could re-activate abandoned and almost forgotten Xavante knowledge and link it to the knowledge of modern life. Children were to give life to the traditional Xavante past by incorporating it into the present and thereby preparing it for the future.

What made this ambitious project innovative and different from the others I knew was the central and strategic position of the children in it – as receptors, conductors and creators of culture and knowledge. The Xavante teachers' perception of culture as a process was in line with Carneiro da Cunha, who said: "What we must guarantee for future generations is not the preservation of cultural products, but the preservation of the capacity for cultural produc-

---

30 For several decades, missionary boarding-schools existed in some of Xavante areas, where Indian children were brought up and kept apart from their families during the school year, and, obviously, from their own Xavante culture. This caused significant cultural and social alienation between the different generations. Gradually, with pressure from Xavante leaders and scholars rising, these boarding-schools were closed (Menezes 1985). School education in the Xavante areas, however, largely remained under missionary control.

tion" (Carneiro da Cunha 1995: 290).[31] The teachers seemed convinced that children were those most able to guarantee this would actually happen.

Blackened faces at the break of dawn

Soon after I arrived in the village and started my fieldwork, the teachers told me with considerable enthusiasm about something called "coal dust game," referring to it as one of the school activities the children enjoyed a lot. The game had been inspired by a Xavante practice recently recalled by the old people and re-arranged to serve a new purpose in school education. According to the elder Xavante people, in times past, when the Xavante were still living a semi-nomadic life, everyone woke up before sunrise and took a bath in a nearby river. This was supposed to maintain one's health and prepare a person for the daily tasks. The older generation still stick to this habit today, but the younger ones have given it up or limited its frequency. The "coal dust game" was intended to recollect this practice and adapt it to new educational purposes. It was carried out as follows:

The children (five to 12 years old) who managed to wake up at daybreak gathered in front of the teacher's house and went along with him from house to house, awakening the other children. To do so they were given little pieces of coal from the fire the night before, which they crumbled into dust, to rub on the faces of their sleeping mates. The latter, caught by surprise, would protest, but – now fully awake – would join the group in their activities. When all children were awake, the game transformed into a mock fight – including a lot of laughter, shouting, and sometimes some tears as well – with all of them rubbing each other's bodies with coal dust. Then they and their teacher all went to take a bath in the nearby river.

This practice of rubbing faces with coal dust has its origin in the gendered division of labour with women in charge of all domestic tasks. They collected fruits and seeds and worked in the small seasonal manioc gardens. Men for their part had to defend the territory and the people. They were in charge of opening clearings in the woods to establish new settlements and engaged in hunting and fishing. In case a man stayed at home for too long, not fulfilling his duty to provide for the family with fresh meat and fish, his wife would protest by rubbing coal dust in his face. To wash himself he needed to go to the river. It was likely for him to be seen by someone who would then spread the embarrassing news that he had not brought home any food for a long time. Through the "coal dust game" the teachers wanted to revive a cultural practice almost forgotten among the younger generation. They managed to do so by furnishing it with new dynamics. At the same time they caused the same kind of shameful feeling among those not able to fulfil their responsibilities – arriv-

---

31 See Clifford (1988) and Sahlins (2000) on the topic of "culture" as anthropology's "disappearing object."

ing at school on time, clean and fresh. What the teachers were not expecting, however, was the children taking the lesson so seriously and becoming so enthusiastic about it that they decided to wake up all sorts of people by rubbing their faces with coal dust. This caused a lot of fun and laughter initially – as well as some protest by the young men – but most of all it initiated a general discussion about the present gendered distribution of work in the village. I will try to explain why.

After settling permanently, the need to clear woods for new settlements decreased substantially. Having to defend one's territory became a thing of the past and the surrounding farms hardly made hunting activities possible. Thus, traditional male tasks became largely obsolete. Apart from their involvement in local politics, which takes up some time, men these days have a lot of spare time.

On the other hand, the increased number of children that need to be taken care of and fed, increased the need to raise crops and collect wood for fires. Furthermore, once clothing had been introduced into their culture by the missionaries, these also had to be washed. As all these activities are traditional female tasks, women – as opposed to the men – had to work more and more. As one result, most women stick to the tradition of waking up before sunrise so as to complete their many tasks. Most men on the other hand – especially the younger ones – do not. It was these younger men who were forced to wake up through the "coal dust effect."

The children's awakening action thus uncovered several social problems in the community at large. It caused the villagers to reflect upon traditional Xavante practices and new practices introduced by school education. For example, people started to talk about the fact that women were gradually withdrawing from participation in dances and rituals, simply because they were too tired from work. People felt this was a serious loss, especially in a society where the older generation need to serve as examples to maintain its cultural heritage. Furthermore, girls stopped going to school at a very early age to help their mothers in their domestic tasks and to look after their younger siblings. People gathered that such an uneven distribution of knowledge would increase problems between the sexes. Women would largely remain illiterate, they would not know Portuguese and thus would have little chance outside the world of the Xavante. They realized that if they let things continue in this way, the Xavante would never manage to establish school education as a means to prepare all of their members – girls and boys, women and men – to interact as equals with one another and with the more widely established Brazilian society and its culture.

Another important discussion the "coal dust game" evoked concerned the question of parents' and teachers' responsibilities for children's education. Being at school on time, for example, was a problem. The teachers did not want to ring the bell to call the children to class, like the missionaries used to do and like city schools still do today. They preferred to rely on their own cultural heritage, inventing the "coal dust game." They succeeded too. I noticed that on the days the "coal dust game" did not take place, some children were late for school, were not clean and had left their school materials at home. Sometimes the teacher had to send them to the school lavatory to wash themselves or back home to get their things. The teachers did not feel at ease doing so because they were afraid to hurt the parent's feelings, who, in their opinion, were the ones who should feel responsible, but some of whom obviously did not.

A number of questions arise: What are the teachers' and the families' obligations in such a differentiated school project that wants to include the whole community? Where are the boundaries between parents' and teachers' duties? Where do these boundaries overlap? Children who have to help their parents while they should be at school have a problem. How is this problem to be solved by those personally and institutionally involved – children, parents, teachers, and the school system? How can the rights guaranteed by the Constitution be put into practice?

Such problems were often discussed at the evening meetings in the *warã*, the central area of the village. Although this is traditionally a male space, it was also frequented by women and children on such occasions. The children used to stay quiet and listen to what was said, playing around a bit. Obviously, finding solutions that satisfied everyone was not easy since there were contradictory opinions and viewpoints, but the teachers tried anyhow. "We are just at the beginning. We still do not understand fully what this differentiated school education is," one of them told me. Another one said: "We have lived under the influence of the missionary school system for 40 years. That is quite a long time. [...] We have to accept that sometimes the community does not understand, does not approve. It is part of it. But I am not going to give up trying other ways. I cannot remain within old patterns forever."

The children's positive response to the "coal dust game" as well as the discussions that ensued confirmed the teachers' conviction that they should go ahead in searching for appropriate new solutions to the developing problems. Besides, the "coal dust game" had many – intended and unintended – positive effects on social life in the community. I could observe not only the discovery of the gender problem through the "coal dust game," but also some attempts to find solutions. For example, the village's truck was made available for women at least once a week to go collect wood. Before, women as well as some of the girls had to walk several kilometres carrying heavy burdens on their backs. I also heard the older men in the village stating that men should help their wives with the work in the fields, which caused some confusion with regard to gender roles and obligations at first. They said, men's help would make it less necessary for girls to help their mothers, which would enable them to attend school. So the old men set an example for the younger ones, an initiative much appreciated by the teachers in charge of the project.

How to value children's participation?

I do not know what the project has achieved since my fieldwork, but I think that the unfolding of the "coal dust game" in this small community serves as a good example of what the Xavante teacher described as giving value to children's participation. In theorical terms: children's experience is perceived as having an impact on social life which is acknowledged as agency. Later, the same teacher explained to me that this to him means paying attention to the signs children give and to gradually completing an educational process taking place both at school and in daily life elsewhere.

This educational process has been affecting the whole community of Idzö'uhu. For example, children took home Portuguese words, but they also showed increasing interest in Xavante mythology. In ethno-science lessons, children learned how to make use of their natural environment in order to improve their own and their families' nutrition, they learned how to find healing herbs and roots and to produce useful tools as well as arts and crafts. As children were learning about almost forgotten cultural practices from the older men and women, who had still experienced a semi-nomadic lifestyle, the intermediate generation eventually recalled them as well, giving them new meanings and using them for new purposes.

As we have seen, combining different forms of knowledge and different ways of communicating knowledge is not an easy task and involves many problems. One needs to combine children's need for regular school education with their family's need for children to partake in domestic activities. Tasks with regard to school education need to be distributed. Xavante women, for instance, do not traditionally have any role in their children's formal education. Therefore it is difficult for people to accept female teachers, difficult to understand that such a female teacher might leave the village for long periods of time to attend courses while her husband takes care of the children. This very woman and teacher with all her expertise and influence will – as a result of the latter – also play an important role in politics concerning indigenous education, a major field of indigenous politics. This fact will likely also encounter resistance in a society, where traditionally politics and public affairs were once the exclusive domain of men.

The project, the implementation of which I observed among the Xavante, needs to be understood as an intercultural process. To do so, one needs to acknowledge that the acquisition and mediation of knowledge in indigenous cultures differs from how this process takes place in non-indigenous cultures. The former is based on specific oral traditions, which differ from one group of people to another, whereas the latter has a written tradition, which is influenced by mass communication resulting in a higher degree of standardization and mutual intelligibility. Nevertheless, it is possible to communicate between indigenous and non-indigenous cultures and their respective traditions. Such an intercultural process would ideally involve communication, exchange and reciprocity on an equal footing between the societies involved. However, my observations show that this is not (yet) the case. Teachers mentioned more than once that school education occupies the space of Indian culture, keeping children away from Xavante culture and its ways of learning about the world. This suggests competition rather than dialogue between the cultures concerned – with the Xavante culture on the losing side. The Indians' search for solutions to such problems – solutions which make sense within their own culture – is of crucial importance here, also because it is a way to identify differences and peculiarities, thus making it easier to deal with them.

An important step in the direction of intercultural education on the part of the non-indigenous society would be the institutional acknowledgement of indigenous schools and teachers by the government as well as that proposals coming from the villages be treated with respect and given support. Here is where anthropologists can give a hand.

The question remains, however, whether those planning differentiated school education for the Indian peoples of Brazil are able to accept and understand what the Xavante teacher from Idzö'uhu said: "Not everyone can bow their head and recognize a child's experience. But it is important to give attention to the wisdom that children have and which we do not know anything about. Instead of going there, where the child has more freedom to be creative, we do not care and say: 'it is just childish.' And that is why we are unable to value what children feel."

The perception of childhood that this Xavante teacher expressed is usually not perceived by the professionals dealing with education questions. It also escapes most social scientists' minds, anthropologists included. When we talk about intercultural dialogue we need to keep in mind that even a single culture is not experienced the same way by all those identifying with it. There are several interacting sub-cultures within any given culture, as well as many cultural identities, one of them being those of children. Within the programmes of indigenous school education, it might be clear and generally accepted that the cultural particularities of each of the indigenous peoples be taken into consideration. What is not so clear and not accepted is that children as members of these indigenous groups of people have an identity of their own, which might be congruent in parts with the rest of the community, but might very well differ from it in others. Such particularities and differences in children's identity within a given culture and society are still not considered in the differentiated school education programmes and curricula. It is still only adults who officially define them. Children's perception of such cultural particularities of the society they live in is still ignored, as is their (sub-)cultural identity.

References

Alvim, Rosilene & Lícia Valadares 1988: Infância e sociedade no Brasil: Uma análise da literatura. *Anpocs/BIB* 26: 3–37.
Capacla, Marta 1995: O *Debate Sobre a Educação Indígena no Brasil (1975–1995)*. Cadernos de Educação Indígena, Vol I. São Paulo: MARI, MEC.
Caputo, Virginia 1995: Anthropology's silent 'others:' a consideration of some conceptual and methodological issues for the study of youth and children's cultures. In: Amit-Talai, Vered & Helena Wulff (ed.): *Youth Culture*. London & New York: Routledge: 19–41.
Cardoso de Oliveira, Roberto 1986: O que é isso que chamamos de antropologia Brasileira. *Anuário Antropológico* 85: 227–246.
Cardoso de Oliveira, Roberto 1998: *O Trabalho do Antropólogo*. Brasília: Paralelo 15. São Paulo: Editora Unesp.
Carrara, Eduardo 1997: *Tsi Tewara: Um Vôo Sobre o Cerrado Xavante*. Dissertação de Mestrado. Universidade de São Paulo: Faculdade de Filosofia, Letras e Ciências Humanas, Departamento de Antropologia.
Centro Brasileiro de Análise e Planejamento (ed.) 1972: *A Criança, o Adolescente e a Cidade*. São Paulo: Relatório de Pesquisa.
Cohn, Clarice 2000: *A Criança Indígena: A Concepção Xikrin de Infância e Aprendizado*. Dissertação de Mestrado. Universidade de São Paulo.
Carneiro da Cunha, Manuela 1992: *História dos Índios no Brasil*. São Paulo: USP, Cia das Letras, SMC e Fapesp.
Carneiro da Cunha, Manuela 1995: Children, politics and culture: the case of Brazilian Indians. In: Stephens, Sharon (ed.): *Children and the Politics of Culture*. New Jersey: Princeton University Press: 282–291.
Clifford, James 1988: *The Predicament of Culture: Twentieth-Century Ethnography, Literature and Art.* Cambridge: Harvard University Press.
Del Priore, Mary (ed.) 1991: *História da Criança no Brasil*. Col. Caminhos da História. São Paulo: Contexto.
Del Priore, Mary (ed.) 2000: *História das Crianças no Brasil*. São Paulo: Contexto.
Emiri, Loretta & Ruth Monserrat (eds.) 1989: *A Conquista da Escrita – Encontros de Educação Indígena*. São Paulo: OPAN/Iluminuras.
Ferreira, Mariana 1992: *Da Origem dos Homens à Conquista da Escrita: Um Estudo Sobre Povos Indígenas e Educação Escolar Indígena*. Dissertação de Mestrado. Universidade de São Paulo: Faculdade de Filosofia, Letras e Ciências Humanas, Departamento de Antropologia.
Ferreira, Mariana 2001: A educação escolar indígena: um diagnóstico crítico da situação no Brasil. In: Lopes da Silva, Aracy & Mariana Ferreira (eds.): *Antropologia, História e Educação: A Questão Indígena e a Escola*. Série Antropologia e Educação. São Paulo: Editora Global, Mari e Fapesp: 71–111.
Ferreira, Mariana (ed.) 2002: *Ideias Matemáticas – de Povos Culturalmente Distintos*. Série Antropologia e Educação. São Paulo: Editora Global, Mari e Fapesp.

Giannini, Isabelle 1991: *A Ave Resgatada: A Impossibilidade da Leveza do Ser*. Dissertação de Mestrado. Universidade de São Paulo: Faculdade de Filosofia, Letras e Ciências Humanas, Departamento de Antropologia.

Giannini, Isabelle 1994: Educação indígena e o manejo socioeconômico dos recursos Florestais: a experiência Xikrin. *Em Aberto* 14 (63): 117–121.

Graham, Laura 1990: *The Always Living: Discourse and the Male Life Cycle of the Xavante Indians of Central Brazil*. 2 Vols. PhD thesis. Austin: The University of Texas.

Graham, Laura 1995: *Performing Dreams: Discourses of Immortality Among the Xavante of Central Brasil*. Austin: University of Texas Press.

Hardman, Charlotte 1973: Can there be an anthropology of children? *Journal of the Anthropological Society of Oxford* 4 (2): 85–99.

Hirschfeld, Laurence 2002: Why don't anthropologists like children? *American Anthropologist* 104 (2): 611–627.

James, Allison & Alan Prout (eds.) 1990: *Constructing and Reconstructing Chidhood: Contemporary Issues in the Sociological Study of Childhood*. Basingstoke: Falmer Press.

James, Allison & Alan Prout 1995: Hierarchy, boundary and agency: toward a theoretical perspective on childhood. *Sociological Studies of Children* 7: 77–99.

James, Allison, Chris Jenks & Alan Prout 1997: *Theorizing Childhood*. Cambridge: Polity Press.

Jenks, Chris 1996: *Childhood*. London & New York: Routledge.

Kaplan, Joanna 1977: Orientation for paper topics and comments to Simpósio Social Time and Social Space in Lowland South American Societies. *Actes du XLIIe Congrès International des Américanistes*, Vol II. Paris.

Lévi-Strauss, Claude 1960: On manipulated sociological models. *Bijdragen* 116: 45–54.

Lopes, Marta 1988: *A Resistência do Índio ao Extermínio: O Caso dos A'uwẽ-Xavante , 1967–1980*. Dissertação de Mestrado em História. São Paulo: Universidade Estadual Paulista.

Lopes da Silva, Aracy (ed.) 1981: *A Questão da Educação Indígena. Comissão Pró-Índio de São Paulo*. São Paulo: Brasiliense.

Lopes da Silva, Aracy 1982: A expressão mítica da Vivência histórica: Tempo e espaço na construção da identidade Xavante. *Anuário Antropológico* 82: 200–214.

Lopes da Silva, Aracy 1983: Xavante: Casa-Aldeia-Chão-Terra-Vida. In: Novaes, Sylvia Caiuby (ed.): *Habitações Indígenas*. São Paulo: Editora da Universidade de São Paulo: 33–56.

Lopes da Silva, Aracy 1986: *Nomes e Amigos: Da Prática Xavante a Uma Reflexão Sobre Os Jê*. Coleção Antropologia, Vol. 6. São Paulo: Faculdade de Filosofia, Letras e Ciências Humanas/Universidade de São Paulo.

Lopes da Silva, Aracy (ed.) 1987: *A Questão Indígena na Sala de Aula*. São Paulo: Ed. Brasiliense.

Lopes da Silva, Aracy 1992: Dois séculos e meio de história Xavante. In: Carneiro da Cunha, Manuela (ed.): *História dos Índios no Brasil*. São Paulo: USP, Cia das Letras, SMC e FAPESP: 357–378.

Lopes da Silva, Aracy & Mariana Ferreira (eds.) 2001a: *Antropologia, História e Educação: A Questão Indígena e a Escola*. Série Antropologia e Educação. São Paulo: Editora Global, Mari e Fapesp.

Lopes da Silva, Aracy & Mariana Ferreira (eds.) 2001b: *Práticas Pedagógicas na Escola Indígena*. Série Antropologia e Educação. São Paulo: Editora Global, Mari e Fapesp.

Lopes da Silva, Aracy & Luis Grupioni (eds.) 1995: *A Temática Indígena na Escola*. Brasília: MEC, Mari, Unesco.

Lopes da Silva, Aracy, Ana Vera Macedo & Angela Nunes (eds.) 2002: *Crianças Indígenas: Ensaios Antropológicos*. Série Antropologia e Educação. São Paulo: Editora Global, Mari e Fapesp.

Martins, José de Souza (ed.) 1993 [1991[1]]: *O Massacre dos Inocentes: A Criança Sem Infância no Brasil*. São Paulo: Ed. Hucitec.

Maybury-Lewis, David 1960: The analysis of dual organizations: a methodological critique. *Bijdragen* 116: 2–43.

Maybury-Lewis, David 1967: *Akwẽ-Shavante Society*. Oxford: Oxford University Press.

Maybury-Lewis, David 1979: *Dialectical Societies. The Gê and Bororo of Central Brazil*. Cambridge. MA.

Mead, Margaret 1975: Children's play style: potentialities and limitations of its use as a cultural indicator. *Anthropological Quarterly* 48 (3): 157–181.

Menezes, Cláudia 1982: Os Xavante e o movimento de fronteira no Leste mato-grossense. *Revista de Antropologia* 25: 63–87.

Menezes, Cláudia 1985: *Missionários e Índios em Mato Grosso (Os Xavante de São Marcos)*. Tese de Doutorado. Universidade de São Paulo: Faculdade de Filosofia, Letras e Ciências Humanas, Departamento de Ciência Política.

Miller, Michael 2004: *Ensuring the Rights of Indigenous Children*. Innocenti Research Center Digest 11. Florence: UNICEF Innocenti Research Center.

Misse, Michel et al. 1973: *Delinquência Juvenil na Guanabara*. Rio de Janeiro, Tribunal de Justiça do Estado da Guanabara, Juizado de Menores.

Monte, Nietta 1996: *Escolas da Floresta: Entre o Passado Oral e o Presente Letrado*. Rio de Janeiro: Multiletra.

Ninuendajú, Curt 1942: *The Sherente*. Los Angeles: Frederick Webb Hodge Anniversary Publication Fund.

Nunes, Angela 1999: *A Sociedade das Crianças A'uwe-Xavante: Por Uma Antropologia da Criança*. Colecção Temas de Investigação 8, Ministério da Educação. Lisboa: Instituto de Inovação Educacional.

Nunes, Angela 2002: O lugar da crianças nos textos sobre sociedades indígenas Brasileiras. In: Lopes da Silva, Aracy, Ana Vera Macedo & Angela Nunes (eds.): *Crianças Indígenas: Ensaios Antropológicos*, Coleção Antropologia e Educação, São Paulo: Ed. Global, Mari e Fapesp: 236–277.

Nunes, Angela 2004: *Brincando de Ser Criança: Contribuições da Etnologia Indígena Brasileira à Antropologia da Infância*. Tese de Doutoramento. Lisboa: Instituto Superior de Ciências do Trabalho e Empresa, Departamento de Antropologia.

Peirano, Mariza 1991: *The Anthropology of Anthropology: the Brazilian Case*. Série Antropologia 110, Brasília: Editora da UnB.

Qvortrup, Jens et al. 1994: *Childhood Matters*. Aldershot: Avebury.

Ricardo, Carlos Alberto (ed.) 2000: *Povos Indígenas no Brasil 1996–2000*. São Paulo: Instituto Socioambiental.

Rizzini, Irene 1997a: *O Século Perdido: Raízes Históricas das Políticas Públicas Para a Infância no Brasil*. Rio de Janeiro: Editora Universitária Santa Úrsula.

Rizzini, Irene (ed.) 1997b: *Olhares Sobre a Criança no Brasil – Séculos XIX e XX*. Série Banco de Dados 5, Rio de Janeiro: Editora Universitária Santa Úrsula.

Rizzini, Irene 2000: *Crianças Desvalidas, Indígenas e Negras no Brasil: Cenas da Colônia, do Império e da República*. Rio de Janeiro: Editora Universitária Santa Úrsula.

Rizzini, Irene (ed.) 2002: *Pesquisa em Acção: Crianças, Adolescentes, Famílias e Comunidades*. Rio de Janeiro: Editora Universitária Santa Úrsula.

Sahlins, Marshall 2000: Ethnographic experience and sentimental pessimism: why culture is not a disappearing object. In: Daston, Lorraine (ed.): *Biographies of Scientific Objects*. Chicago: University of Chicago Press: 158–293.

Seeger, Anthony, Roberto Da Matta & Eduardo Viveiros de Castro 1979: A construção da pessoa nas sociedades indígenas Brasileiras. *Boletim do Museu Nacional, Nova Série Antropologia*, 32.

Stephens, Sharon (ed.) 1995: *Childhood and the Politics of Culture*. New Jersey: Princeton University Press.

Tassinari, Antonella 2001: Da civilização à tradição: Os projectos de escola entre os índios do Uaçá. In: Lopes da Silva, Aracy & Mariana Ferreira (eds.): *Antropologia, História e Educação: A Questão Indígena e a Escola*. Série Antropologia e Educação. São Paulo: Editora Global, Mari e Fapesp: 157–195.

Toren, Christina 1993: Making history: the significance of childhood cognition for a comparative anthropology of mind. *Man* (N.S.) 28: 461–478.

Contributors

Nadina Christopoulou, PhD in Social and Political Sciences. Researcher at the Greek Council for Refugees in Athens, Greece. Main interests: diaspora issues, migration, refugees.

Violeta Davoliute, PhD in Comparative Literature. Researcher at the Centre for Comparative Literature at the University of Toronto, Canada. Main Interests: cultural aspects of travel and forced migration, Central and Eastern European literature, memory and history, life stories, The Gulag and its literary aftermath.

Heike Drotbohm, PhD in Anthropology, Lecturer at the Department of Social Anthropology at the University of Freiburg, Germany. Main interests: urban anthropology, migration studies, anthropology of childhood and youth, anthropology of religions. Regions of research are The Caribbean and West-Africa.

H. Julia Eksner, M.A. in Anthropology and African Studies, PhD candidate at Northwestern University in Evanston, USA. Main interests: developmental and cultural context of learning, influence of immigration experiences on the learning of adolescent refugees in the USA.

Marjorie Faulstich Orellana, PhD in Education, Associate Professor in the Graduate School of Education and Information Studies at the University of California in Los Angeles. Main interests: daily lives and language practices of the children of immigrants in urban schools and communities.

Jacqueline Knörr, PhD in Anthropology, Head of Research Group at the Max Planck Institute for Social Anthropology in Halle, Germany. Main interests: migration, creolization, urban anthropology, integration and conflict, political anthropology, gender, childhood. Regions of research are West Africa, Indonesia and Germany.

Sonja de Leeuw, PhD in Film- and Television Studies, Professor at the Department of Theatre, Film and Television Studies at Utrecht University, The Netherlands. Main interests: Dutch television culture in an international context, TV's role in the construction of cultural identity, media and cultural diversity, diasporic media, representation of ethnicity.

Sabine Mannitz, PhD in Anthropology, Senior Researcher at the Peace Research Institute in Frankfurt on Main, Germany. Main interests: migration and national identity, social construction of alterity, socialization processes in modern society.

Angela Nunes, PhD in Anthropology, Research Associate at PINEB (Research Programme on the Northeastern Brazilian Indians), University of Bahia (UFBA), Brazil. Main interests: childhood, intercultural education, ethnic minorities, migration, gender, human rights policies.

Jan C. Oberg, PhD in Anthropology, Research Associate at the Institute for Cultural Studies (BIK), University of Bremen, Germany. Main interests: field research, chilhood and migration, maritime culture in coastal societies.

Jana Pohl, PhD student (Slavonic Philology) at Greifswald University, Germany. Main interests: images of migration and topography in North American children's literature, Jewish American children's literature.